10.2.02 Happy Birthday

Diana —

to a Post modern women

on her next adventure in life

love you

Maddie

Postmodern Ceramics

Postmodern Ceramics
Mark Del Vecchio

with 327 illustrations, 247 in color

Thames & Hudson

This book is dedicated to my parents, Anthony and Katharine Del Vecchio, for a lifetime of love and support.

© 2001 Mark Del Vecchio
© 2001 Garth Clark

First published in hardcover in the United States of America in 2001 by Thames & Hudson Inc., 500 Fifth Avenue, New York, New York 10110

Library of Congress Catalog Card Number 2001087462
ISBN 0-500-23787-5

Printed in Hong Kong
by H & Y Printing Ltd

The following are all details.

Frontispiece (p. 2)
Kohei Nakamura
resurrection, 1991

Chapter 1
frontispiece (p. 26)
Bodil Manz
Cylinder, 1995

Chapter 2
frontispiece (p. 40)
Wouter Dam
Blue Shape, 2000

Chapter 3
frontispiece (p. 56)
Ralph Bacerra
Untitled Platter, 1988

Chapter 4
frontispiece (p. 68)
Gwyn Hanssen Pigott
Still Life #2, 1995

Chapter 5
frontispiece (p. 80)
Babs Haenen
Les Collines d'Anacapris, 1993

Chapter 6
frontispiece (p. 92)
Ah Leon
Vertical Log Teapot, 1992

Chapter 7
frontispiece (p. 104)
Richard Notkin
Pyramidal Skull Teapot: Military Intelligence III—Yixing Series, 1989

Chapter 8
frontispiece (p. 122)
Kurt Weiser
Lidded Vessel (Side A), 1992

Chapter 9
frontispiece (p. 132)
Akio Takamori
The Fallen Angel (Homage to Duane Michals), 1990

Chapter 10
frontispiece (p. 146)
Kukuli Velarde
Isichapuitu, 1998, Installation at the Clay Studio, Philadelphia

Chapter 11
frontispiece (p. 164)
Ken Price
Green Glow, 1996

Chapter 12
frontispiece (p. 176)
Steven Montgomery
Thermal Decline, 1999

Contents

In selecting work to be included in this book I have set up certain criteria. Firstly, all of the work discussed and illustrated, aside from the artworks in Garth Clark's introduction, is drawn from the 1980s and 1990s, the belle époque of postmodernism. Secondly, I have tried to focus mostly on younger artists who came into their own during the 1980s and 1990s. This has proven problematic. Setting an age limit of sixty did not work because some older artists such as Gwyn Hanssen Pigott came to postmodernism later in life and this aspect of their work is still young, so to speak. Others such as Viola Frey, Ken Price, and Betty Woodman have played, and continue to play, too important a role in postmodernism's current development to be excluded. So I have compromised. The focus is still primarily on a younger generation, but with a few mature artists whose exclusion would have skewed this narrative. Thirdly, I wanted to focus on artists who are still working today. Again, this proved difficult in practice. AIDS, cancer, and other causes took away some exceptional talents in early or mid-career—notably Howard Kottler, Rick Dillingham, Angus Suttie, and Art Nelson—and their omission would have distorted the style's true historical record.

Preface

6

Fourthly, and here I have been able to keep to my original concept, all the work included had to be consciously postmodern. To put it in other terms, I wanted work that actively, rather than passively, explored this language. There is a difference between work that contains a chance element of postmodern vocabulary, such as decoration, for instance, and work that deliberately uses decoration in a postmodern context. An example is the work of Betty Woodman. Before she became part of the Pattern and Decoration movement (P and D) her decorated pottery was lively and vital, but not postmodern. In the late 1970s, after she became involved in P and D, her work changed dramatically in its scale, its ambition, and its context, and became postmodern. The artists shown here are all activists in a sense, dealing with one or another of postmodernism's many agendas in a literate and convincing manner. They are aware when their work transgresses modernist edicts or is in abeyance of modernism's intent and they do so deliberately with an understanding of the consequences of their stance aesthetically, perceptually, and philosophically. Many of the artists work in a variety of styles which means they could be included in more than one chapter, but for the sake of saving space, I have limited my selections to those works that best fit the chapter outlines I have created.

One will detect something of a weighting towards the USA and Britain in the selection, but this is not a personal bias. They are the two nations with the greatest role in defining the movement and the number of their artists represented is merely reflective of this formative role. However, thirty nations are represented in this study. Surveys are judged as much by omission as inclusion. Limitations of space require artists to be excluded even though the quality of their work and the subject matter makes a good fit. When faced with choosing between artists of equal importance, I have selected those whose work I know more intimately. This may seem limiting, but I have had wide experience after two decades in the world of ceramics and so it is not as much of an impediment as it might seem. The reason for this is that I wanted to avoid the feeling of armchair research that so often pervades broad surveys. As a non-academic, I hope to convey conviction of intimacy with these magical objects, so that their real-life qualities can be communicated, a duty owed less to myself than to the readers of this book.

Mark Del Vecchio, New York City

**Meaning and Memory:
The Roots of Postmodern
Ceramics, 1960–1980**
By Garth Clark

'Too much of a good thing is often wonderful!'
Mae West

'Too much is never enough!'
Morris Lapidus, architect of the 1950s
Miami Beach hotels, Eden Roc and Fountainbleu

Introduction

Postmodernism and ceramics is a marriage made in artworld heaven. This particular nirvana, shielded from modernism's disapproving scowl, is brightly patterned, unconcerned about reverence for authorship or originality, ready to quote styles from the medium's long past at the drop of a slip brush, and prepared to mine every semiotic meaning inherent in clay, glaze, pottery, and utility. This has liberated ceramics, allowing it to express its historical literacy, its humor, and its relationship to both everyday life and the decorative arts. In the process, ceramics has come alive as never before, it is more diverse, literate, adventurous, and ambitious than at any other time. There is even the room and the encouragement for those who have chosen to remain in the modernist camp. This may sound a touch over exuberant, but the enthusiasm should be read against the background of ceramics' previous relationship to modernism in which much of the ceramic tradition was kept firmly closeted to avoid censure.

To describe the union of ceramics and modernism as a 'relationship' is probably pushing the meaning of the word to its limit. It was unconsummated, antagonistic, and demoralizing. Several factors made ceramics unwelcome at this minimal steel and glass table. Ceramics derived from low art rather than high art, it participated in pagan activities such as decoration and ornamentation and its two primary form types, vessels and figures, were both considered ill suited to the modernist canon. Figuration was thrown out with all realism and representational art, and replaced by abstraction. The vessel posed a different kind of problem. It was too complex, loaded with too much meaning, was too domestic, evoked too many associations both in the past and present. It was simply too messy for modernism to deal with as an art form. It could, however, be redeemed through industry—creating tableware simple in shape, glazed white, and with no decoration or any other outward sign of individuality.

This produced some strange policies. The Museum of Modern Art in New York, for instance, could accession, say, a teapot into their collection if it was machine made, but not if it was hand made, even if the latter reflected better design principles.

On the surface, the reasoning behind this was really quite logical. Industry could better serve the proletariat than crafts. At heart, modernism was a socialist movement and the enemy was the bourgeoisie and their decadent taste. Even though the Arts and Crafts Movement was one of the foundations of modernist philosophy, it was felt that handcrafted objects would be relatively costly to make compared to industrial production, and so would sell to an affluent audience and further encourage bourgeois taste. To an extent this was true. Even the socialist William Morris admitted that his Arts and Crafts Movement had ended up making 'bibelots for the filthy rich.'

However, the argument does not hold water, to use a vessel metaphor. Firstly, it was the *progressive-minded* bourgeoisie who were the primary supporters of the new modernists. These doctors, lawyers, architects, psychiatrists, and other professionals were the boosters who bought modernism's expensive leather and metal furniture, after it was rejected by the working class. The same class still buys this furniture today. Secondly, this attitude about craft materials was not applied to fine art. If industry was the perfect delivery system in modernist utopia then surely all sculpture and paintings should be reproduced industrially as well, in posters and replicas. But modern fine art did not want to change the exclusive, elitist market that had been so carefully nurtured over the centuries, it just wanted to take over the power and run the show. So the aesthetics of art changed, but the high-art mechanisms of control and canonization remained the same.

Either way this meant that aside from producing some superb ceramic designs for industry, ceramics and modernism never really had the chance to dance together, a loss to both parties. Exclusion from the modernist community had an impact on ceramics between the two world wars. Mostly, this was negative. It pushed ceramics into the arms of the anti-modernists, such as Bernard Leach, who argued a regressive non-art position that has hobbled ceramics for decades and which, remarkably, still holds some sway today. It also encouraged a decorative movement, derived from the French

Art Deco potters, of charming, but ultimately shallow, decorated pottery, figures, and figurines that had a veneer of modernist styling. Very little high art was made in the ceramics movement between 1920 and 1950. Cynically, one could argue that this only proved modernism correct, but the embargo kept ceramics from growing and taking part in one of the great art movements of all time, isolating it from modernism's intelligence, and, by forcing it to the right, gave a victory to the least avant-garde elements in the crafts.

These potters were every bit as narrow, intolerant, puritanical, and despotic as the modernists. For ceramists, excluded from modernism, they provided an authoritarian regime to rebel against. Until quite recently they retained a strong voice in the ceramics world. Some have even tried to make the point that such artists as Leach are actually modernists in traditional clothing. Paul Greenhalgh's provocative essay on this subject 'Maelstrom of Modernism' in *Crafts* (May/June 1992) makes particularly interesting reading, but is ultimately unconvincing. They shared elements with modernism such as a very narrow path of approved history (almost all decorative pottery, except for early slipware which was viewed as primitive, proletarian, and therefore 'pure,' was excluded) and they adopted the same reverence for objective functionalism as the modernist architects. For many ceramists, removed as they were from the fine arts mainstream, these traditionalists replaced modernism as the enemy and much of the ceramic rebellion that led to postmodernism was in reaction to Leach rather than to modernism itself. Interestingly, the end result was much the same.

After World War II (1939–45) the paradigm started to change. At that point a generation of young ceramists began to take matters into their own hands and, marginalized or not, made powerful art, more or less within a modernist framework. Lucie Rie, Hans Coper, and Ruth Duckworth in Britain (all three émigrés) worked in a contemporary style that was loosely modernist, influenced by the lineages of Constantin Brancusi, Alberto Giacometti, and Henry Moore. In the USA, Peter Voulkos and John Mason led the modernist charge in Los Angeles with the so-called Abstract Expressionist Ceramics Movement from the mid-1950s, followed soon thereafter by Robert Turner, Karen Karnes, and David Weinrib at Black Mountain College, North Carolina, Ruth Duckworth at the University of Chicago, Richard DeVore at the Cranbrook Academy of Art, Michigan, and many others. Although they came late to the modernist movement, at heart they shared the movement's values—truth to materials, purity of concept, originality, authorship, a commitment to abstraction, a rejection of decoration, and a number of other principles that make them members of this camp.

Postmodernist ceramics has its roots in the USA during the 1960s and in Britain during the 1970s. It is at this point that the long simmering rebellion against modernism's puritanism began to boil over. Ceramics, held back for years, was a player in the postmodernist movement from the start, unusual for a medium that has tended to move with glacial caution, trusting evolution rather than revolution. However, before we look at this in detail it is necessary to explain a little more what postmodernism means in the larger sense of the term. This is no easy task. As Eric Fernie wrote in *Art History and its Methods* (1995), postmodernism is 'intentionally difficult to define.'[1] In an article in the *New York Times*, entitled 'Modern and Postmodern, the Bickering Twins,' writer Edward Rothstein takes this a step further and remarks that, 'Postmodernism is almost impossible to pin down; like a blob of mercury, it slips away under pressure, only to pop up again in its original form.'[2]

Postmodernism is a big tent. In the visual arts, both applied and fine, it has produced a host of styles, theories, and approaches to art. This includes post-minimalism, maximalism, appropriation, post-industrialism and, as much as its adherents deny this paternity, deconstructivism as well. It popularized the conceptual tool of semiotics. It brought about a return to pattern and decoration, allegory, narrative, figuration, and a new type of historicism. It has spawned scores of mini movements, experimental design firms, and workshops such as S.I.T.E.S. and the Memphis group. It both facilitated and exploited the contemporary crafts revival.

While there are references to postmodernism before World War II—in the writings of the literary critic Federico de Onis in 1928 and historian Arnold Toynbee in 1938—they are unrelated to its current definition. Joseph Hudnot uses the term in *Architecture and the Spirit of Man* (1949), but it is not until 1977 that the first major book on the subject arrived, *The Language of Postmodern Architecture*, written by Charles Jencks, an American architect living in London. Later he succinctly defined the movement as, 'fundamentally the eclectic mixture of any tradition with that of its immediate past: it is both the continuation of Modernism and its transcendence.'[3] However, the stage was set for Jencks in 1966 by another American architect, Robert Venturi, whose book *Complexity and Contradiction in Architecture* provided the movement with its battle cry, 'Less is a Bore'—an upending of Mies van der Rohe's modernist diktat, 'Less is More.' Venturi urged for ambiguity and a 'messy vitality' to replace the purity and order of modernism. Aldo Rossi in 1966's *L'architettura della città* was also influential, particularly on the subject of memory, but only after its translation into other languages in the 1980s. On the subject of postmodernism in its broader philosophical context, Jean-François Lyotard's *La Condition postmoderne* (1979) was the most influential text.

The fact that postmodernism's most influential writing came mainly from architecture was a good fit with ceramics as both disciplines have their roots in the applied arts. Jencks' book is notable for its fierce critique of modernism's failures, in particular that its buildings had no memory and no communication skills. The lack of memory is easily explained. By this Jencks meant that modernism's paranoia about revivalism, which led to the banishment of almost all historical references, cut architecture off from its past and vacated its memory. Therefore its buildings had no connection to the continuum of time. One of the great benefits of postmodernism was that it reconnected artists and designers with their past.

Hans Ibelings explores this in a slender, but compelling, book, *Supermodernism* (1998), writing that, 'Parallel with the discovery of memory as a medium for channeling meaning in architecture, was the discovery of architecture's own memory. One aspect of postmodernism is its (re)discovery of history as a value-free source of inspiration and as an inexhaustible repertoire of forms, types, styles, and so on, that everyone is free to re-cycle at their own discretion. Simply put, the modernists regarded the past—with the exception of the particular line in history from which they claimed descent—as just so much dead weight. For postmodernists the past was the natural starting-point for the creation of something new. What is more, they discovered an infectious delight in the past, for it turned out that there was so much more to discover than the Palladio-Ledoux-Schinkel line of descent. One of the lasting salutary effects of postmodernism is that a good deal of previously neglected architectural history is now the subject of research.'[4] What is fascinating about this statement is that with a few adjustments (replace 'architecture' with 'pottery' and the 'Palladio-Ledoux-Schinkel line of descent' with the 'Sung, Japanese teaware-and-medieval-slip line of descent') it applies exactly to ceramics as well.

Claiming that modern buildings had no communication skills may seem a less obvious criticism. This refers to the growing interest in semiotics or semiology in the late 1960s. Semiotics is a branch of structuralism that examines the meaning of signs rather than words. These signs comprise a language system—iconic, indexical, and symbolic—that enables a building or an object to become what semiologists term, 'a bearer of meaning.' Ornament, the primary means of presenting signs in architecture, had been banished and this inhibited modernism's ability to communicate. Semiotics now plays much less of a role and much fun has been made of this concept of architecture 'speaking,' notably Tom Wolfe in his acidly pointed critique, *From Bauhaus to our House* (1993). But in fact ornament does allow a building to signal information: for the function of a building to be made more clear, for its relationship to the buildings that surround it to be 'discussed,' for traffic to be directed, and for buildings to be made texturally warmer, friendlier, and more accessible.

Postmodernism's arguments were not restricted to aesthetics. At the heart of the postmodernist rebellion lay a deeper issue that is dealt with in the separate, but related, field of postmodernist philosophy. By 1960 there was a growing sense of ennui about the modern dream. In the light of the Cold War, urban unrest, ecological concerns, and the Vietnam War critics began to question the modernist ideal of progress. As art writer Robert Atkins comments, 'The ecological revolt that dawned during the 1960s signaled a loss of modern faith in technological progress that was replaced by postmodernist ambivalence about the effects of that progress on the environment.' Atkins points out that postmodernism reflects a fundamental change in the techno-economic structure of the major developed countries, 'Just as modern culture was driven by the need to come to terms with the industrial age, so postmodernism has been fueled by the desire for accommodation with the electronic age.'[5]

This is a significant point. Postmodernism is mainly the product of a generation reared on electronic entertainment, with television being the most influential. Music Television (MTV), founded in 1981, has influenced the optical sense of the postmodern generation. Its staple, the music video, developed an audience that could accept visual information at breakneck speed. This is a group that is visually literate without necessarily being informed. Through these videos they have been exposed to the work of Old Master painters and classic photographers which has been referenced in otherwise low-art videos to sell the music. So when they see R.E.M.'s video 'Losing My Religion' done stylistically in the look of the famous Czech photographer Jan Saudek or watch Madonna play with Horst P. Horst's classic photograph in the music video 'Vogue,' they are being taught about appropriation. In this case the audience is different from that of the educated art world where it is assumed that the audience knows in advance from whence the artist is 'outsourcing his images.' In the case of MTV, the process is reversed. Later they may encounter the original source and make the connection. As they begin to realize how the game is played they look more carefully for these connections. An audience has emerged whose sophistication in processing layered, rapid-fire imagery, and content is second to none in the history of man. Appropriation looms large in other electronic fields—such as 'sampling' in hip hop and rap music, another distinctly postmodern phenomena of taking short chords of classic popular music and making entire choruses.

More radically, digital imagery allowed makers of music, film, music videos, and television advertising to employ memory in ways not imaginable a generation ago. One of the groundbreaking images in this regard was the Hoover advertisement showing a famous Fred Astaire film clip where a broom he dances with has been seamlessly replaced by a modern vacuum cleaner. Personal computers have created a remarkable democracy of access, whereby almost every kind of artistic creation by man can be photographed, transcribed into 0s and 1s, downloaded, altered, e-mailed anywhere in the world in a matter of seconds, and incorporated into the work of the contemporary artist. This, in turn, can be made available on the Internet where millions can take these images and re-appropriate them in their own work. With this flood of data and information, modernism could not hold to its narrow aesthetic view of life.

Ceramics first began to tweak modern reticence in the 1960s with the arrival of Robert Arneson, the maverick father of the ceramic Funk Movement and one of the major ceramic artists of the twentieth century. Bridling at both the wall-to-wall dominance of the Abstract Expressionists in American art at that time and the deathly conservatism of the ceramics movement (with the notable exception of Peter Voulkos and company whom Arneson admired), he took a stand in 1961. While demonstrating throwing techniques at the California State Fair he threw a bottle shape, sturdy but inelegant, more or less in the shape of a soda bottle, impressed the legend 'No Deposit,' and then sealed it with a hand-made bottle cap. At this moment the postmodern battle in ceramics had been enjoined.

Although this object now seems tame—certainly when compared to the scatological work that followed in which Arneson encrusted toilets and urinals with ceramic vaginas, penises, breasts, and feces—even this small gesture managed to enrage both modernists and anti-modernists alike. *No Return* (1961)—now in the collection of the Los Angeles County Museum of Art—was exhibited later at the M.H. De Young Memorial Museum in San Francisco where it provoked considerable criticism. A reviewer for *Crafts Horizons*, Alan Meisel, wrote peevishly, 'if the purpose of including this in the exhibition was to irritate the reviewers, it did.'[6]

Funk can most easily be described as an inversion of Pop art. It has the same elements as Pop, but turned inside out to reveal a visceral interior. Both movements used 'commercial' craft. Both were related to consumerism. Pop took its techniques from advertising art and Funk from the hobbyist shop. Both used banal everyday images. But Pop was clean and Funk was dirty. Where Pop was cool, neat, and detached, Funk was hot, messy, and confrontational. Both used humor. Pop was sly, subtle, and ironic, while Funk was sophomoric, offensive, and obvious. This is best explored by comparing the work of Robert Arneson and Claes Oldenburg.

Oldenburg's toilets are made of white canvas, pristine and even elegant in their droll, deflated presence. Arneson's toilets, made at about the same

Robert Arneson
Herinal, 1965
Ceramic
h 5 ft, w 6 ft
h 1.5 m, w 1.8 m
Courtesy the Estate of Robert Arneson, Licensed by Vaga,
New York, NY and George Adams Gallery, New York, NY

time, are flowing with a lava of store-bought glazes, puddles of unmentionable liquids and solids, and containers of all known varieties of human sexual organs. One provokes wry amusement, the other a much darker humor. Needless to say, when this work first appeared in the early 1960s, Arneson and Oldenburg were equally offensive to both the art world and the lay public, albeit for different reasons.

After an outpouring throughout the 1960s of excrement, genitalia, and disturbing and offensive subjects of every description—telephones with breasts, hands reaching out of electric toasters, penis handles on boxes—Funk could not get any dirtier without moving beyond the pale. The Super-Object, a term that I coined in the late 1970s, was the next step.[7] Arneson's younger students took the commercial glazes, the popular culture images, and the low-fire techniques from Funk, cleaned up the act, and refined the end product. The Super-Object arrived more or less simultaneously during the late 1960s in the Bay Area of Northern California (San Francisco, Berkeley, Oakland, and their environs) and in Seattle. In California its leading exponent was Arneson's student, Richard Shaw. Howard Kottler led the charge in Seattle with a group of artists which included Patti Warashina, Fred Bauer, and later Mark Burns and Michael Lucero.

The Super-Object is high craft. Its technical finesse reminds one of Boehm birds or Lladro figurines—over priced, over crafted porcelain atrocities from the kitsch industry—an association that these artists happily acknowledged and parodied. Clay's ability to mimic materials such as wood, cloth, leather, or metal was an important part of the vocabulary. The Funk artists had used this mimetic technique, but so crudely that it provoked humor rather than illusion. In the hands of the Super-Object makers, the imitation of other media was so convincing that one often had to touch the object to convince oneself that it was indeed fired clay.

In particular, Marilyn Levine was a master of this technique, creating leather objects in high-fired stoneware that defied the eye, right down to the details of chrome-plated studs and steel zippers, all ceramic. Harold Rosenberg observed that Levine's

work 'was essentially a conceptual art, that brings to the eye nothing not present in nature but instructs the spectators that things may not be what they seem.'[8] This was in tune with a growing super-realist movement amongst painters at the time. Ceramics considered this work to be heretical, a bucket of slip thrown in the face of both the crafts and modernism, assaulting the one principle that both these movements shared and revered, truth to materials. As the art critic Kim Levin observed, 'Old time illusionistic art has collided with the future becoming as literal as minimal forms...form has redissolved into content—Pygmalion is back in business.'[9]

Richard Shaw's work was not solely dependent upon illusion, but invested in a kind of visual poetry derived both from the surrealist object and earlier realist paintings of curious still-life assemblages by American painters such as John F. Peto. Shaw used discards from consumer society—broken pencils, tins that had held canned food, which he then cast and painted to build composite figures or assemblages. Howard Kottler, on the other hand, was more of an appropriationist, long before the title existed and achieved its legitimacy through artists such as Sherrie Levine and Mike Bidlo. Kottler's breakthrough body of work was a series of witty plates in the late 1960s and early 1970s. They were factory-made, white-glazed porcelain to which he applied colored ceramic decals that were either store bought or custom made for him by other artists. There are thousands of these plates and no record as to how many were produced. He mischievously parodied the multiples market, giving the sense that they were part of a carefully monitored edition by sometimes using a decal on the foot that read, '2 of 10,' the only edition number he ever used.

Above, left
Claes Oldenburg
Soft Toilet, 1965
Paper (Gemini G.E.L.)

Above, right
Patti Warashina
Kiln Car, c. 1979
Porcelain, wood, plastic
l 36 in., 91.4 cm

The subjects were unashamedly populist: the American flag, pink roses, and portraits of the Pope. Mainstream art images were also used—Thomas Gainsborough's *The Blue Boy*, Leonardo da Vinci's *The Last Supper* and *Mona Lisa*, and Grant Wood's *American Gothic*. He boxed some plates in sets and lavished more craft on the 'packaging' than the 'product,' another neatly presented irony. These sets dealt with specific themes, such as four plates in wood-grained leather envelopes resting in a pine box and dedicated to Wood's painting *American Gothic*. Kottler, a homosexual, plays havoc with the all-American family virtues that this painting represents, mixing and matching genders with transgressive glee. In another set, with the plates sexily enclosed in reddish pink leather, Kottler took Gertrude Stein's famous line, 'Rose, is a rose is a rose,' as his starting-point—the images were made up from decals of pink roses and then titled with a wicked sense of camp. These plates are a perfect early expression of the appropriationist impulse in postmodernism. They replicate high art in a decidedly low-art format and are cool, industrial, populist, witty, and subversive.

It was 1977 when Kottler's work really struck home in the ceramics community. A sculpture he made in that year, *The Old Bag Next Door is Nuts*, was reproduced in *Ceramics Monthly*, the primary professional journal for ceramic artists in the USA. Subscribers noted that the work, which was literally comprised of a molded house and a paper bag full of nuts, was made directly from two commercial molds that were available from Duncan Ceramic Products. Letters of outrage flowed into the magazine. The response of Ms. Poris, a ceramist from Farmington Hills, Michigan, was typical. She noted the page numbers on which the molds were illustrated in the Duncan catalog and then fumed that her sense of 'justice, honesty, integrity and aesthetic feeling [has] been affronted. The piece is cynical and dishonest, stretching originality beyond my level of acceptance.'[10]

Kottler's stance challenged both the ceramist's belief in the sanctity of the hand and the modernist notion of originality. There was an additional irony in that those most offended by Kottler were adherents of the Bernard Leach/Warren MacKenzie school whose hands were busy at work mimicking wares originally made by Chinese and Korean potters seven hundred years ago. That they, of all potters, should pillory Kottler for his 'lack of originality' was absurd and part of the theater that his work was meant to provoke.

In a later statement regarding the outrage over his work, this super-mannerist stated unapologetically, 'I am lazy, I use images already available—casting is simpler and faster than molding—I purchase molded pieces already cast, use prepared glazes, in fact, I seldom touch clay. I use other people's molds, other people's ideas and other people make my ceramic decals. I just assembled the parts.'[11] In a letter to Ms. Poris he had acknowledged that even the title was not his, but was suggested by his students Michael Lucero and Alice Sundstrom: 'In fact the only element that is mine was the concept for the sculpture and hopefully, Ms. Poris, you will permit me this one small glory.'[12]

Not surprisingly, Los Angeles was the other center of postmodern invention. The West Coast was isolated from the establishment on the East Coast and felt freer to reject the orthodoxies of the day. Los Angeles contributed two important artists to the emerging postmodern aesthetic in the 1960s, Michael Frimkess and Ken Price. Both artists were 'graduates' of Peter Voulkos's so-called Abstract Expressionist Ceramics Movement. Neither actually fitted this description, although both Frimkess and Price did do work during the 1950s that superficially fitted the style of the action painters.

In the mid-1960s Frimkess began to work in a Pop format. He drew comic-book imagery onto classic ceramic forms such as Chinese ginger jars, Greek amphoras, and Zuni Native American bowls, terming these cultural forms his 'melting pots.' The work was funny and smart; black- and red-figure cyclists peddled across the surfaces of Volute Krater amphora, Uncle Sam chased naked women of various nationalities around the voluptuous volumes of ginger jars, jazz bands played riffs on Kang H'si vases. These works began to seduce the ceramic community, softening their feelings about some of the new styles that were then percolating. They were still hand made (in fact, painfully so as Frimkess

threw them dry because he believed that this was how the ancients had made their pots, but it caused his fingers to split and bleed) and they could get the joke between the street and the museum, pitting comic-book imagery against iconic stature of forms devised by potters two thousand years ago.

Ken Price came from a school which is variously termed 'Fetish-Finish' and 'The L.A. Look.' Fetish-Finish was a high-process approach to art often using advancing materials such as resins and plastics. The end result had a somewhat industrial feel and was finely crafted and included the minimalism of Robert Irwin, Edward Ruscha's billboard-like paintings, the linoleum-like splatter paintings of Ron Davis, Craig Kauffman's serene Plexiglas wall reliefs, and Billy Al Bengston's meticulous air-brushed paintings. Price's work in the 1950s was not particularly memorable, but in the early 1960s he found his voice with his remarkable cups and ceramic 'eggs.' Unglazed, the egg forms could have passed as Arp-like modern sculpture, but it was Price's vivid, primary palette that transformed them into sexy postmodernist works. Furthermore, he irreverently substituted automotive lacquer for glaze, imbedding a slyly abstract reference to popular culture and consumerism.

Between 1972 and 1974, Price created a series of 'Architectural Cups.' These neo-cubist, neo-constructivist objects are three- to five-inch (8–13 cm) high postmodernist trophies and amongst the most sought-after of all American ceramics. Their bright commercial colors, their playfulness, and insouciance does not detract from their presence as serious, intelligent works of art. Exhibited

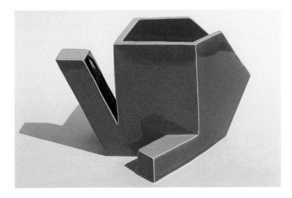

extensively in the 1970s both in New York and London, these brilliant objects had considerable influence. The British artist, Richard Slee, another important postmodernist, was just one of the artists for whom they were a revelation.

In the 1960s, Ron Nagle, the enfant terrible in Voulkos's Berkeley circle (he was only twenty years old), found himself growing more sympathetic to the Los Angeles art scene than to what was happening in the San Francisco Bay Area. Between 1960 and 1965 he frequently visited Irving Blum's Ferus Gallery on La Cienega Boulevard in Los Angeles where many of the 'L.A. Look' artists exhibited, including Ken Price. He found Price's 'little Grandma wares' a revelation. He was expecting some heavy macho Abstract Expressionist clay, but instead 'here is this guy making boxes with cups and lace and stuff and it blew my mind.'[13] But the gallery also showed a number of East Coast artists (Andy Warhol had his first gallery exhibition there) and European artists as well, including Giorgio Morandi. The combination of Price's cups and Morandi's exhibition of austere still-life paintings proved to be an epiphany. 'If Morandi could spend his life painting half a dozen objects on a tabletop then I could devote mine to the cup,' he decided.[14] Nagle was deeply invested in popular culture. In addition to his ceramics, he was a musician and a composer of pop music, writing songs for Barbra Streisand, amongst others, and producing the sound effects for the movie *The Exorcist*. He therefore had the inside track on pop as a hands-on practitioner and was not an academic slumming in the streets of the everyman.

Nagle was able to pack an immense amount of information into his small forms. His cups were an amalgam of mixed resources, a love of Japanese Momoyama tea wares, a fascination with 1950s and 1960s automobile design, and with the 'splash and drip' decoration on early plastic and linoleum kitchen surfaces. Sometimes his cups drew their texture and sometimes their form from the 1930s San Francisco 'deco-stucco' houses in which he had grown up. He began to work with decals and china paint, both considered hobbyist materials and occasionally did away with the bottom of his cups so that they were just hollow, tube-like cylinders.

Above, left
Michael Frimkess
Covered Jar, 1968
Stoneware, glazed over
with over-glaze painting
h 23³/₄ in., 60.3 cm

Above, right
Ken Price
Untitled Cup, 1973
Porcelain, glaze, paint
h 3³/₄ in., 9.5 cm

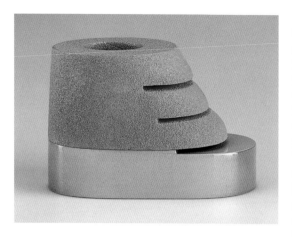

The handle became a vestigial sculptural element, sometimes organic and, at other times, precisely geometric. He worked through one series after another and it is difficult to select any one work to represent his polychromatic genius, but his *Untitled Cup (Guggenheim)* of 1975 was certainly one of his most amusing and succinct early American postmodernist works. This cocky piece rises to its full height of $3^1/_8$ inches (8 cm) and takes on and satirizes the giant presence of Frank Lloyd Wright and his most controversial piece of architecture—the Solomon R. Guggenheim Museum in New York.

In the 1970s the focus shifted to a group of students from the Chouinard Art Institute in Los Angeles. Its beginnings were not auspicious. Had one visited the school while Ralph Bacerra, Adrian Saxe, Peter Shire, and Elsa Rady were all students, one would have found them making work that, while accomplished and stylish, was quasi-Asian and tilted towards the conservative look of the anti-modernists. But they soon began to take a turn to the left, while retaining their impressive technical facility. Bacerra, who became the head of the department, developed exceptional skills at pattern and decoration. His works, an unlikely amalgam of the decoration on Japanese Imari, the princely Nabeshima wares, the optical art of M.C. Escher, and the flat stylized paintings and prints of Andy Warhol, were gloriously hedonistic, a complementary mix of decorative excess and disciplined craft.

Shire began to work with bright primary colors and create playful forms out of neo-constructivist geometry that led him to join Ettore Sottsass' influential Memphis group. Rady created cut-wing bowls, as crisp and sharp as a Coco Chanel suit, which were the apex of an Art Deco spirit that had invaded postmodern ceramics. Lastly, there is Saxe, with his informed, multi-layered response to court porcelains as instruments of power and privilege. This large, manic, red-haired iconoclast has had an extraordinary influence internationally. Erudite, impassioned, and controversial, he decisively reshaped the rules of engagement for the ceramic arts in the last quarter of the twentieth century. He took on the eighteenth-century porcelain factory wares of Meissen, Sèvres, Nymphenburg, and Chelsea, an aspect of ceramics that everyone— from modernist to anti-modernist and all in between—had dismissed as irredeemable. His erudition at explaining why this body of work fascinated him and his ability to validate its aesthetic integrity won converts and brought this once despised ceramic inheritance into the fold.

Saxe was crossing a line in taste that the ceramics community had drawn between the 'cottage aesthetic,' which was honest, direct, and 'pure,' and what Kottler, a decade earlier, had identified as the 'palace aesthetic,' which was (at least from the viewpoint of the cottage) effete, decadent, derivative, hyperbolic, excessively decorated, and, given its overtones of aristocratic privilege, politically incorrect. Most ceramic art by the modernists was raw, organic, and rustic in its feel and look (i.e., cottage). So, too, was the work of the anti-modernists. In this they were united against postmodernism. The use of gold and silver, not in an ironic context to imitate metal as with the Funk and Super-Object artists, but to express the beauty of the most opulent and sensuous of these surfaces, was the third rail in ceramic art politics. No one up to this point had dared touch or defend it.

Kottler had played with this, but used humor and a commercial treatment to take out the sting. The use of gold by Saxe was semiotic as well as

Ron Nagle
Untitled Cup
(Guggenheim), 1975
Cast earthenware, glaze,
multi-fired china paint
h $3^1/_8$ in., 8 cm

aesthetic. His glazes were as exquisite as any of the 'approved' glazes such as tenmoku or celadon. He meant viewers to be seduced by the overt allure of the surfaces at the same time as the symbolism of wealth and dynastic privilege made them feel uneasy about their apostasy. As Peter Schjeldahl, now the art critic for the *New Yorker* has written, this guilty pleasure makes Saxe's pots 'glamorous and untrustworthy, like a pedigreed dog that has been known to bite.'[15] He created some pots with surfaces that comprised as many as five different gold glazes, each one more refined and magnificent than the other, and then rudely contrasted this with plastic toys which became finials or hung from brocaded swags. He also put street language on his pots, the intrusion of a lower class into the palace context which many found disturbing.

Saxe is not an appropriationist, however. His work does not look like Meissen or Sèvres, or any other court porcelain, but he uses their lush palette, has appropriated some of their glazes, directly molded handles and ornaments from original models at Sèvres, and ended up making his objects even more outré than the originals. His approach to history, as Schjeldahl notes, is not imitative but 'enraptured and cannibalistic.'[16] It is not surprising that when two Australian art historians, Justin Clemens and Mark Pennings, decided to create a symposium in 1996 for Craft Victoria entitled 'Cultural Theory and Craft Practice,' which explored the place of crafts in postmodernism, they chose Saxe to be their poster boy.

The work of Saxe, Richard Notkin, who deals with political subject matter, Anne Kraus, who explores dreams and narrative, and Cindy Kolodziejski, who creates bizarre 'historical' vessels loaded with perverse sexual imagery, all belong to a kind of vessel that Schjeldahl has dubbed 'the smart pot.' In a catalog essay about the work of Saxe he defines this kind of vessel as: 'an academic object positing an imaginary academy, the brains of an imaginary all-embracing civilization. The smart pot is so removed from innocence, so thoroughly implicated in every received notion of nature and culture, so promiscuous in its means and ends that it is almost

innocent all over again... The smart pot x-rays the hoary art/craft distinction to reveal its confusion of values: values of prestige fouling up values of use.'[17]

In the late 1970s a group of New York-based artists, many of them originally from California, gathered for a series of meetings at the studio of the painter, Robert Zakanitch. They discussed the inherited resistance to decoration, its importance in feminist art, and its significance in non-Western art. From these meetings a movement, Pattern and Decoration (P and D), was born with the agenda of building credibility for artists who worked in this genre, including Robert Kushner, Ned Smyth, and Miriam Schapiro. The movement's voice was the gifted art historian Amy Goldin who argued that 'while decoration can be intellectually empty, it does not have to be stupid.'[18]

The ceramic involvement was limited, but significant, namely the ceramist Betty Woodman and the tile muralist, Joyce Kozloff. The breakthrough came in a series of exhibitions beginning with curator John Perreault's 'Pattern and Decoration' in 1977 at P.S. 1 in New York and 'Decorative Impulses' at the ICA in Philadelphia in 1979. The Solomon R. Guggenheim Museum in New York lent credence to the movement when it chose five P and D artists for its survey 'Nineteen Artists: Emergent Americans' in 1981. What P and D managed, through the fledgling Holly Solomon Gallery in New York (which took on the cause) and the breakthrough museum exhibitions, was to empower indirectly those in ceramics who had long worked with pattern and decoration. Suddenly decoration had a new respectability after years of being considered the ultimate fine-art pejorative.

P and D contributed some good writing to the painfully small list of published material on postmodernism and ceramics, in particular the paper 'Ceramic Decorations and the Concept of Ceramics as Decorative Art' by George Woodman, himself a P and D painter and the husband of Betty, which was presented at the 1st International Ceramic Symposium in Syracuse, New York, in 1979. This oft-quoted manifesto explained in the most lucid and convincing terms a role for decoration that was neither passive nor secondary. 'Among sensitive young potters,' he wrote prophetically, 'there appears to be a dawning awareness that the decorative stance is one of the strongest and most appropriately taken in ceramics. Attempts to avoid, disguise or transform the "minor" arts into "real" art are the result of a misconception of the nature of decoration in part brought about by the critical assumptions underlying an increasingly attenuated and artificial framework of cultural values.'[19]

Betty Woodman, in turn, also became one of clay's most controversial and effective ambassadors for P and D ceramics, giving new life to an ancient, persistent style. An indefatigable exhibitor, her shows influenced artists throughout the USA and Europe. Her pots at this point were 'playing a kind of sneaky game with function. They are to be used and used with a sense of decorative ebullience and not some mean notion of the function of eating and life at table.'[20] George Woodman was correct about the groundswell of interest in decoration and in the 1980s this came to life with a vengeance from Ralph Bacerra's over-the-edge palace wares to Phillip Maberry's room-sized installation for the 1983 Biennial at the Whitney Museum of American Art in New York, the city's most controversial showcase for groundbreaking art.

Lastly there is the matter of the ceramic figure. This, too, was once verboten. To be fair to the modernists, there were few strong artists working

with the clay figure in the years between the two world wars. The saccharine quality of most ceramic figuration during this period quite understandably made the teeth of the modernists ache. It still has that effect today on anyone with a dislike of doe-eyed sentimentality. There were exceptions such as Lucio Fontana who was working actively in figurative ceramics from 1925 onwards and 'visitors' from other media who briefly took on ceramics—Elie Nadelman, Isamu Noguchi, Louise Nevelson, and others. Arneson's arrival on the scene, and the more neo-classical Stephen De Staebler, began to encourage figuration in the 1960s. Margaret Israel, Patti Warashina, Michael Lucero, Peter VandenBerge, and Jack Earl are amongst a host of artists who worked figuratively in ceramics during the 1960s and 1970s. Some continued into the 1980s and are represented in this book by their later work.

The one artist who deserves special mention in the rise of the postmodern figure is Viola Frey. She had been dealing with the figure since the 1960s. Another Bay Area artist, she was influenced by Arneson, but was not a Funk artist and most of her early work identified as being of this style ends up being more Pop in character. In the early 1970s she began to play with eerie animal sculptures that at first seemed comical in their appearance, but carried a discomforting and edgy 'human' quality achieved at times by placing a rendering of her own readily identifiable mouth in place of the animal's. Then she moved to the human figure. Some were modeled by hand as original works, while others were what Claude Levi-Strauss terms 'bricolage,' mixed assemblies of 'cultural detritus'—both hand-modeled pieces and works molded directly from dime-store figurines. Frey obsessively collected these figurines, attending the huge outdoor Alameda Flea Market in San Francisco over weekends and acquiring new pieces for her ever-growing hoard.

In Frey's mind the flea market was her 'church' and sight of these cheap, sentimental and simply made chotchkahs, laid out on the endless tables of the market, graced by the sunlight, had for her an almost religious quality. Even when she was creating her huge ten-foot (3-meter) high figures, Frey still had the ideal of the figurine in her mind

Phillip Maberry
Paradise Fountain, 1983
Ceramic and multimedia
Installation at the 1983
Biennial, Whitney
Museum of American
Art, New York

educationally based, and often obsessive about process—will survive in the boundary-less world of postmodernism.

Whether postmodernism is now at its end after a run of nearly forty years is a good twenty-first century question. After all, most movements last on average only seven to ten years. Certainly, there is enough criticism. For some, postmodernism is symptomatic of all the evils of globalization, consumerist at heart, and with its revivalist license, creating inter-cultural creolization. Chris Baldick, writing in *The Concise Oxford Dictionary of Literary Terms* (1990), certainly manages to encapsulate most of the concerns about postmodernism's significance. Calling postmodernism 'a cultural condition prevailing in the advanced capitalist societies since the 1960s' he views this phenomena as a 'culture of fragmentary sensations, eclectic nostalgia, disposable simulacra, and promiscuous superficiality, in which the traditionally valued qualities of depth, coherence, meaning and originality are evacuated or dissolved amid the random swirl of empty signals.' He notes that the 'posties'—a derogatory term for the movement's supporters, see a certain salvation and egalitarianism in the fact that the movement has flattened the hierarchy of high and low art, but Baldick feels that this has come at great cost and that many now regard the movement 'as a symptom of irresponsible academic euphoria about the glitter of consumerist capitalism and its moral vacuity.'[22]

Of course Baldick is correct, but he is also incorrect. Postmodernism has produced the most heinous explosion of trite and often misinformed historical quotations, it has encouraged all the 'isms,' from feminism to conceptualism, to play havoc with aesthetics in the name of postmodern content-based art, most of which has a lack of profundity and has subjected us to tedious artworld lectures on morality, political correctness, and even the meaning of life. It has resulted in an often incompetent and manipulative assimilation of the crafts. It has blighted the skylines of many a city with its pink, blue, and gray miasma of crudely proportioned buildings, seemingly made from giant children's toys. Postmodernism at its worst is admittedly much more of a visual catastrophe than modernism which,

at its lowest ebb, resulted in a boring, featureless sterility which can more easily be ignored; although it should be noted that some feel that modernism's post-1950s blight has been enormously corrosive. Prince Charles, Britain's reactionary royal architectural critic, went on record as saying that modernism had done greater damage to London than the bombing during World War II.

Postmodernism, being easy to mimic, is, at its worst, horrifyingly ugly and gruesomely vulgar, particularly in architectural scale. But the opposite is true as well. Postmodernism has been a tonic. Color has flooded back into our lives. Memory has been restored, often with remarkable insight and freshness. Society's love of decoration—seemingly an innate sensibility of the human being—has been revived. Architecture is free to be individualistic again. The concept of beauty is making a cautious re-entry. But finally what makes postmodernism great is that one really cannot generalize about it because it has no singularity or hard boundaries and as a result it can never become the formidable, intolerant, and restrictive academy that grew out of modernism. Its practitioners are too diverse, its theory too broad, its freedoms too boundless to be able to install a regime and police the arts. As Eric Fernie states, it 'represents the principle of no principles'[23] and so it defies centralized theory and dogma. It is a bit like the Internet, limitless in its boundaries and finally impossible to control or regulate fully. It will die its own death at some point, but not just yet. It may well only be halfway through its raucous life. At this moment we are still enjoying many of its fruits. The ceramic ones are documented here, but the movement has also resulted in the current revival of design innovation, the most significant advance in this once becalmed field since 1960.

Then there are those who believe that postmodern is not an independent activity at all, but simply a sub-culture of modernism itself. As Edward Rothstein remarks, 'Is it possible then that the culture is still immersed in Modernism? Po-Pomo may turn out to be just another variety of Mo.'[24] Certainly modernism is resilient and is re-emerging in a traditionally progressive mood in movements

Jeff Koons
Pink Panther, 1988
Porcelain
h 54 in., 137.2 cm

such as super-realism, neo-modernism or what Charles Jencks terms 'New Moderns.'[25] This movement is based partly on the concept that modernists were not able to realize fully their aesthetic ideals because the technology of building had not yet matched their ambitions and so the physical realization of their designs was imperfect. Now that there is a wide range of new materials and systems to create seamless, transcendent, and transparent structure, modernism can return in a more ambitious and perfect form.

For ceramics, postmodernism is certainly still laden with unexplored opportunities. It has changed the entire paradigm that once oppressed the medium. As Justin Clemens states in his paper 'Postmodernity, or The Shattering of the Vessels' which he delivered in 1999 at the 'Ceramic Millennium: Leadership Congress for the Ceramic Arts' in Amsterdam, postmodernity has exposed the fact that art was always more dependent on craft than the other way around—'craft was a fundamental *condition* of art— and not simply its aesthetically degraded shadow.' Clemens believes that 'postmodernity has caused a dislocation of both art and craft in which art is de-capitalized and dispersed through new arts such as "video art" and "sound art" while the old arts of painting and sculpture have lost their traditional centrality and legitimacy. Craft based art on the other hand is in ascendancy gaining increasing clarity and relevance within the arts.'[26]

This is an historic opportunity and one which has only been partially seized. 'There is now a chance,' says Clemens, 'for ceramic art (and new practices and poetics) that are not simply submitted to the regimes of technologies for reproduction, nor identified in their essence with the logics of the hand, nor opposed nor subordinated to the dictates of other arts. Ceramics is in a singular situation, at once perhaps the most archaic and genuinely global of all the arts, it...finds itself at the cutting edge of aesthetico-technical innovation.'[27] This moment may indeed be not the apex of a movement, but the thin edge of a new and bold ceramic wedge.

Nowhere is this issue clearer than in Del Vecchio's last chapter, post-industrialism. This is the emerging of a new order in ceramic art. The environmental term 'ecotone' describes an area where two adjacent ecosystems overlap, say, a wetland and a forest. In a sense this is true of these works where the line between old-fashioned craft and industrial technology meet. It is producing new visions and new processes that draw from the strengths of both. This has been of growing fascination to younger craftspeople, but is now moving out of the margins and is on its way to becoming an aesthetic mainstream for ceramic art.

This book takes a particular view of the postmodern era and the ceramic art it has produced, mainly specialist makers, mainly highly crafted, mainly artists under sixty years of age. It has been assembled by an author who has had remarkable intimacy with this artwork. He and I co-founded the first ceramics gallery to devote itself to a new generation of postmodern artists. This has given Del Vecchio a hands-on contact with the product of two decades of creativity. All too often these surveys are the result of armchair research by authors who know work only through slides. This book is unique because Del Vecchio has personally handled just about every object reproduced in this book, he knows its heft, its scale, and its texture. There are exceptions, but they are few. Most of the pieces have also been part of almost four hundred exhibition installations in galleries, museums, and public spaces which Del Vecchio has designed, lit, and supervised. His reputation amongst artists for the sensitivity of his displays is without peer mainly because he feels that the work of the installer should be invisible and the art itself should dominate. This experience shows in the book in many ways, in the excellent choice of representative images and in the structure of the book itself, which flows with the same structure and logic as an authoritative exhibition—Del Vecchio is sensitive to what objects do and say in proximity to each other and is always striving to reveal as much about the artist as possible. Given this pragmatism and lack of academicism, *Postmodern Ceramics* is likely to be the practical reference point to this movement for decades to come.

Footnotes

[1] Eric Fernie (ed.), *Art History and its Methods* (London: Phaidon, 1995), p. 351

[2] Edward Rothstein, 'Modern and Postmodern, the Bickering Twins,' *New York Times* (Saturday October 22, 2000)

[3] Charles Jencks, *The Language of Post-Modern Architecture* (London: Academy Editions, 1977), p. 48

[4] Hans Ibelings, *Supermodernism: Architecture in the Age of Globalization* (Rotterdam: Netherlands Architecture Institute, 1998), p. 21

[5] Robert Atkins, *Artspeak: A Guide to Contemporary Ideas, Movements, and Buzzwords, 1945 to the Present* (New York and London: Abbeville Press, 1997), p. 152

[6] Alan Meisel, 'Robert Arneson,' *Crafts Horizons* (September, 1964), p. 64

[7] See Garth Clark, *A Century of Ceramics in the United States, 1878–1978* (New York: E.P. Dutton, 1979) and for a revised view of the Super-Object by the same author, *American Ceramics: 1876 to the Present* (New York: Abbeville Press, 1987)

[8] Harold Rosenberg, 'Reality Again,' in Gregory Battcock (ed.), *Super Realism: A Critical Anthology* (New York: E.P. Dutton, 1975), p. 120

[9] Kim Levin, 'The Ersatz Object,' *Arts Magazine* 49 (February 1974), p. 12

[10] The piece was illustrated in the September 1977 issue of *Ceramics Monthly*. Two letters from Ruth Poris were published in *Ceramics Monthly*, the first in November 1977, p. 7, and the second in March 1978, p. 7

[11] Howard Kottler, quoted by Elaine Levin in the exhibition catalog *Illusionistic Realism Defined in Ceramic Sculpture* (Laguna Beach, CA: Laguna Beach Museum of Art, 1977), unpaginated

[12] Letter from Howard Kottler to Ruth Poris, dated March 3, 1978

[13] Ron Nagle quoted in Barbaralee Diamonstein, *Handmade in America: Conversations with Fourteen Craftmasters* (New York: Abrams, 1983), p. 169

[14] Ron Nagle in interview with author, May 1999

[15] Peter Schjeldahl, 'The Smart Pot: Adrian Saxe and the Post-Everything Ceramics,' in Jeff Perrone and Peter Schjeldahl, *Adrian Saxe* (Kansas City: University of Missouri, 1986), p. 11

[16] Ibid.

[17] Ibid.

[18] Quoted in George Woodman, 'Ceramic Decorations and the Concept of Ceramics as Decorative Art,' in Garth Clark (ed.), *Transactions of the Ceramics Symposium 1979* (Los Angeles: Institute for Ceramic History, 1980), p. 106

[19] Ibid., p. 110

[20] Ibid.

[21] Peter Fuller, 'Review: Textiles North,' *Crafts*, March/April 1982, pp. 49–50

[22] Chris Baldick, *The Concise Oxford Dictionary of Literary Terms* (London and New York: Oxford University Press, 1990), p. 212

[23] Eric Fernie, op. cit., p. 351

[24] Edward Rothstein, op. cit.

[25] See Charles Jencks, *The New Moderns: From Late to Neo-Modernism* (New York: Rizzoli, and London: Academy Editions, 1990)

[26] Justin Clemens, 'Postmodernity or the Shattering of the Vessels,' in Dawn Bennett, Garth Clark, Mark Del Vecchio (eds), *Ceramic Millennium: Transactions of the 8th International Ceramics Symposium* (New York: Ceramic Arts Foundation, 2000), p. 83

[27] Ibid.

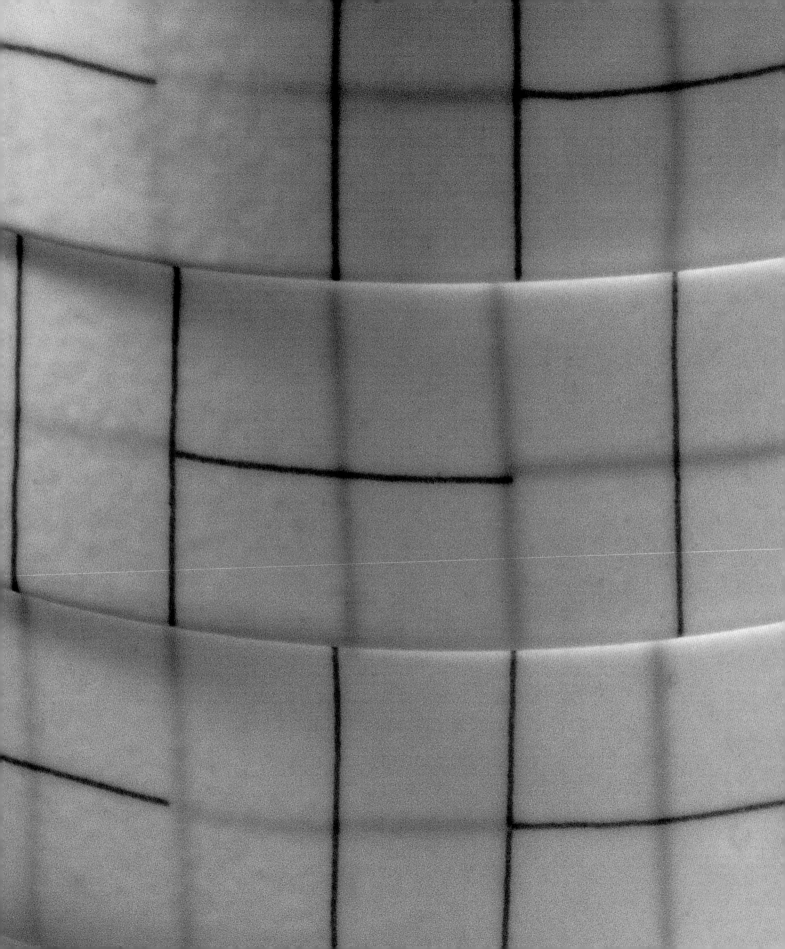

Chapter 1
The Postmodern Look

Peter Shire
Michael Duvall
Art Nelson

Judith Salomon
Roseline Delisle
Martin Bodilsen Kaldahl
Bodil Manz

Elsa Rady
Howard Kottler
Ron Nagle

Most people think of postmodernism as a particular style or 'look' that is colorful, pop, geometric, self-aware, smart, planar, and playful. This 'look' uses panels and bands of bright color, playful forms, is friendly to pattern, and overtly stylish. It is a kind of sophisticated romper-room aesthetic for adults. The underlying structure is clearly derived from modernism and despite the color and irreverence, its foundations are built on the examples of Gerrit Rietveld, Richard Neutra, Le Corbusier, Mies van der Rohe, Walter Gropius, and others from the canon of international-style architecture. The overall style is most clearly defined by certain postmodern architects, namely Ettore Sottsass, Alessandro Mendini, Matheo Thun, Robert Venturi, and Michael Graves. While all of these architects have designed ceramics for industry, some with great distinction, the finest ceramic art from this genre comes from studio ceramists.

Peter Shire was a member of Sottsass' famed Milan-based Memphis group, the definitive postmodern collaborative which included many of the architects mentioned above. Shire made both furniture and ceramics for Memphis and influenced the group's approach to clay and kiln. This Los Angeleno compiles vessels from discrete parts, reflecting his love of Russian Constructivist art, amongst other influences. This can be seen clearly in one of his signature pieces, the *Pan Pipe Scorpion* (1984). **Michael Duvall** (p. 30), one of the best exemplars of the style, also captures the architectural character of the 'look', using planes of color to define geometric constructions with great élan.

The notion of a romper room with visions of brightly colored, snap-together toys, which are now so ubiquitous in children's play schools and nurseries, certainly comes to mind in the Bay Area artist **Art Nelson's** *Meta-Vessels* (p. 31). These large, double-walled forms, a tour de force of throwing skill, are pots within pots. The stacks of vessels invite play, challenging one to recompose these totems. Similarly, the vessels of fellow American artist **Judith Salomon** (p. 31) have the same kind of innocence and youth, and at first glance have the unpretentious appearance of having been made from colored construction paper. But close inspection reveals just how wonderfully liquid and vibrant her use of colored glazes is on these slab and assembled pieces.

Canadian-born **Roseline Delisle** (p. 32) works with a restricted palette of Yves Klein blue, black, and the white of the porcelain. Her linear vision and anthropomorphic forms recall both the 1920s futuristic ballet designs of Oskar Schlemmer at the Bauhaus, in Germany, and the 1956 ceramic designs of Sottsass' *Rocchetti* series. The Dane **Martin Bodilsen Kaldahl** (p. 33) also has a penchant for line. Whereas Delisle's works suggest figuration, Kaldahl's work evokes architectural structure. He allies two volumes in one vessel. One part is monochrome and rises vertically like a tower, while the other moves out horizontally with the bold stripes enhancing the duality of these complex vessels.

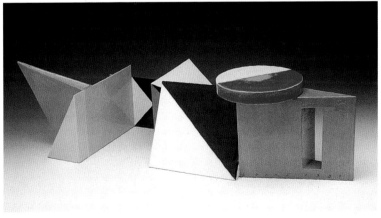

Top
Peter Shire
Pan Pipe Scorpion, 1984
Whiteware
h 16¹/₄ in., w 24¹/₂ in.,
d 12 in.
h 41 cm, w 62 cm, d 30.5 cm

Right
Peter Shire
Around the Corner, 1986
Whiteware
h 9¹/₂ in., w 12 in.
h 24 cm, w 30.5 cm

Michael Duvall
Lidded Construction
'Transformer,' 1986
Whiteware
h 18 in., w 10 in.
h 45.8 cm, w 25.5 cm

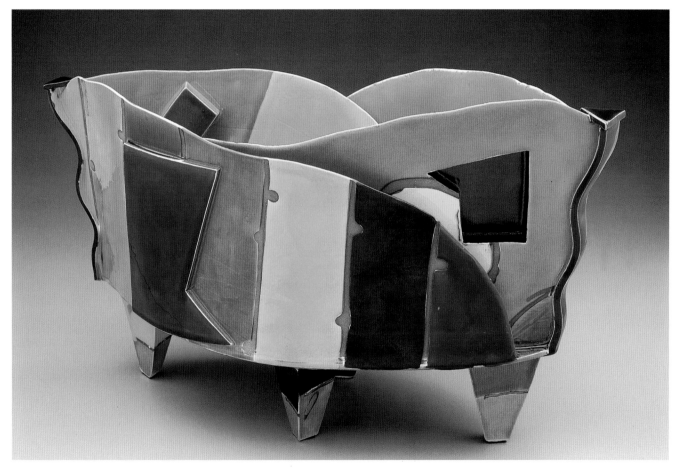

Top
Art Nelson
Meta-Vessel, 1983
Whiteware
h 15 in., diam. 17 in.
h 38 cm, diam. 43 cm

Above
Judith Salomon
Orange Envelope Vase, 1987
Whiteware
h 10 in., w 18 in., d 9 in.
h 25.5 cm, w 45.8 cm, d 23 cm

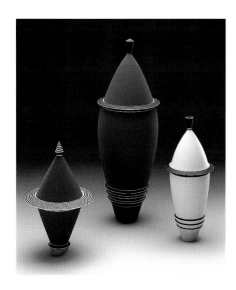

Top
Roseline Delisle
Left to right: *Fusiforme 14*,
h 6 in., 15.3 cm; *Série
Pneumatique 45*, h 11 in.,
28 cm; *Série Pneumatique
42*, h 7 in., 17.8 cm, 1988
Porcelain

Above
Roseline Delisle
Installation at Garth Clark
Gallery, Los Angeles, 1994
Drawings on paper with
three porcelain vessels

Top
Martin Bodilsen Kaldahl
Sculptural Vessel Yellow,
1997
Stoneware
h 10 1/2 in., w 21 in.
h 26.8 cm, w 53.3 cm

Above
Martin Bodilsen Kaldahl
Sculptural Vessel Striped,
1995
Stoneware
h 10 in., w 19 in.
h 25.5 cm, w 48.3 cm

Fellow Dane **Bodil Manz** combines all of the issues raised above and more. Her work is exceptionally refined, the walls on some of her porcelain cylindrical vessels are so thin and translucent that they resemble wax paper. The fragility is deceptive. The forms are strong and resilient, but Manz does exploit their extraordinary translucence. Part of her pattern is placed on the outside surface and part on the inside. The inner decoration shows through as a ghost on the outside, drawing the viewer's eye through from the outside to the inside. For some time her forms were simple, sturdy cylinders which are slip cast and yet distort so much in the firing that no two look alike. But the shapes of her vessels have become more complex, as has the surface activity. Manz's lines, blocks of color, patterns, and geometric schematics are all placed on the surface by cutting and applying custom-made decals as she wants to keep the surface decoration graphic in feel and not have the sensibility of drawing or painting.

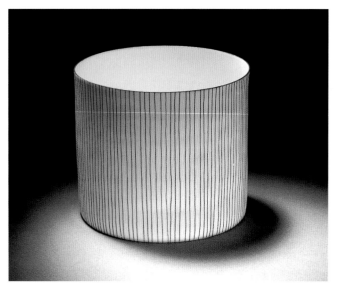

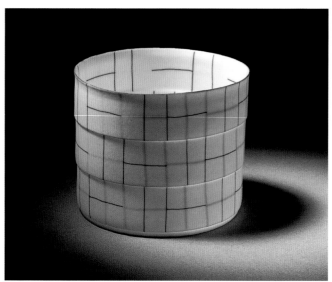

Above, left
Bodil Manz
Cylinder, 1993
Porcelain
h 8¹/₄ in., diam. 8 in.
h 21 cm, diam. 20.3 cm

Above, right
Bodil Manz
Cylinder, 1995
Porcelain
h 8¹/₂ in., diam. 9¹/₂ in.
h 21.5 cm, diam. 24 cm

Ron Nagle
Walking with Sadie, 1998
Earthenware and overglaze
h 3$\frac{1}{8}$ in., w 7$\frac{1}{8}$ in.,
d 1$\frac{5}{8}$ in.
h 8 cm, w 18 cm, d 4.1 cm

Chapter 2
Post-Minimalism

Alev Ebüzziya Siesbye   Fritz Rossmann   Ken Eastman   Sueharu Fukami
Wouter Dam   Barbara Kaas   Martin Smith   Masamichi Yoshikawa
Thomas Naethe   Michael Cleff   Magdalene Odundo   Geert Lap
Nicholas Rena

While some give the starting-point of postmodernism as the 1950s, others see the movement as emerging later, following the 1960s minimalist art of Tony Smith, Carl André, and Donald Judd. I believe both views are correct. The minimalists do constitute modernism's last hurrah. At the same time there is work from the 1950s, Ettore Sottsass' ceramics in particular, which puts in place all the style elements of what would later become identified as postmodernism. This minimalism was one of the strongest influences on the postmodern style, although taken on with somewhat promiscuous license. As a result post-minimalism is one of the most satisfying of all the aspects of postmodern ceramics, as the following works attest.

Ceramists have always had an affinity for the 'less is more' approach. Sometimes it reflects the primal nature of the process—pots made in villages with simple technology and little time for embellishment, forcing an economy of appearance without sacrificing beauty of form. For modern potters, however, this reductive aesthetic arrives through careful control. The fire has a tendency to release the expressionist qualities in materials—ash flashing, kiln tears, metallic lusters, orange flashes, changes of color where the glaze 'breaks' on the edges of a pot. All of this can create exactly the kind of richly exuberant surface that minimalists abhor. This has to be carefully suppressed. The balance is crucial—withhold too much and the work is stillborn and lifeless—allow the materials too much freedom and the tension and purity is lost.

The cosmopolitan **Alev Ebüzziya Siesbye** (raised in Turkey, trained in Denmark, and with a studio in Paris) was one of the first 'new' minimalists. In the 1960s she shocked her Danish colleagues with the severity of her work and her commitment to the primacy of one form, her signature bowl shape which she has used with only slight modifications throughout her career. Then there is the minuscule foot (no more than an inch and a half, 4 cm, in diameter, even on the largest forms) which allows her bowls to float in a kind of stasis. However, she is not as severely reductive as Dutch artist Geert Lap and does celebrate just the touch of the raw, expressive quality of her material. This is something orthodox minimalists would prefer to neutralize, but is one of the ways in which postmodernism had altered the rules of this game. Siesbye allows one thin band, sometimes two, of exposed stoneware clay to show between the neck and the lip, celebrating the textured sensuality of the grogged, stoneware clay.

Above, left
Alev Ebüzziya Siesbye
Turquoise Bowl, 1984
Stoneware
h 6¹/₂ in., diam. 8¹/₂ in.
h 16.5 cm, diam. 21.5 cm

Above, right
Alev Ebüzziya Siesbye
Untitled Bowl with Stripes, 1986
Stoneware
h 8¹/₂ in., diam. 10¹/₂ in.
h 21.5 cm, diam. 26.8 cm

Opposite, left
Wouter Dam
Black Shape with White Lines, 2000
Stoneware
h 10¹/₂ in., w 11¹/₂ in.
h 26.8 cm, w 29.2 cm

Opposite, right
Wouter Dam
Blue Shape, 2000
Stoneware
h 12 in., w 13 in., d 10 in.
h 30.5 cm, w 33 cm,
d 25.5 cm

Wouter Dam, from the Netherlands, uses a similar device. His vessels are glazed with strong monochrome-saturated color, but he allows the clay to show through at the edge, providing the formal climax to the form. What makes his work different is that he has given up the classical vessel format. His vessels are turned onto their side and the foot of the pot has disappeared, leaving a tube-like shape, open ended at both sides. It still deals, as do all vessels, with the enclosure of space, except that one can enter this enclosure at either end. He also allows elements of anthropomorphism, sensually hinting at body parts without ever crossing the borderline from abstraction to the literal.

Thomas Naethe (pp. 44, 45), who works in Utzerath, Germany, makes one aware of the distinctive presence of a stoneware aesthetic by showing uncovered clay, but celebrates this with a rougher, more assertive, textural presence.

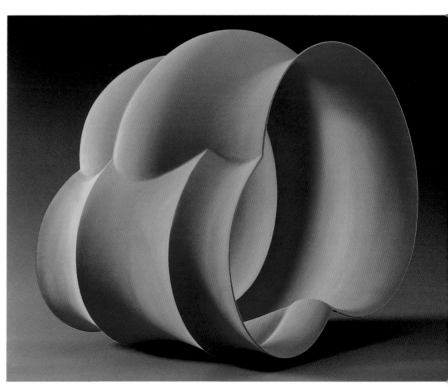

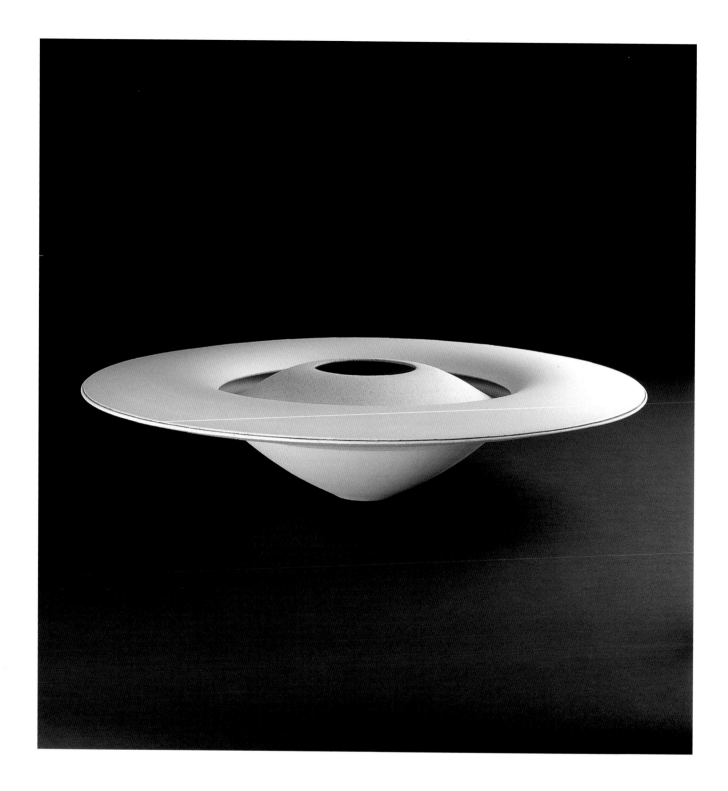

Above
Thomas Naethe
Vessel Nr. 2, 1995
Stoneware
h 5^1/$_2$ in., w 25^1/$_2$ in.
h 14 cm, w 64.7 cm

Opposite
Thomas Naethe
Vessel Nr. 4, 1999
Stoneware
h 10^1/$_4$ in.
h 26 cm

Fritz Rossmann is a member of Germany's highly successful clay collaborative Keramikgruppe Grenzhausen, a group of six young artists who have established a complex of studios, a gallery, and other shared facilities. The group often exhibits together and while they do not adhere to a common aesthetic, their work is decidedly complementary when seen together. Several of the group members are included in this survey. Rossmann takes his minimal approach one step further by working with black and white and in so doing he adds another level of reduction—the removal of color with all of its emotional associations, and the cultural and historical baggage that certain glazes imply. These works are intelligent meditations on form, surface, and material.

Fritz Rossmann
Amphoren, 1998
Stoneware
Left: h 20^1/$_2$ in., diam. 10 in.
h 52 cm, diam. 25.5 cm
Right: h 13^1/$_4$ in., diam. 6 in.
h 33.6 cm, diam. 15.3 cm

Magdalene Odundo burnishes her pots. This creates a similar effect to Rena's, except that Odundo's ancient technique involves polishing the surface with a smooth stone or other tool. She, too, is a British potter and an alumna of the Royal College of Art, London, but she draws from her African roots (she was born in Kenya) and her pots have the traditional purity and elegance that is so admired in the elegant coil-built vessels of sub-Saharan Africa. However, she does not dwell on either the ethnic or the historical association. From that point on, she abstracts, simplifies, and exaggerates to change formal relationships between the foot, belly, shoulder, neck, and lip of her pots. At one stage she used pit firing to create rich, textured, lustrous surfaces, but now focuses on very even monochromatic surfaces, mainly pumpkin and black.

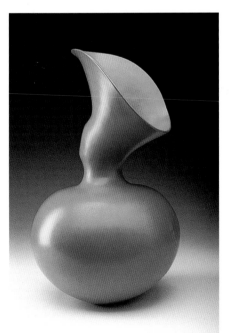 

Sueharu Fukami
Installation at Togakuda
Gallery, Kyoto, Japan,
1995

Celadon began life in the Sung dynasty in China, with mimetic intent. It was invented to resemble jade, a semi-precious stone treasured by the Chinese. The best celadon is the Sung dynasty porcelains which are unadorned and vibrate with a transcendent, translucent depth, as powerful a statement in minimalism as has ever been made. Color-wise, celadon comes in a score of tonal shifts from near clear glaze with just a hint of gray, green or blue to much deeper coloration—jade greens, light sky blues, and smoky, moody grays. The Japanese took celadon from both the Chinese and the Koreans and soon exceeded them as masters of this glaze. **Sueharu Fukami** and **Masamichi Yoshikawa** are two of Japan's finest contemporary celadon masters. Fukami seeks a pure surface on slab-built bowls and vases, as well as large sculptures he calls 'blades' and other totemic structures. His vessels are as rigorously minimal as his glazes are determinedly flawless. Nothing leaves his studio which has even the slightest flaw to interrupt the flowing silk of his surfaces. Yoshikawa makes bowls that are structurally complex and draws from cubist and constructivist inspiration. Yet the calming celadon flowing over the white porcelain structures creates unity and diminishes the complexity of the form.

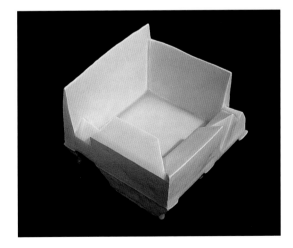

Above
Sueharu Fukami
Imagining the Box (Going),
1995
Porcelain
h 7⁷/₈ in., w 5¹/₈ in., d 4³/₄ in.
h 20 cm, w 13 cm, d 12 cm

Right
Masamichi Yoshikawa
An Open Space, 1998
Porcelain
h 6 in., w 12 in., d 12 in.
h 15.3 cm, w 30.5 cm,
d 30.5 cm

Many ceramists revere **Geert Lap** as the ultimate minimalist potter. His work is coveted and acquired as much by fellow artists as it is by collectors, a sure sign of esteem in his community. His admirers are as diverse as Ellsworth Kelly (a likely connection) and Claes Oldenburg (a less likely one). This Amsterdam-based artist has done for the vessel form what Donald Judd has done for sculpture. Personally unassuming and discretely private, he has never proselytized his style or tried to encourage a school based on his aesthetic. Nonetheless, he has acquired a commanding importance in this field through the example of his work and the deep regard that the ceramic community feels for his achievement. Working in stoneware, the forms are thrown with exacting precision—often dozens of pots are destroyed before one finally has the clarity of shape he demands. He colors the clay to match the terrasigillata surface (a fine suspension of slip which acts almost as a glaze), so that the integrity of the color is felt throughout the work as integral and not seen as an applied surface.

Above
Geert Lap
Untitled Blue Vessel, 1991
h 18¹/₂ in., 47 cm
Untitled Yellow Vessel, 1991
h 17¹/₂ in., 44.5 cm
Stoneware

Right
Geert Lap
Black Vase, 1993
Stoneware
h 12 in., diam. 8³/₄ in.
h 30.5 cm, diam. 22.2 cm

Opposite
Geert Lap
Massive White Vessel,
1997
Stoneware
h 31 in., diam. 30 in.
h 78.7 cm, diam. 76.2 cm

Chapter 3
Pattern and Decoration

Betty Woodman   Alison Britton   James Lawton
Joyce Kozloff   Rick Dillingham   Gary DiPasquale
Phillip Maberry   Gustavo Perez   Ralph Bacerra
Jacqueline Poncelet   Junko Kitamura

Above
Betty Woodman
*Somewhere Between
Denver and Naples*
Installation at the
Institute of Contemporary
Art, Philadelphia, PA,
1992

Opposite, left
Betty Woodman
Edo Fashion Pillow Pitcher,
1997
Whiteware
h 24 in., w 28 in., d 22 in.
h 61 cm, w 71 cm, d 56 cm

Opposite, right
Betty Woodman
Ostia, 1986
Whiteware
h 26$^{1}/_{2}$ in., w 17 in., d 17 in.
h 67.3 cm, w 43 cm,
d 43 cm

The exhibitions 'Pattern and Decoration' at P.S. 1 in New York in 1977 and 'Decorative Impulses' at the Institute for Contemporary Art in Philadelphia in 1979 changed the world for pattern and decoration. The acknowledgment that the decorative could also be serious art was perhaps one of the largest postmodern leaps over the bastion of modernist dogma. If there was one thing which united modernists it was their dislike of the decorative. Ceramics had never given up on this fanciful language and was one of the elements which kept this medium marginalized by the fine arts community. So this endorsement of the notion of decorative fine art, once thought to be a contradiction in terms, gave the decorative a new contemporary legitimacy and a future.

Pattern and Decoration was a formal movement founded by a group of artists in the 1970s and its founders included painters Robert Kushner, Miriam Schapiro, and Robert Zakanitch. Known as 'P and D', the movement also had a feminist edge, creating a sympathetic mood for the crafts in general and in particular those activities seen as women's crafts. Although not a member of the group, Judy Chicago's controversial, but populist, success, *The Dinner Party* (1979), a large collaborative installation work, with its china painted dinner plates and embroidered table runners, was a revisionist look at the role of women in history and was a beneficiary of this new freedom.

Two New York members of P and D, **Betty Woodman** and **Joyce Kozloff** (p. 60), work in ceramics. Woodman's husband, George, was one of the artists in the 'Nineteen Artists: Emergent Americans' exhibition at the Solomon R. Guggenheim Museum in New York (1981) and a convincing speaker and writer for the decorative cause. Until the mid-1970s he also decorated his wife's pottery, but then Woodman took this role on herself. Woodman's work was at first devoted to relatively traditional vessel forms, reflecting her functionalist background. The 'Pillow Pitcher', a large, round-bottomed vessel of Mediterranean origins, is her signature form, which was introduced in the late 1970s and is still part of her current form vocabulary. The 'spinach and egg' glazing of Tang pottery provided an initial impetus for her multi-hued surfaces. But she soon began to dissect the vessel and move it from the pedestal to the wall, taking a position somewhere between painting and sculpture.

In her annual exhibitions at the Max Protetch Gallery in New York, Woodman first placed her vase forms on wall-mounted plinths, then she removed the handles from the vessels, stylized them and nailed them to the wall. The handles spawned more complex environments of flat clay, painted with bright glazes which surrounded the central vessel. Indefatigable, Woodman's peripatetic exhibition program, both in the USA and abroad, and her ambitiousness to see ceramics appreciated alongside the highest canon of art, has had an enormous impact on the field. Kozloff also prefers to work on the wall. Aside from a few collaborative pottery forms produced together with Woodman, she has worked exclusively within the tile mural format, taking on large, ambitious public art projects.

Another of the leaders in the late 1970s and early 1980s was **Phillip Maberry**. For a while he and Woodman exhibited in the same New York gallery, the pioneering Hadler/Rodriguez, before her move to the Max Protetch Gallery. From the start Maberry was interested in placing his decorative ceramics in large installation settings. His gallery-sized work *Paradise Fountain* was one of the highlights of the 1983 Biennial at the Whitney Museum of American Art, New York. He was one of the few ceramists to have been invited to participate in this regular, high-profile survey of new art. He has continued to make both individual works, tendril-handled vases often on ceramic pedestals, and larger tile installations. The largest and the latest of these works was a 25,000 square foot (2,250 sq m) installation in a private home in Massachusetts in 1998.

Joyce Kozloff
Wilmington, Delaware
Train Station, 1984
Glazed ceramic tile
30 x 20 x 15 ft
9.1 x 6 x 4.5 m

Above
Phillip Maberry
Installation at Garth Clark
Gallery, New York, 1988

Right
Phillip Maberry
Sister Dimension, 1989
Earthenware
h 24¹/₄ in., w 25 in.
h 61.5 cm, w 63.5 cm

61

Jacqueline Poncelet and **Alison Britton** are both graduates from the Royal College of Art, London, one of the hotbeds of postmodernist insurgency during the early 1970s. These RCA students, several of whom are in this study, took a decidedly irreverent stance, rejecting both the limitations placed on them by modernism and the conservative stylistic expectations of the powerful Bernard Leach and his Anglo-Oriental school of vessel making. Poncelet's 1970s work was a series of groundbreaking bowls, small, but powerful, forms made from thinly cast bone china, over which flowed a variety of ceramic stains, taking on a special vitality on these translucent forms. She shifted to stoneware in the 1980s and the forms became larger and more assertive. While nominally vessels, they were certainly non-traditional, standing on the floor and leaning against the wall. But the decorative theme continued in their brilliantly hued glazed surfaces. Britton's work on angular slab-built forms was an important part of the 1980s growth of a tough new decorative aesthetic. She drew her inspiration from action painters such as Jackson Pollock.

Top
Jacqueline Poncelet
Form with Three Limbs and a Tail, 1984
Inlaid colored clay, painted with slips,
glazed and enamel painted
h 14 in., w 29 in., l 34 in.
h 35.5 cm, w 73.6 cm, l 86.4 cm

Above
Alison Britton
*Blue and White Two-part
Vessel*, 1987
Earthenware
h 13 in., w 24 in.
h 33 cm, w 61 cm

Rick Dillingham was both a student of and a dealer in rare Native American pottery. He was accustomed to studying and viewing many of these works reassembled from shards found in archaeological digs. This act, rebuilding a pot that has been destroyed, has a conceptual edge. It suggests that it is a cultural artifact which is worthy of rescue. Dillingham co-opted this system of assembling cultural evidence. His broken pots do not come apart by accident, but are carefully cut and scored before firing and then broken along precise lines, painting planes of color, panels of decoration and gilding certain elements, and reconstructing the parts. Mexico's great potter, **Gustavo Perez**, approaches the cutting of the vessel surface more with the feel of tribal mutilations and then turns them into rhapsodic plays with line and pattern, while making us acutely aware of the 'skin' that makes up the outer wall of every pot.

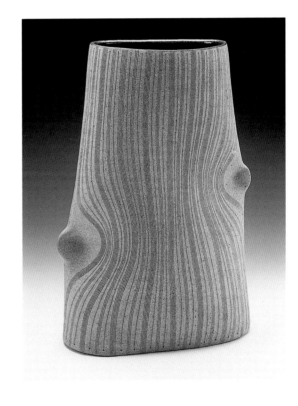

Above
Rick Dillingham
Large Globe, 1987
Raku, gold leaf
h 11 in., d 16 in.
h 28 cm, d 40.6 cm

Right
Gustavo Perez
Untitled Vase, 1995
Stoneware
h 12¹/₄ in., w 8¹/₂ in.
h 31 cm, w 21.5 cm

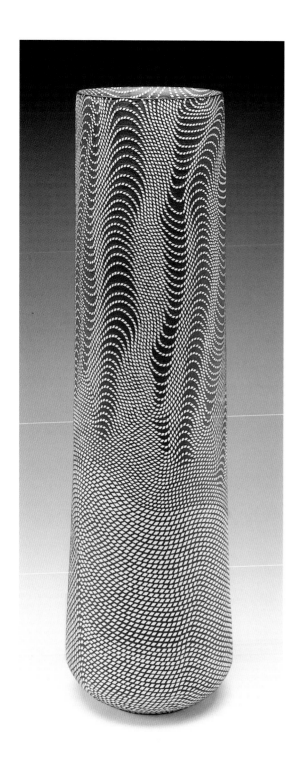

Above
Junko Kitamura
Untitled Vessel #8, 1993
Stoneware
h 21 in., d 5¹/₂ in.
h 53.3 cm, d 14 cm

Right
James Lawton
Teapot with Script, 1989
Terracotta
h 11 in., w 11 in., d 3¹/₂ in.
h 28 cm, w 28 cm, d 9 cm

Junko Kitamura pursues exacting craft in her studio in Kyoto, Japan. She pierces the surface of her pots with hundreds of tiny holes and then inlays white clay into the surface, an adaptation of the famous Mishima slip and rope impression technique from Korea's Koryu Dynasty; at the same time they suggest the swirling free-form drawings in the sand gardens of Buddhist temples. **James Lawton** works with raku, a technique developed by the early Japanese tea-bowl makers, which allows for a richness of color and immediacy of craft. Unlike other types of firing, which are lengthy, the raku forms are first bisque fired (unglazed) and then the glaze firing takes a matter of minutes in a special kiln. But Lawton does not rely upon the unpredictable nature of raku firing. His works are meticulously planned and controlled to get an even, brilliant finish. **Gary DiPasquale's** work is forthright and playful. He creates unique pieces and also makes handmade wares in large quantities for the design shops and stores such as Barneys in New York (where he lives), constantly evolving his surfaces, palette, and decorative style.

Gary DiPasquale
Striped Bottle, 1985
Stoneware
h 18 in., w 7¹/₄ in., d 6³/₄ in.
h 45.8 cm, w 18.4 cm,
d 17.1 cm

Ralph Bacerra is one of the leading decorative ceramists in the world today. This gifted potter derives his aesthetic mix from a diverse group of influences. Japanese Imari-style decoration is the root, but then he adds optical art both from princely seventeenth-century Edo Period Nabeshima wares and the dazzling virtuosity of M. C. Escher's interlocking imagery. Even Andy Warhol's paintings find their place in his work, particularly this pop artist's flower series which can be seen emerging through the many layers of jewel-colored overglaze in Bacerra's vessels. His works are first fired and glazed, usually with a plain white surface. Then they return to the kiln up to ten times, each time adding a layer of overglaze painting and firing in strict descending order of temperature. This is a complicated process, fraught with kiln accidents which result in a high mortality rate. But when they emerge successfully they are a dazzling brocade of rich color and texture which is without peer. As Ken Johnson, art critic for the *New York Times*, wrote in 1999, 'Sometimes one wishes avantgarde art could be so unashamedly sumptuous.'

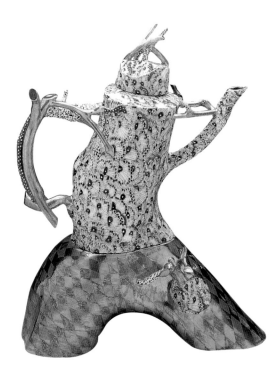

Opposite
Ralph Bacerra
Portrait Vessel, 1994
Whiteware
h 32¹/₂ in., w 18 in.
h 82.5 cm, w 45.8 cm

Above
Ralph Bacerra
Untitled Platter, 1988
Whiteware
diam. 22 in.
diam. 56 cm

Right
Ralph Bacerra
Branch Teapot, 1990
Whiteware
h 17 in.
h 43 cm

Chapter 4
The Multiple Vessel

Andrew Lord   James Makins   Jeanne Quinn
Gwyn Hanssen Pigott Bobby Silverman Emil Heger
Elsa Rady   Kim Dickey   Piet Stockmans

The notion of a serial aesthetic in ceramics is inborn. As Omar Khayyám (1048–1131) wrote, 'along the wall stood pot after pot,' adding a critical note, 'some were articulate and some were not.' Potters, particularly those who work on the wheel, tend to work in series, making large numbers of identical or similar forms at a single sitting. This is partly because of the process of ceramics. Firing a single vessel is rarely cost effective so the unfired forms gather like squads of soldiers awaiting their call to the kiln. Also, repetitive forming of the same shape again and again allows the potter to understand the form more intimately, and in so doing, achieve an effortless eloquence. Then there is a tradition of the painted still life. From Pablo Picasso to Giorgio Morandi, Vincent Van Gogh, and Georges Braque, pottery has tended to be the visual anchor of most still-life compositions. Contemporary ceramists have begun to reverse the compliment and draw inspiration from the paintings in which these pots appear, returning them to the three-dimensional realm, but retaining some painterly associations.

British-born **Andrew Lord** was not the first artist to see the promise in reversing the still-life process. Lucio Fontana, for instance, had done this in the 1940s. But Lord is the artist who radicalized the concept and took it further than anyone before or since. Interested in the way vessels were abstracted by the painters and by the play of light which enhanced the abstracting process, he began to haunt museums and carefully studied these compositions. He experimented in the 1970s, creating vessel groupings of two or three pots and lighting them so that there was a specific play of light on the work (morning, afternoon, natural, artificial). Lord then painted the chiaroscuro of light and shade with glaze on the surface. In his 1980 American debut at Blum/Helman, a pace-setting New York gallery, Lord entranced the critics with a masterful show which filled the gallery's cavernous space. In response to his later 1986 exhibition, Christopher Knight, then the art critic of the *Los Angeles Herald Examiner*, wrote, 'Pictorial traditions of painting constitute the realm from which Lord's sculptures have forthrightly emerged. Formally, he is amongst a handful of artists who have been slowly but surely rescuing pictorial sculpture from the hell of exhaustion and redundancy to which it had been consigned for more than twenty years.'

By this stage Lord's groupings had grown beyond the tradition of the modest, tasteful accumulations he had researched and they now comprised as many as sixty vessels in a single work. Over the years his treatment of the surface has altered. Now his surfaces are not painterly, but more visceral, dealing with primal experience such as touching, biting, and smelling.

Andrew Lord
Five Pieces. Fist. Tin., 1992
Ceramic, epoxy, gold leaf,
and encre de chine
Base: h 1 ft, w 8 ft, d 4 ft
h 30 cm, w 2.4 m, d 1.2 m

Andrew Lord
Twelve Mexican Pieces,
First Round, 1995–98
Ceramic, epoxy, gold leaf
and encre de chine
various dimensions

Australian potter **Gwyn Hanssen Pigott** came to the still life by a more banal route. An accomplished functional potter (she worked with the pioneering workshop potter Michael Cardew in Britain and with traditional stoneware potters in France), she made exceptionally beautiful porcelain bowls and bottles, but found that when shown individually in exhibitions, these beautiful vessels were ignored, seemingly too traditional. In one exhibition she spontaneously decided to exhibit the work in a carefully composed grouping and quite suddenly it was noticed. Realizing that she was invading the still-life tradition, she began to delve into painters who specialized in this work and in the process fell in love with the work of Giorgio Morandi, an artist who spent his life painting a handful of bottle and bowl forms on a small tabletop. The delicate coloration of Pigott's wood-fired porcelains—soft tans, creams, mochas, and off-whites—perfectly matched Morandi's muted and limited palette, and a kind of posthumous marriage was born between painter and potter.

Elsa Rady refers to her multiple vessel groupings as paintings, making her intended relationship to the still life very clear. In these works she brings the same sweep of movement of her earlier forms. **James Makins** makes some of the finest contemporary functional wares in the ceramics world (this is still a field dominated by conservative potters working in the Anglo-Oriental Leach school). These wares were exquisitely made with the accentuated throwing rings spiraling up the walls of his teapots, cups, pitchers, bowls, vases, and candlesticks. When he decided to make a more sculptural statement he massed thin-necked bottles, the white porcelain body stained in bright acid greens, yellows, and blues, and assembled them on a large platter, all of the surfaces swirling with throwing lines like demented candy-colored dervishes.

Above, left
Gwyn Hanssen Pigott
Still Life #2, 1995
(7 pieces)
Porcelain
h 10 in.
h 25.5 cm

Above, right
Gwyn Hanssen Pigott
Dark Still Life, 1993–94
Porcelain
h 10¹/₂ in.
h 26.8 cm

Above
Elsa Rady
Still Life #59, 1999
Porcelain and steel shelf
h 21 in., w 18 in., d 12 in.
h 53.3 cm, w 45.8 cm,
d 30.5 cm

Right
James Makins
Scrovegni, 1992
Porcelain
h 11 in., diam. 20 in.
h 28 cm, diam. 50.8 cm

73

Bobby Silverman
Installation at
Farrell/Pollack Fine Art,
Brooklyn, NY, 2000

Chapter 5
Organic Abstraction

Claudi Casanovas

Jean-François Fouilhoux

Lawson Oyekan

Angus Suttie

Kathy Butterly

Babs Haenen

Irene Vonck

Tony Marsh

Steve Heinemann

Chris Gustin

Geo Lastomirsky

There is an unfounded belief that organic form is the 'natural' response to clay. Many ceramists argue against this popular notion saying that the only natural clay is that which man has not yet mined from the ground. Everything we do to clay thereafter is unnatural and a process of deliberate manufacture, including filtering, throwing, firing, and glazing. This is true. Clay, as we will discover later, is the ultimate plastic chameleon and can be many things of which organic form is but one option. But organic form and clay do have a long and special history. Clay easily takes on surfaces and shapes of the natural world and potters have exploited this affinity for millennia.

Man's first pots were gourds, frequently inspirations for the earliest ceramic vessels. At times they even served as molds for shaping these vessels. Pots were also modeled from baskets, themselves made from woven reeds, leaves, twigs, and bark. Throughout time, potters have sought to create man-made ceramic forms which echo the sensibilities of nature, sometimes by mimicking nature or through stylization and abstraction. The history of ceramics is filled with organic masterpieces—the lidded Sung dishes in the shape of a melon, flower-encrusted potpourri containers from Meissen and Sèvres, the cabbage, cauliflower, and pineapple teapots of mid-eighteenth-century Staffordshire, and the delicate erotic undulations of art-nouveau style flowers and plant forms by Alf Wallender at Rörstrand, Hector Guimard at Sèvres, and other fin-de-siècle potters.

This style comes across as a kind of deistic collaboration between 'the maker and The Maker' as Garth Clark notes in his catalog essay, 'Rising Above the Polemic,' for 'Pandora's Box,' an exhibition curated by the late Ewen Henderson and organized in 1995 by the British Crafts Council in London. 'Organic Abstraction creates less of a confrontation between the viewer and the artist's ego,' he argues. 'When a pot is covered with glazes whose textures are torn from nature and the palette is drawn from the colors of rocks and plants, the viewer tends to see the work as not being solely the result of the artist's skills but as part of a partnership with nature's gifts. It matters not to the viewer that the seemingly spontaneous trickles, bubbles and flowing melding colors took as much intervention and conscious artfulness to create as Barbizon School china painting on a ceramic basket.'

Above
Claudi Casanovas
Large Swirl Plate, 1991
Stoneware
diam. 56 in.
diam. 142 cm

Opposite
Claudi Casanovas
Pedra Foguera—L'Afrau, 1996
Stoneware
h 29 in., w 47 in.
h 74 cm, w 120 cm

Tony Marsh from Long Beach, California, and Canadian Steve Heinemann (p. 90) take on the organic with more of a sense of distance and reduction. There are no ragged edges, no allusions to volcanoes, no chunks of ice, or beckoning floral sexuality. The basic form is symmetrical, almost classical, and, if anything, both use vessel shapes which recall early wooden Polynesian serving bowls. Marsh has two faces to his work, one is the white pierced vessels which seem to be drilled from salt-rock, while his other work presents what seem to be 'paleo-botanical' fossil collections in archaic muffin tins. Heinemann evokes nature in a very sophisticated and controlled vessel, combining the strict geometry that underlies all of nature's life forms with beautifully painted surfaces which resemble everything from layers of schist to rusting metal as it oxidizes and returns to the elements.

Tony Marsh
Reliquary, 1995
Earthenware
h 5 in., w 28 in., d 24 in.
h 12.7 cm, w 71 cm,
d 61 cm

Steve Heinemann
Untitled, 1998
Earthenware with
multiple firings
h 6 in., w 6 in., l 13 in.
h 15.3 cm, w 15.3 cm,
l 33 cm

Two Americans, **Chris Gustin** and **Geo Lastomirsky**, have both created organic-cultural hybrids. Gustin's vessels, with their sand-blasted, satin-glazed surfaces, take on the unlikely form of a Peruvian stirrup pot, and yet intimate that it has arrived as the consequence of nature rather than by the intervention of man. Lastomirsky's teapot takes on two Chinese art traditions at once. Firstly, it is in the tradition of the Yixing teapots, the production and design of which was supported by the late Ming Chinese literati. He has merged this with another aesthetic pursuit of the literati, scholar's rocks. These were rocks selected by connoisseurs for their aesthetic beauty and treasured as art objects. Lastomirsky seemingly removes the handle and spout so that their function is secondary to their presence as natural objects.

Above, left
Chris Gustin
Stirrup Pot, 1995
Stoneware
h 14 in., w 12 in., d 10 in.
h 35.5 cm, w 30.5 cm,
d 25.5 cm

Above, right
Geo Lastomirsky
Teapot #34, 1997
Terracotta, unglazed,
mixed media
h 7 in., w 9^1/$_2$ in., d 6^1/$_2$ in.
h 17.8 cm, w 24 cm, d 16.5 cm

Chapter 6
The Real/Super-Real

Marilyn Levine   Stefano Della Porta   Lu Wen Xia
Paul Dresang   Luis Miguel Suro   Zhou Ding Fang
Richard Shaw   Frank Steyaert   Ah Leon

The Real/Super-Real

Above, left
Marilyn Levine
HRH Briefcase, 1985
Ceramic, zipper, metal rings
h 16 in., w 17 in., d 6³/₄ in.
h 40.6 cm, w 43 cm,
d 17.1 cm

Above, right
Marilyn Levine
Bob's Jacket, 1990
Ceramic, zipper, metal rings
h 33¹/₂ in., w 21 in., d 7³/₄ in.
h 85 cm, w 53.3 cm, d 19.7 cm

Opposite
Paul Dresang
Untitled, 1998
Porcelain
h 17 in.
h 43 cm

Realism, another orphan from the modernism wars, returned to fine-art respectability in the 1960s by making itself more real than life. In a final paradox, by challenging the eye to believe the manufactured evidence, this simultaneously made the work feel disturbingly unreal and so provides it with its inherent tension and content. Critic Edward Lucie-Smith writes that in worldly terms it is the only innovative style to achieve a marked commercial success in the late 1960s and early 1970s, although that success was more with collectors than the museums who remained skeptical of its popularity. The style was known variously as super-realism, hyper-realism, sharp focus realism, photo realism, photographic realism, illusionistic realism, and, in ceramics, the Super-Object.

The new super-realist painters used the trompe-l'oeil technique to render images startlingly three dimensional as they seemed to leap from canvases. Other painters recorded imagery with the meticulous fidelity of the camera. Malcolm Morley (who coined the term super-realism for his style) was one of the pioneers together with Richard Estes, Mel Ramos, Audrey Flack, and others. In sculpture, it was John De Andrea's nudes, exact down to bristling underarm and pubic hair, and Duane Hanson's startling portraits of seemingly alive Miami tourists, hippies, and security guards. The ceramic star of the movement was **Marilyn Levine** whose leather objects made from stoneware challenged the mind to refuse the evidence presented to the eye.

The concept was not new to ceramics. Levine's clay-into-leather transition has been explored since medieval times when leather vessels were copied, complete with stitching marks. The realism at that stage was crudely rendered. By the nineteenth century, ceramic novelty items such as copper-rimmed 'leather' jugs were being manufactured in ceramics by England's Royal Doulton factory in Stoke-on-Trent with eye-popping exactness. Levine's work took this a step further so that the pieces became a kind of conceptual art form. Some admirers validate her art as being about the 'human histories' recorded by the wear and tear on leather, but this does not ring true. While leather does retain the history of its use, Levine could have communicated this more satisfactorily and with greater tactile conviction by taking the actual leather objects she so closely copies and placing them on a pedestal rather than making them in clay. The work is not about history, it is about transition from one state to another, while retaining the disguise of its former life. **Paul Dresang** approaches leather from a decidedly different angle, playing with zippers, phallic elements, and sexual undercurrents to introduce leather's erotic S & M associations.

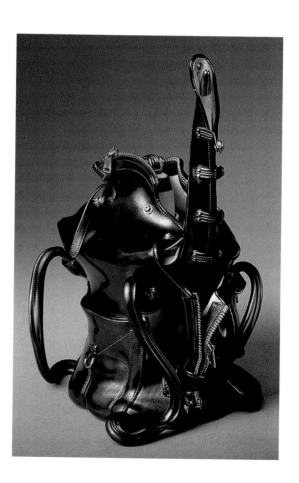

Richard Shaw mimics a wide range of objects and materials, using both the clay and painted faux finish to make his point. His work is a mix of subject matter we find in the American realist paintings of nineteenth-century masters John F. Haberle and John F. Peto and the virtuoso craftsmanship of eighteenth-century porcelain factories such as Niederviller, which produced entire dinner services in faux wood surface with renderings of what seemed to be paper prints attached to and peeling off the surface. Shaw is the leader of what Garth Clark labeled in 1979 as the Super-Object school and remains one of its most gifted practitioners. Like Levine, he lives and works in San Francisco's Bay Area, one of the centers, together with Seattle and Los Angeles, of the Super-Object.

Richard Shaw
Seated Figure with Gray Head, 1985
Porcelain
h 33 in.
h 83.8 cm

Italian artist **Stefano Della Porta** and Mexican sculptor **Luis Miguel Suro** (pp. 98, 99) both find the 'super' in super-real through increasing the scale of their work. Della Porta's work, gigantic ashtrays filled with cigarette butts, and pills, are at once beautiful because of their superb craftsmanship and horrific because they dramatize addiction blown up to giant proportions. Suro also makes larger than life statements, strewing galleries with giant ear swabs, sperms, antacid tablets, and other identifiable objects of hygiene, procreation, and indigestion.

Above
Richard Shaw
Canton Lighthouse, 1985
Porcelain
h 25¹/₂ in.
h 64.7 cm

Right
Stefano Della Porta
Anxiety, 1999
Ceramic
h 12 in., diam. 29 in.
h 30.5 cm, diam. 73.6 cm

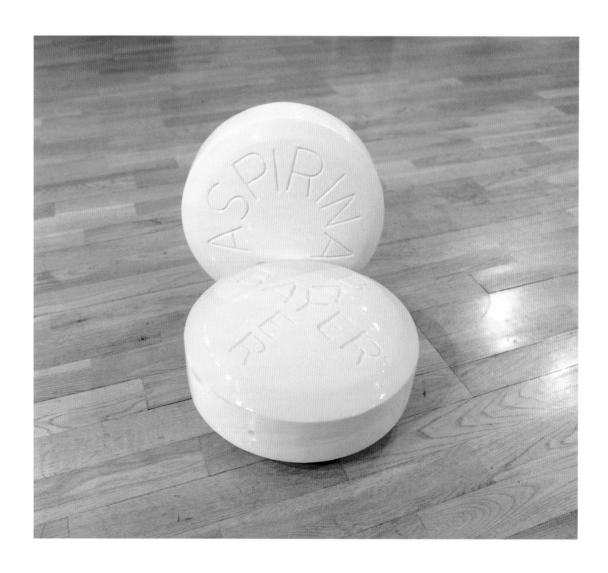

Above
Luis Miguel Suro
Aspirina, 1998
Ceramic
h 12 in., d 6 in.
h 30.5 cm, d 15.3 cm

Opposite
Luis Miguel Suro
Daily Plagiarism, 1999
Installation at Leonora
Vega Gallery, New York,
1999

Belgian artist **Frank Steyaert's** sculpture of wrecked ships explores the decay of wood translated through clay and kiln. They are made both as individual works and as parts of impressive large landscapes such as the massive and memorable exhibition of Steyaert's work at the Vlaams Cultureel Centrum de Brakke Grond which was one of the highlights of the Ceramic Millennium Arts Festival in Amsterdam, 1999. The boats are made with precision, almost plank by plank, but at the same time the artist puts the work on a cusp between mimicking wood and celebrating clay, something of a time-honored passion in ceramics.

Frank Steyaert
Untitled, 1998
Stoneware
h 22¹/₂ in., w 17 in., d 52³/₄ in.
h 57.2 cm, w 43 cm, d 134 cm

Frank Steyaert
Composed Group, 1990
Stoneware
h 6¹/₄–30¹/₄ in. each
h 16–76.8 cm each

Top
Left: **Zhou Ding Fang**
On the Edge, 1999
Stoneware, h 4$^1/_2$ in., 11.4 cm
Right: **Lu Wen Xia and Lu Jiangxin**
Melting Bamboo, 1999
Stoneware, h 9 in., 23 cm

Above
Ah Leon
The Bridge, 1997
Installation at Arthur M. Sackler
Gallery/Freer Gallery of Art, Smithsonian
Institution, Washington, DC
l. 60 ft, 18 m

Steyaert's mimetic game is well known to China's Yixing potters who have been using clay to present faithful replicas of nuts, rocks, fabric, bamboo, and tree trunks for about five hundred years. Two of the current masters of the trompe-l'oeil style of Yixing wares are the young women artists **Lu Wen Xia** and **Zhou Ding Fang**. They live and work in this pottery town and use the fine-grained beauty of Yixing's distinctive stoneware clays to imitate burlap, bamboo, leather, and other materials.

Ah Leon (his Chinese name is Ching-Liang Chen) lives and works across the Formosa Straits of Taipei, Taiwan, but has his roots in the traditions of Yixing pottery. As is suggested by the title of a recent book on his work, *Beyond Yixing: The Ceramic Art of Ah Leon*, he believes he has outgrown this connection. Certainly he has outgrown any scale restraints that Yixing, known for its intimate two to four inch (5–10 cm) high teapots, might have imposed. *The Bridge* (1997), a three-year labor of love, was first shown in its entirety at the Arthur M. Sackler Gallery/Freer Gallery of Art, Smithsonian Institution, Washington, DC, and then traveled through the USA. The piece is described by Garth Clark in *Beyond Yixing* as, 'arguably the most monumental and mesmerizing work of trompe l'oeil ceramics ever made.'

Sixty foot (18 meters) in length, it is an amazing sight. Every piece from the seemingly metal nails to the hundreds of wood planks is modeled by hand, using a needle to striate and imitate weathered wood grain. As with his tree-trunk teapots, Ah Leon refuses to mold his work from actual pieces of wood, even though it would speed up the process dramatically, saying that if he did this he would not 'own' the work. It is important to him that he invent each piece of wood and its history. As a Bonsai master, Ah Leon can point to any section of his wood look-alikes and be able to explain how the weathered surface would have been created in nature, whether the erosion came from wind or rain and how many years it would take for such a surface to make its appearance. This intimacy of knowledge about both the reality of wood and his grasp of clay's mimetic power is what gives him his mastery of the super-real.

Above, left
Ah Leon
Vertical Log Teapot, 1992
Stoneware
h 17 in., w 15 in.
h 43 cm, w 38 cm

Above, right
Ah Leon
Double Spouted Branch Teapot,
1992
Stoneware
h 8 in., w 32 in., d 6 in.
h 20.3 cm, w 81.3 cm, d 15.3 cm

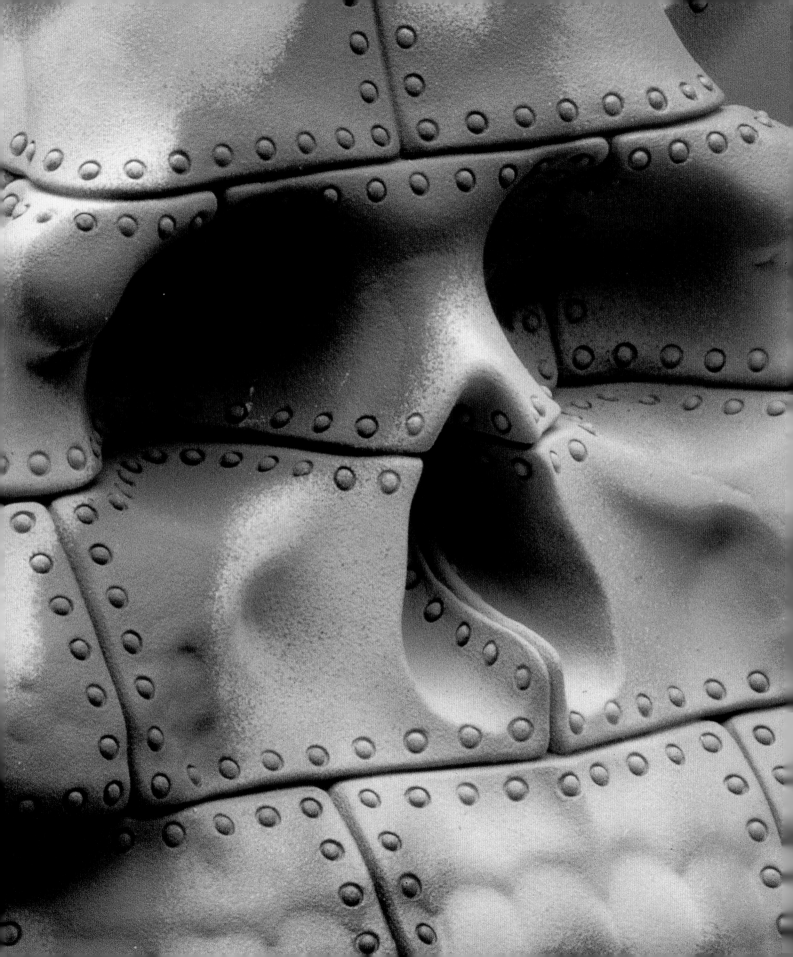

Chapter 7
History, Culture, and Time

Richard Notkin   Robert Dawson   Cindy Kolodziejski
Hilbert Boxem   Paul Scott   Léopold Foulem
Richard Slee   Richard Milette   Kohei Nakamura
Charles Krafft   Grayson Perry   Adrian Saxe

One of the main goals of modernism was to brush off the dust of the past and to create something entirely new. In part, this was disgust with historicism which had been responsible for an enormous outpouring of mindless, decadent art and decoration. This was made worse by the ability of industry to manufacture pastiches of past styles in enormous quantities. So the modernist's deliberate ban on quoting directly from the past was understandable and necessary. As modernism progressed, however, it was clear that no artist works without connections to his or her past, nor without inspiration from the history of art and that finally, 'newness' was in itself something of a myth. New styles do not arrive overnight by immaculate conception, but are the result of an evolution of ideas over time. The potter Bernard Leach was fond of quoting William Blake, who said that in order to innovate, the artist must first 'drive horse and cart over the bones of the dead.'

One of the most distinctive and controversial aspects of postmodernism is appropriation. At its most extreme end appropriation can involve the exact remaking of a work by an artist, such as Sherrie Levine's drawings in the style of Kazimir Malevich or Mike Bidlo's remake of Marcel Duchamp's *Fountain*, which seem nearly identical to the originals. More usually appropriation is akin to sampling in rap music where the artist lifts identifiable elements and incorporates them into their work, but within a new context which can be humorous, instructive, ironic, or satiric.

Appropriation has allowed ceramists to play with their long 30,000-year-old history. Dipping into this treasure chest has always been a passion for the ceramist. The interest is twofold. The ceramist is fascinated by the style and social context of earlier work, but is also challenged by trying to re-create the processes that brought that work to life—the clays, glazes, and firing techniques.

Yixing is a well spring for this approach. The most important artist in the revival of Western interest in Yixing is the American **Richard Notkin** who became obsessed by the intelligence, beauty, and communicative power of the small Yixing teapots. The first of these teapots were made around 1526 during the late Ming period. The potters of Yixing were the first in China to make teapots and the first to become known as individual artists, ending the anonymity of the Chinese potters by signing the work with their 'chop', an impressed character seal. In addition, they collaborated with the Chinese intelligentsia—poets, actors, writers, connoisseurs, scholars—who designed some teapots themselves, wrote poems to be inscribed on their sides and debated the beauty, symbolism, and meaning of these finely crafted, hand-built vessels.

Notkin is a junkie for politics. He had a satellite dish installed so he could watch the gavel to gavel debates of the US congress on C-Span. Notkin felt that he could take the universal symbolism of the Yixing teapot as its form had meaning to the Chinese, such as a peach for longevity, a Buddha's hand citron for good luck, or a pomegranate covered in nuts to promise numerous offspring, and give it a contemporary edge. His symbols dealt with the USA's questionable nuclear energy programs, foreign policy, and military adventures. He chose symbols which communicated readily, avoiding closed-shop art world esotericism. For instance, his inclusion of dice meant gambling with lives. He used nuts differently from the Chinese to mean literally 'nuts', as in insane. Mushroom cloud finials on top of teapots shaped like nuclear cooling towers explain the dangers of the energy source that even the least informed viewers could understand.

All Notkin's forms have their roots in traditional Yixing teapots. The heart teapots were inspired by the Buddha's hand teapot, a form based on the citron fruit which also resembles a human heart with its ventricles and clavicles. His hearts are presented as small tabletop monuments of man's inhumanity to man, playing to the Western symbolism of this organ as the source of the human conscience. Notkin's work has not only been a source of inspiration and delight to the Yixing potters themselves, but also to many other artists from Taiwan's Ah Leon to the USA's Geo Lastomirsky.

Above, left
Richard Notkin
Cooling Towers Teapot (variation #2)—Yixing Series, 1983
Stoneware
h 6 in., w 9 in., d 3³/₄ in.
h 15.3 cm, w 23 cm, d 9.5 cm

Above, right
Richard Notkin
Hexagonal Curbside Teapot (variation #17)—Yixing Series, 1988
Stoneware
h 5 in., w 7⁷/₈ in., d 4 in.
h 12.7 cm, w 20 cm, d 10 cm

Above, left
Richard Notkin
Heart Teapot: Mace II–
Yixing Series, 1988
Stoneware, luster
h 6 in., l 40 in., d 6¼ in.
h 15.3 cm, l 101.6 cm, d 16 cm

Above, right
Richard Notkin
Pyramidal Skull Teapot: Military
Intelligence III–Yixing Series, 1989
Stoneware, glaze
h 6 in., w 9⅛ in., d 7 in.
h 15.3 cm, w 23.2 cm, d 17.8 cm

Dutch sculptor **Hilbert Boxem** has recently completed a series of works which abstract high points in ceramic history—Greek attic vase painting, Hispano Moresque luster decoration, the graphic beauty of Chinese and Delft blue and white. He then creates a surreal twisted form in which fragments of the particular style, in this case the classical Greek vase, are distorted and converted from vessel to pure sculpture. **Richard Slee**, one of the most persistently inventive postmodern artists in Britain, worked with the eighteenth-century Staffordshire tradition of the toby jug in the early 1990s. Toby jugs were novelty vessels in the form of a human figure which have remained popular since the late eighteenth century and are still in production today. Often they were portraits of known personalities. But Slee shifts them out of time and place by making them monumental (four to five times their usual scale) and combining them with both highbrow and lowbrow influences. His toby jugs are presented in a variety of modernist styles, from Cubism to Abstract Expressionism, and in one of his masterpieces, *Acid Toby* (1993), a 'happy face' masks the face of the jug, referencing both pop culture and the photo montages of the artist John Baldessari.

Top
Hilbert Boxem
*The Open Container
Greece I*, 1999
Earthenware
h 9 in.
h 23 cm

Above, near right
Richard Slee
Acid Toby, 1993
Earthenware
h 19 in.
h 48.3 cm

Above, far right
Richard Slee
Fuzzy Toby Jug, 1994
Earthenware
h 16 in.
h 40.6 cm

Blue and white is the most popular form of decoration in the entire history of ceramics and the eighteenth-century blue willow pattern which draws from this tradition is the most successful single pattern ever devised for ceramic ware, still in production in massive quantities today. So when one sees this distinctive surface it evokes any number of connections from one's grandparents' dinner service, to Chinese Ming blue-and-white export wares, eighteenth-century Dutch Delft, or more commonly today, those nasty little airport souvenirs at Schipol Airport, Amsterdam, of little clogs in blue-and-white ceramic. No other style of decoration is more ubiquitous or more relentlessly popular.

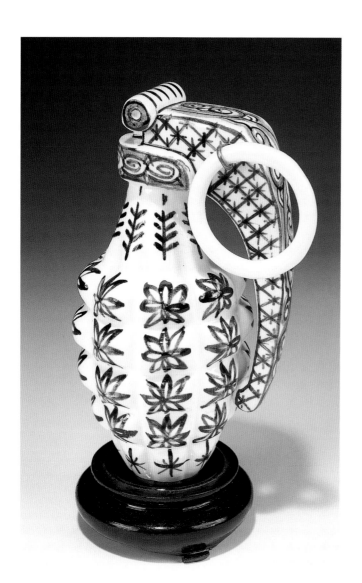

History, Culture, and Time   **Charles Krafft**
*Porcelain War Museum
Project: Frag Grenade*,
2000
Porcelain
h 5^1/$_4$ in., w 2^1/$_2$ in.
h 13.3 cm, w 6.4 cm

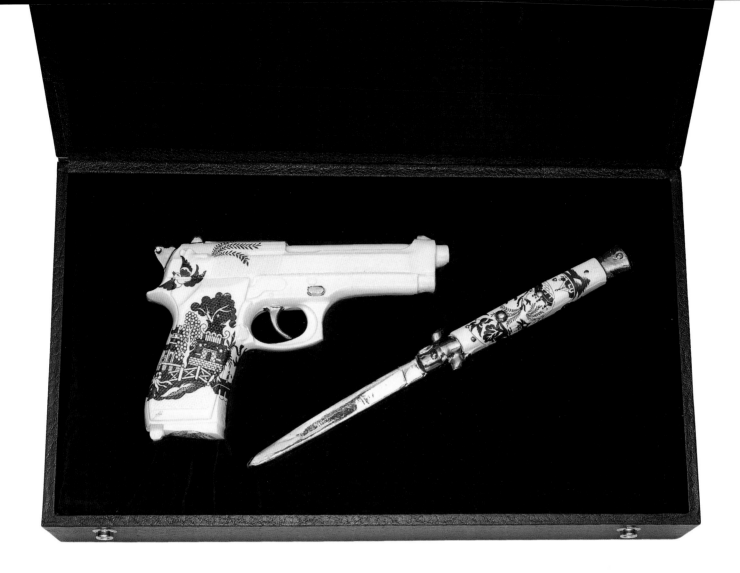

Charles Krafft
Porcelain War Museum
Project: Assassination Kit,
2000
Porcelain
Box: h 2 in., w 14³/₄ in., d 8 in.
h 5 cm, w 37.5 cm, d 20.3 cm

In this chapter, four artists are discussed who have appropriated blue and white for their own purposes— **Charles Krafft** (pp. 110, 111), who is American, **Robert Dawson** and **Paul Scott**, who are British, and the French Canadian member of the Quebecois Clay group, **Richard Milette**. Each has something different to say. Krafft is one of the USA's most seditious artists and plays difficult, uneasy games with content and culture. His blue-and-white works began in earnest with his 'Disasterwares' which satirized the common souvenir plate. They 'celebrated' tragic events such as the bombing of Dresden in the Second World War and the sinking of the Titanic with tongue-in-cheek adherence to populist style. Around 1998 he began to make replicas of East European weaponry, which was used by the Communist secret police, for his Porcelain War Museum Project held at the Ministry of Defense in the Republic of Slovenia in 1999, decorating the weapons with the friendly domesticity of blue-and-white decoration, disturbingly at odds with the forms of death they embellished.

Above, left
Robert Dawson
In Perspective, 1996
Bone china
diam. 10¹/₂ in., 26.8 cm

Above, right
Robert Dawson
Can you walk from the garden,
does your heart understand, 1996
Bone china
diam. 10¹/₂ in., 26.8 cm

Opposite, above
Paul Scott
The Scott Collection, Sellafield, Cumbrian
Blue(s) (from The Beckermet Road), 1997
Screen print. Inglaze blue decal on
bone china
diam. 9³/₄ in., 24.8 cm, edition of 10

Dawson uses blue-and-white decorated plates as the subject matter for his own plates, but is inventive in the way in which he gives these appropriated plates a sense of movement and dimension within his plate. Scott makes plates that comment on the fact that blue and white was a staple of the ceramic industry, painting landscapes of industrial gloom which are very different from the bucolic scenes that these factories placed on their own wares. Lastly, there is Milette who invokes blue and white as 'cultural treasure' in his mantelpiece garniture set of vases. The handles are grand and gilded, but the vessels are made up of blue-and-white shards and suggest an archaeological, museum context.

Right
Richard Milette
Garniture with Blue and
White Shards, 1995
Ceramic
Middle: h 17 in.; the set: w 25 in., d 5 in.
Middle: h 43 cm; the set: w 63.5 cm, d 12.7 cm

Grayson Perry and **Cindy Kolodziejski** both have a fascination with Victorian über-kitsch. Perry explores this in his own way with a deliberate sense of the amateur or, at the very least, an outsider to the ceramic arts. Even though there is a sly magic in his use of ceramics, it reveals no overt virtuosity at all. The forms are a little lumpen, the handling of the clay suggests folk craft, rather than a sophisticated artist who actually lives and works in London, until one begins to put together all the elements—drawings, relief modeling, decals, lusters, and increasingly beautiful glazes. Then it becomes apparent what a remarkable vision is being presented. The drawings that cover the surface are often obscene and provocative. To this is added a plethora of related decal images, mostly overly decorative and of a regressive taste. His subject matter includes family histories (both his own and that of the royals), incest, the lives of the super-models, and Perry's personal involvement in gender-bending, all competing to evoke the crowded, fussy milieu of Victorian decorative arts.

Above, left
Grayson Perry
Revenge of the Alison Girls, 2000
Earthenware
h 26 in., w 10$^1/_4$ in., d 10$^1/_4$ in.
h 66 cm, w 26 cm, d 26 cm

Above, right
Grayson Perry
Language of Cars, 2000
Earthenware
h 15$^3/_8$ in., w 11 in., d 11 in.
h 39 cm, w 28 cm, d 28 cm

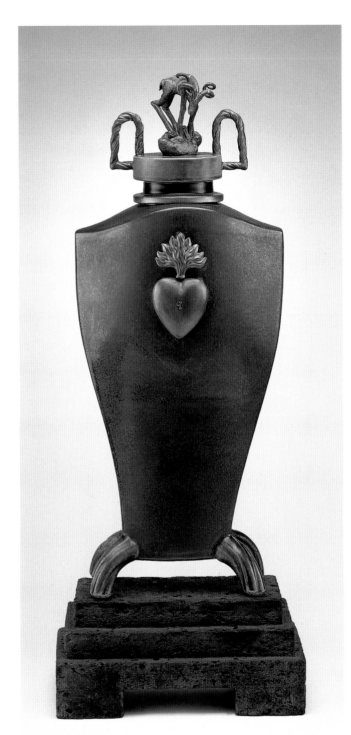

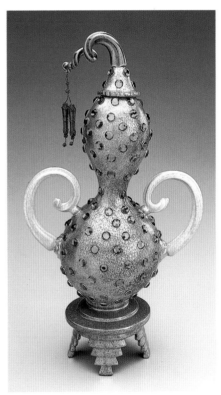

Above, left
Adrian Saxe
*Untitled Covered Jar on Stand with
Antelope Finial*, 1984
Porcelain, raku, and stoneware
h 26¹/₂ in., w 10¹/₂ in., d 5¹/₂ in.
h 67.3 cm, w 26.8 cm, d 14 cm

Above, right
Adrian Saxe
Post-Bungee Grin, 1990
Porcelain
h 13¹/₄ in., w 7¹/₂ in.
h 33.6 cm, w 19 cm

History, Culture, and Time **Adrian Saxe**
Virgule, 1990
Porcelain and wood
h 23³/₄ in., w 37 in.
h 60.3 cm, w 94 cm

Above, and right (detail)
Adrian Saxe
Installation for
'Departures: 11 Artists at
the Getty' at J. Paul Getty
Museum, Los Angeles,
2000

Chapter 8
The Image and the Vessel

Anne Kraus   Edward Eberle
Matt Nolen   Daniel Kruger
Kurt Weiser   Lidya Buzio

The use of imagery with story content is one of the threads that makes 1980s ceramic art different from that of earlier periods in the twentieth century. The modernist ideal of pottery was of simple shape with a monochrome glaze devoid of pattern and any literal imagery. This was revenge on the Edwardian regime of pink rose decals which Grayson Perry so mischievously exploits. Plain surfaces, flowing abstract glazes, and unspecific marks were acceptable, but imagery was considered regressive which makes the 1960s breakthrough work of Michael Frimkess and Howard Kottler all the more impressive and courageous. This allowed for the narrative to return to ceramics, a long-term role for the humble pot going back 2,000 years to the days when Greek black-figure painters illustrated scenes from mythology, titillated by recording sexual practices, and captured other everyday moments of life. Much of the understanding of the Olympic games, for instance, comes from sports illustrations on Greek pots.

In the work of **Anne Kraus** imagery takes on an unusually personal and emotional content. Kraus came to ceramics as a painter. On visits to the Metropolitan Museum of Art in New York she would linger over the German and French court porcelains and marvel at their beauty, while at the same time disliking the fact that the exquisitely painted images on them had no emotional depth, what Léopold Foulem denounced as 'scenes of insipid heterosexuality'. She began to conceive of using the pot as a vehicle for recording highly personal moments. As the filmmaker Karel Reisz comments, collecting her work is like having illicit access to a private diary, each pot another page torn from her life.

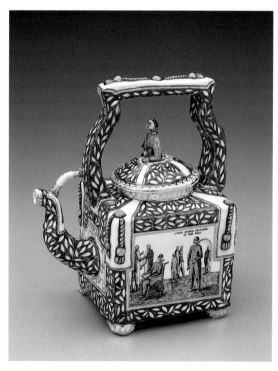

Above, left
Anne Kraus
Heroes Teapot, 1989
Whiteware
h 8 in., w 6$^{1}/_{2}$ in., d 4 in.
h 20.3 cm, w 16.5 cm,
d 10 cm

Above, right
Anne Kraus
The LKS/NKS Vase, 1991
Whiteware
h 9$^{1}/_{2}$ in., w 6 in.
h 24 cm, w 15.3 cm

Opposite
Anne Kraus
*China Cup Motel (Double Vase
with Base)*, 1999
Whiteware
h 14$^{1}/_{2}$ in., w 14 in., d 8$^{1}/_{2}$ in.
h 36.8 cm, w 35.5 cm, d 21.5 cm

The notion of a diary is very close to Kraus' way of working. She keeps a dream diary at her bedside which forms the core of her subject matter, delving into painful issues—crises of confidence, unrequited love, uncomfortable images of humiliation represented both in words and images and rendered surreal by the dream state. What makes her work so effective is that it is presented in a style that is decorative and unthreatening. It is only when one picks up her teapots, cups, bowls, or plates and reads the tiny hand-printed text that one realizes that the subject matter is often emotionally raw, not the content one anticipates in this context. As the *New York Times* critic Ken Johnson writes about her work, 'More than just amusing essays in postmodern pastiche, her works are little monuments to significant moments or crises in the artist's spiritual biography.'

Matt Nolen, living and working in New York City, also uses language with his images. The work is visually and textually complex, almost to the point of overload. They are wry statements on the human condition as in the piece *Holy Grail No. 1: Money* (1993) which deals with foreign exchange, greed, and the almighty dollar. **Kurt Weiser** gives a contemporary twist to china painting. This technique was used extensively in Western court porcelains and in the late nineteenth and early twentieth centuries became the rage of lady hobbyists, who bought 'blanks' (fired, glazed, but undecorated porcelain wares) which they then decorated and fired in small muffle kilns. China painting clubs still exist all over the world. As a result it had not been thought of as a medium for a serious artist. The Super-Object makers in the 1960s were amongst the first to bring it back to respectability, using it mainly to paint faux surfaces on their work. Ron Nagle uses layer upon layer of china paint to obtain the intense color on his abstracted cups. But Weiser uses china paint in the same way as Meissen's court painters, to produce exquisite imagery.

Matt Nolen
Holy Grail No. 1: Money,
1993
Porcelain
h 16 in., w 11¹/₂ in.
h 40.6 cm, w 29.2 cm

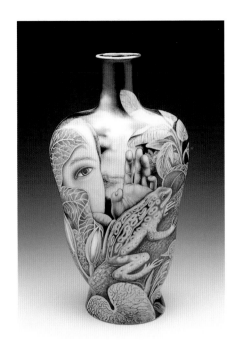

Weiser also made some changes in the process. The scale of the images he paints is much larger than the china painted wares of the past. He occasionally paints vignettes within reserve areas, but prefers to cover the entire vessel from back to front with one continuous image. His imagery is rooted stylistically in pre-1950s Magic Realism and is inspired by his trips in the 1980s to Thailand, reproducing the country's tropical flora and fauna alongside nude figures and surreal faces. Other works draw on famous paintings which he reprises in his own format—from those of the Hudson River School to those of the German romantics, which are his favorite period styles. He achieves a remarkable depth, polychromatic range, and luminosity in his painting over white, glazed, porcelain vases, lidded jars, and teapots, creating images with lush eroticism which is quite unlike any other body of china painting.

Top
Kurt Weiser
Untitled Vessel, 1992
Porcelain
h 17^1/$_2$ in., w 9^3/$_8$ in.
h 44.5 cm, w 23.8 cm

Above, near right (side A)
and above, far right (side B)
Kurt Weiser
Lidded Vessel, 1992
Porcelain
h 17 in., w 10 in.
h 43 cm, w 25.5 cm

Edward Eberle, on the other hand, eschews color. Occasionally a lick of gold appears in his work, but for nearly two decades he has been developing his distinctive style of black drawing and painting on large, white porcelain forms. Inspired initially by Native American Mimbres pottery, his drawing style quickly evolved from this rudimentary abstraction towards the complexity of painting on ancient Greek and Minoan pottery and the drawing style of the Old Masters. The most immediate impact of Eberle's art is his draughtsmanship, which has no equal in contemporary ceramics. His massing and layering of figures is masterful, using a mix of gray washes, sgraffito, painted and drawn figures. Equally impressive is his handling of porcelain. This is not the most plastic or giving of clay bodies, yet in Eberle's hands the thrown, articulate, thin-walled forms, with their finely modulated throwing rings, seem to defy gravity. He inserts a number of small flourishes with each piece, corners that are elegantly collapsed and folded, beautifully detailed, but with tiny handles, tall, square columnar feet with minute drawings every bit as complex as those on the main form. In places, he deliberately throws the porcelain so thin that the surface is abraded, becoming nearly transparent or in other cases breaking through the surface to allow access to the inner volume.

Edward Eberle
re Solutio, 1991
Porcelain
h 11¹/₂ in., w 6¹/₂ in., d 6¹/₂ in.
h 29.2 cm, w 16.5 cm, d 16.5 cm

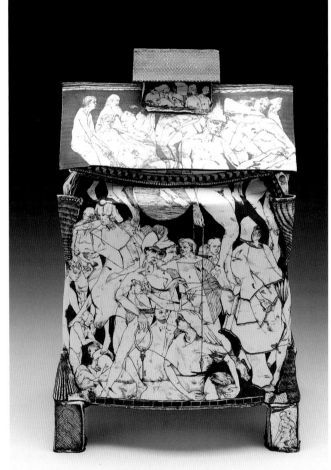

Above, left
Edward Eberle
Sentinel, 1995
Porcelain
h 17 in., w 16 in., d 16 in.
h 43 cm, w 40.6 cm,
d 40.6 cm

Above, right
Edward Eberle
*Twenty-five Years to
Bachelard*, 1995
Porcelain
h 18 in., w 12 in., d 8 in.
h 45.8 cm, w 30.5 cm, d 20.3 cm

The photographic decal allows **Daniel Kruger**, the South African-born artist who now lives and works in Germany, to create a new kind of portrait vase with the male nude as subject matter. One hesitates to describe the works shown here as homoerotic, although there are some aspects of Kruger's output that would fit this term. These nudes are so frank, innocently frontal and good-natured that they lack a sexual edge. The images are taken from a German magazine where each month a man is selected to photograph himself nude, the image appearing next to an interview. As can be seen, the men are holding a shutter release device to take the photograph, so their exposure is happily self-inflicted. Reproduced on thin sheets of porcelain and resembling photographic paper, they are attached to classical vase forms.

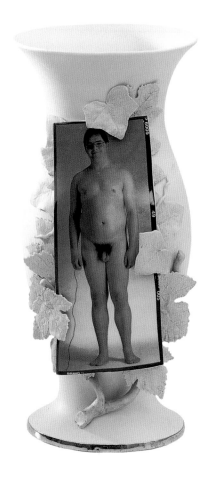

The Image and the Vessel

Above, left
Daniel Kruger
Untitled, 1997
Porcelain
h 12 in., w 6 in.
h 30.5 cm, w 15.3 cm
From the Europees Keramisch
Werk Centrum series

Above, right
Daniel Kruger
Untitled, 1997
Porcelain
h 12 in., w 6 in.
h 30.5 cm, w 15.3 cm
From the Europees Keramisch
Werk Centrum series

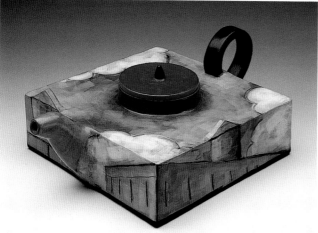

Lastly, there is the work of **Lidya Buzio** who grew up in Montevideo, Uruguay, in the studio of the great South American modernist, Joaquín Torres García (1874–1949). Although Torres García died a year after Buzio was born, the studio continued under his son, Horacio Torres, who married Buzio's sister. The studio was a magnet for South American artists and provided Buzio with an exciting, unconventional education. Initially her work was figurative, responding to the painterly influence of Horacio Torres and the ceramic style of Jose Collell, but when she moved to New York City in 1972 she found herself drawn to the strangely Italianate skyline of SoHo and began to do roofscapes. She was responding to the city's architecture in a similar way to Torres García fifty years before when he first visited the city and began to fill his notebooks with drawings of cityscapes. Her work was not imitative of Torres García—it is more realist and has the delicate translucent sensibility of a Roman fresco.

The late Philip Rawson, one of the field's most distinguished writers on ceramics and aesthetics, spoke instructively about her work in an unpublished address at the 3rd International Ceramics Symposium in Kansas City in 1983: 'one of the most splendid uses of "potter's space" seems to me to be Lidya Buzio's pots. The tension between the curved surface which subtend the independent potter's volume and the superficially banal perspectives of the cityscape that she paints onto them seems to be what generates their extraordinary enigmatic atmosphere... One volume content flows into another to make a beautifully modulated content of space: something carvers or makers can never achieve, only potters.'

Top
Lidya Buzio
Untitled Roofscape Vessel XXXIX, 1986
Burnished earthenware
h 15¹/₂ in., w 12 in.
h 39.4 cm, w 30.5 cm

Above
Lidya Buzio
Untitled Roofscape Teapot, 1993
Burnished earthenware
h 4 in., w 11¹/₂ in.
h 10 cm, w 29.2 cm

Chapter 9
The Vessel As Image

Elizabeth Fritsch   Nicholas Homoky   Anthony Bennett
Linda Gunn-Russell   Claude Bouchard   Greg Payce
Susan Shutt Wulfeck   Paul Mathieu   David Regan
Michael Sherrill   Akio Takamori

There is the second approach to the vessel and the image, treating the entire pot *as* an image or a drawing, a development which was first noted and defined by Garth Clark in his 1986 article for *Crafts*, entitled 'The Pictorialization of the Vessel.' This is one of the few visual approaches to come from postmodernism which is without substantial historical precedent. It is, in effect, a new way of perceiving vessel form. This is perhaps best explained by looking at the work of **Elizabeth Fritsch**, the artist who was the first to define this approach (although photography of the objects tends to make the illusion all the more real). Fritsch was a student at the Royal College of Art, London, in the early 1970s and was strongly influenced by her teacher, Hans Coper, who was then making forms which were flattened and oval. Fritsch realized that she could play with our perception by taking the vessel shape, flattening the volumes until they were just a couple of inches deep and then, by using drawing techniques such as foreshortening, make them appear to the eye to be full and round.

Fritsch did this by 'drawing' the mouth of the pot so that the back of the rim was built up higher than the front, giving the optical illusion of a wide-mouthed pot when in fact the vessel was only a couple of inches in depth. The foot was shaped in such a way that it echoed the perspectival exaggeration of the mouth. The exquisite engobe-painted patterns further enhanced this effect. Fritsch was working in what can be best described as two-and-half dimensions, part real volume, part drawn illusion of volume. The idea was a revelation and Fritsch's work was widely influential. In the 1980s **Linda Gunn-Russell**, another British potter, took this on and went a step further, playing with perspective on vessel forms which were only an inch or so in depth and had practically no volume at all.

Elizabeth Fritsch
Optical Cup and Saucer and
Night Boat with Music, 2000
Ceramic with slips
Left: h 8 in., w 7 in., d 3 in.
h 20.3 cm, w 17.8 cm, d 7.6 cm
Right: h 7 in., w 13 in., d 4 in.
h 17.8 cm, w 33 cm, d 10 cm

Above, left
Linda Gunn–Russell
Vessel, 1984
Earthenware
h 9 in., w 6 in., d 2 in.
h 23 cm, w 15.3 cm,
d 5 cm

Above, right
Linda Gunn–Russell
Teapot, 1984
Earthenware
h 8 in., w 8 in., d 2 in.
h 20.3 cm, w 20.3 cm, d 5 cm

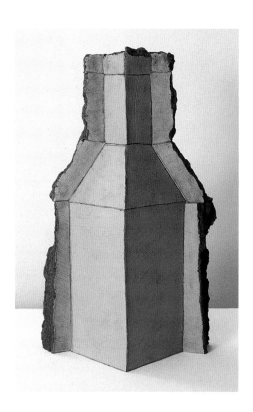

Above, left
Susan Shutt Wulfeck
Untitled/Light (Gray Bottle), 1984
Earthenware
h 16 in.
h 40.6 cm

Above, right
Michael Sherrill
Swoon Tea, 1996
Porcelain
h 28 in., w 18 in., d 7 in.
h 71 cm, w 45.8 cm,
d 17.8 cm

American artist **Susan Shutt Wulfeck** does not pretend to preserve volume. Her pots stand upright, single slabs of clay cut into the shape of cups and vases, drawn on the surface in slip. **Michael Sherrill** uses color to draw his vessels with remarkable freedom on flattened forms. Like many artists in this section, he particularly favors the teapot because its linear elements, the handle and spout, lend themselves so well to this kind of draughtsmanship. **Nicholas Homoky** has left his forms full and round and at first they are as blank as a sheet of white drawing paper. Then he draws images of vessels on the white porcelain in black or blue inlay, creating a graphic art which dominates the form. **Claude Bouchard**, a Frenchman, also treats his pots as graphic inventions. His are a little different to those of Homoky as the edge of every vessel he makes is drawn with a black line, often ragged and seemingly quick and spontaneous, as though they are pen-and-ink drawings that have come to life.

Above, left
Claude Bouchard
Tara, 1998
Porcelain
h 6–10 in.
h 15.3–25.5 cm

Above, right
Nicholas Homoky
Group of Five Teapots,
1981–83
Porcelain
h 4–6^1/$_2$ in. each
h 10–16.5 cm each

Two other artists have radicalized this self-referential 'vessel as image' approach—Quebecois artist **Paul Mathieu** and Japanese-born **Akio Takamori** (pp. 140, 141). They do two things at once—treat the vessel as a drawing, but use it as the canvas for images of figures and other subjects as well. Mathieu uses layered vessels, one on top of the other. At the bottom of each work he has painted the full image. As the dishes are piled one on top of the other, the drawing becomes more and more sculptural and three-dimensional. For instance, if one removes the actual cup in *My Cup of Tea* (1986) one finds that the same cup is drawn on the plate underneath, and the one beneath that. This is a clever game in which the essential 'drawing' remains the same, becoming more or less three dimensional, depending upon whether pieces are added or removed. Drawing and form are one interlocking concept in Mathieu's work.

Takamori's 'envelope' pots had the same impact on American ceramics as Fritsch's coil-built pots had in Britain. He used a similar device to that of Fritsch, making a wide, flat vessel, raising the back of the pot's mouth higher than the front to suggest depth. But in his case the entire pot becomes a drawn figurative silhouette. The idea came to him from looking at Japanese erotic prints and realizing that the couples in these woodblock images, one lying in front and the other lying behind, together enclosed space, and so became a kind of conceptual vessel. These pots, with their unique vision, innovative approach to drawing and erotic content are now amongst the most sought-after works of the 1980s.

Paul Mathieu
The Arrows of Time, 1990
Porcelain
h 13 in., w 14 in., d 14 in.
h 33 cm, w 35.5 cm, d 35.5 cm

Paul Mathieu
My Cup of Tea, 1986
Porcelain
h 6 in., w 11¹/₂ in.
h 15.3 cm, w 29.2 cm

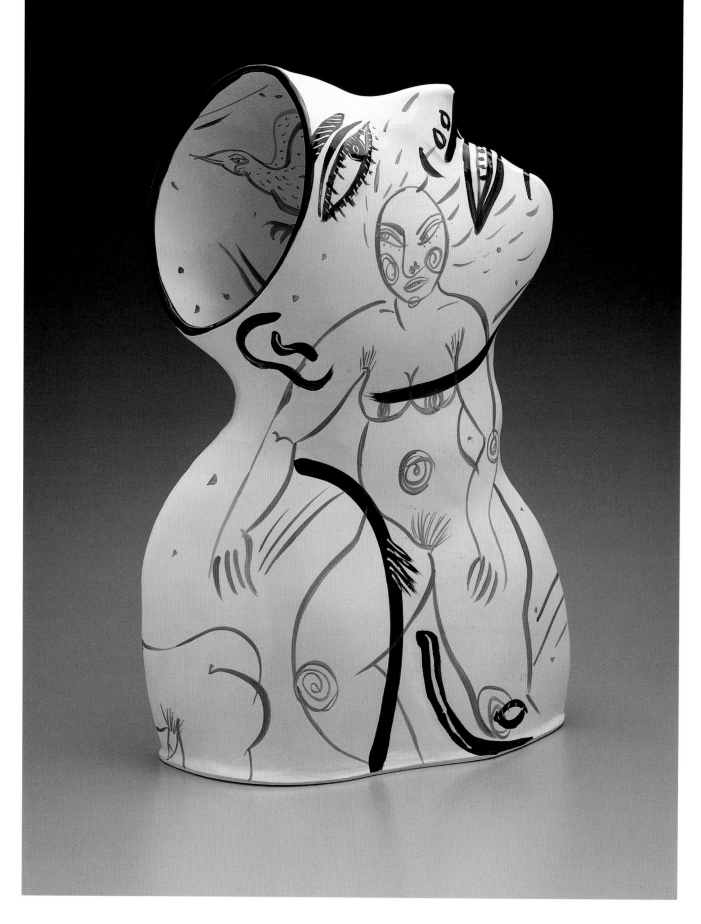

Opposite
Akio Takamori
Portrait of Mr. W, 1986
Porcelain
h 24 in., w 16 in.
h 61 cm, w 40.6 cm

Above, left
Akio Takamori
The Fallen Angel (Homage to Duane Michals), 1990
Porcelain
Bust: h 21 in., w 16 in., d 8 in.;
Torso: h 21 in., w 10 in., d 6 in.
Bust: h 53.3 cm, w 40.6 cm, d 20.3 cm;
Torso: h 53.3 cm, w 25.5 cm, d 15.3 cm

Above, right
Akio Takamori
Aphrodite and Eros, 1991
Porcelain
h 11¼ in., w 21 in.
h 28.5 cm, w 53.3 cm

Anthony Bennett, from England, brings a three-dimensional cartoon sensibility to this concept. The vessels take on the shape of people or animals, partly drawn, partly in relief, and partly sculptural. Canadian artist **Greg Payce** literally pulls the figure out of his vases in the throwing. Working with two or more vessels, the negative space between the vessels replicates a human form, giving a new meaning to the belly, foot, shoulder, and lip of the pot. The idea is not new. The Imperial War Museum in London has a dramatic example of this approach in a ceramic profile of Mussolini (c. 1935) by Giuseppe Bertelli. Payce has refreshed and advanced the idea by creating serial imagery stringing along processions of figures formed by the silhouettes of his pots.

Above, left
Anthony Bennett
Three Running Man Teapots, 1994
Colored earthenware
h 12 in., w 10 in.
h 30.5 cm, w 25.5 cm

Above, right
Greg Payce
Wane, 1999 (6 parts) (detail)
Earthenware
h 10¹/₂ in., w 30 in., d 7 in. each
h 26.8 cm, w 76.2 cm,
d 17.8 cm each

Greg Payce
Apparently, 1999 (2 parts)
Earthenware
h 36 in.
h 91.4 cm

America's **David Regan** makes tureens different in style, but similar in their means. His tureen forms take on the shape of a figure, fish or animal, but then he carves through a black surface to the white porcelain below. The effect is distinctly that of a wood-block print which has come to life.

David Regan
Feathers Tureen, 1996
Porcelain, sgraffito
h 11 in., w 19 in.
h 28 cm, w 48.3 cm

David Regan
Snake Tureen, 1997
Porcelain, sgraffito
h 11 in., w 28$^1/_2$ in.
h 28 cm, w 72.4 cm

Chapter 10
Sculpture: The Figure

There are two golden chords that run throughout the millennia-long history of ceramic art—the vessel and the figure. The oldest ceramic rendition of the human figure is a small, roughly modeled female form, from what is now Slovakia, which is twenty-seven thousand years old. Until the Second World War classically trained sculptors still learned to model in clay as part of their academic training, either for the purpose of making maquettes or to make finished terracotta sculptures. In the 1930s and 1940s, the Great Depression in the USA, and later the war, caused a number of major sculptors to turn to ceramics because it was, compared to marble or bronze, an affordable and accessible material. Lucio Fontana, Arturo Martini, Isamu Noguchi, Louise Nevelson, and Henri Laurens were amongst the many sculptors who made their finished works in clay. But then the tradition began to disappear as modernism turned against the figure and, in particular, the detailed, realistic modeling of the terracotta tradition.

Above
Viola Frey
Untitled July IV, 1982
Whiteware
h 87 in. each
h 221 cm each

Right
Michael Lucero
Anthropomorphic Seated Male Figure, 1996
Earthenware with glazes
h 19¹/₂ in., w 12 in., d 6 in.
h 49.5 cm, w 30.5 cm, d 15.3 cm

Around 1960 the figurative movement began to revive. Impetus came primarily from the USA where West Coast artist Robert Arneson was leading a revolution in form and content. He rejected the decorative figurine tradition and the modernist abstraction for raw, objectionable subject matter which was confrontational. While some ceramists actually copied Arneson's style, his major contribution is broader in that he opened the doors to a tougher sense of what the clay figure could be in art terms. The Bay Area provided us with Stephen De Staebler's craggy abstracted modernist figures and the distinctly postmodern sculpture of **Viola Frey**.

Rather than rejecting the commercial figurine, Frey embraced and collected them, made molds from them and placed the cast figures in tableaux, as well as using them as subjects for her paintings. Her next step was to increase their scale, rising from five inches (13 cm) to five feet (1.5 meters), eventually topping ten feet (3 meters) in height. When asked at a conference why she made such huge work (the artist is of modest height), she replied that she was raised on a vineyard in Northern California and was always shorter than the vines. 'Perhaps I am finally trying to look over the vineyards,' she mused. From 1980 onwards Frey has been one of the most significant influences on figurative ceramics, and has exhibited extensively in the USA, Europe, and Japan.

Michael Lucero's brilliant 'shard figures' of the late 1970s were one of the signs that the ceramic figure was making a dramatic return. He moved to New York from Seattle and produced his *Dreamers*, a series of huge heads laid on their side, with their dream imagery painted on the surface in bright primary colors. The 1990s saw two of his most important bodies of work—Pre-Columbian figures which reinvented this cultural icon and gave it a new polychromatic life, and his *Reclamation* series, in which he took damaged objects, ranging from actual African art to valueless, broken concrete garden statuary, and then 'reclaimed' the piece by replacing the damaged sections with ceramic additions. In a sense this made the work whole again, a definitive postmodernist gesture acknowledging time and history. The work shown here has another element of note and that is the homage to the maverick turn-of-the-century American potter, George E. Ohr, imitating the way the form has been thrown and then ruffled and collapsed as in *Female Roman Statue* (1996).

Michael Lucero
Grayhouse Dreamer, 1984
Earthenware with glazes
h 20 in., w 24 in., d 22 in.
h 50.8 cm, w 61 cm, d 56 cm

Michael Lucero
Female Roman Statue, from *Reclamation*
series, 1996
Ceramic, glazes, plaster, paint
h 47¹/₂ in., w 16¹/₂ in., d 12 in.
h 120.7 cm, w 41.9 cm, d 30.5 cm

The Russian artist **Sergei Isupov** uses a similar palette to that of Lucero, bright, sunny, primary colors which are generally quite joyous (although Isupov can occasionally descend into darker tonalities). Also, in common with Lucero, he paints images on forms which take on the shape of human figures or fantastic animals.

Above
Sergei Isupov
The Time is Coming, 1997
Porcelain, ceramic stain
h 14^1/$_2$ in., w 11^1/$_4$ in., d 8 in.
h 36.8 cm, w 28.5 cm, d 20.3 cm

Right
Sergei Isupov
Invisible Support, 1997
Porcelain, ceramic stain
h 13^1/$_2$ in., w 9^1/$_2$ in., d 9^1/$_2$ in.
h 34.3 cm, w 24 cm, d 24 cm

American artists **Mark Burns** and **John deFazio** both approach the figure with a Punk edge. Burns and deFazio (who was a student of Burns) deal with highly sexual, fetishistic, and, at times, scatological references. An explanation of the content of these artists' work is always provocative and frequently X rated. DeFazio, whose work was shown at the 1993 Venice Biennale, assembles his sculptures from commercial and hobbyist ceramic molds, playing with the lowest rung of working-class kitsch. His portrait of Elvis Presley in *King's Throne* (1998) uses an actual toilet with the familiar commercially produced 1960s Presley bust, a comment on his death on the john. With this background in pop culture, deFazio was perfect for the commission of the boardroom table and chairs for Music Television's (MTV's) headquarters in New York City, a complex set of relief sculptures under a glass top, replete with images of the network's denizens, Beavis and Butthead. Burns uses no molds, but rather fashions by hand his smooth shapes of cartoonish figures having deviant sex, with frosting and cherries to sweeten the experience.

New Yorker **Toby Buonagurio** and Dutch artist **Hans van Bentem** are both influenced by Japanese Manga. Manga is the Japanese comic tradition of the 'robot-as-pall' such as Testuwan Atom (known as Astro Boy in the West), who has a nuclear reactor for a heart and rockets in his shoes.

Above
John deFazio
King's Throne, 1998
Whiteware
h 60 in., w 30 in., d 36 in.
h 152.4 cm, w 76.2 cm,
d 91.4 cm

Right
Mark Burns
Pies Men Like, 1989
Stoneware, earthenware,
paint, glaze, found objects
h 48 in.
h 121.9 cm

Opposite, left
Hans van Bentem
Warrior Angels, 2000
Ceramic
h 83–84 in. each
h 210.8–213.4 cm each

Opposite, right
Toby Buonagurio
Bionic Toby with Pet Boa, 1982
Ceramic with diverse surfaces
h 25 in., w 23 in., d 12 in.
h 63.5 cm, w 58.4 cm,
d 30.5 cm

Van Bentem's goal is to create an original fantasy world where culturally we all unite in saving the world. *New York Times* art critic Grace Glueck wrote of van Bentem's 2000 New York exhibition, 'Influenced by the friendly sci-fi monsters of Japanese comic strips, they are composed of techy and creaturely parts, with an eye on mythology, anthropology and today's pop mystique of medieval knighthood too. Monstrous as they are, they inspire affection rather than terror. But both the figures, done with an admirable command of glazes and large-scale ceramic construction, score by virtue of their bold size.' Buonagurio's self-portrait robot sculptures are among the earliest of the postmodern figures, having first explored this world in the mid-1970s. A mixture of flocked, painted, and glitter surfaces, and just the right amount of *Barbarella*, her work has a sexy sci-fi fantasy bent.

153

Americans **Jan Holcomb, Beverly Mayeri,** and **Marilyn Lysohir** are all as much painters as they are sculptors. This trio tends to use acrylic paint on fired clay rather than glaze. This approach results in surfaces that are different from those that come from slip and glaze and which can be controlled and modulated more finely. All three artists deal with surreal views of the human condition. Holcomb's figures occupy landscapes that are lonely yet serene, reflecting his own isolation in coping with multiple sclerosis. Mayeri deals mainly with distortion of the human form through elongation and surface treatment. Lysohir's tableaux replicate figures to explain an ongoing process, like a serial illustration, and to suggest clones (long before the sheep Lucy made her appearance) with a mood of enforced anonymity.

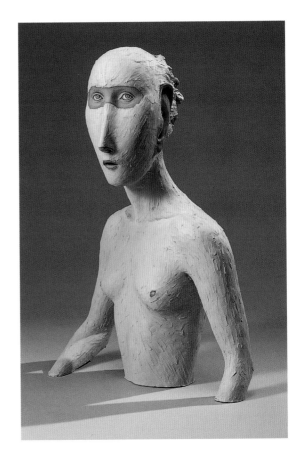

Top
Jan Holcomb
At the Crux, 1986
Stoneware, oil paint
h 32 in., w 28 in.
h 81.3 cm, w 71 cm

Above, left
Marilyn Lysohir
The B.A.M.s, 1980
Clay and plastic
h 4 in., w 12 in., d 4 in.
h 10 cm, w 30.5 cm,
d 10.2 cm

Above, right
Beverly Mayeri
Under Scrutiny, 1984
Ceramic, acrylic paint, ceramic stain
h 15 in., w 11 in., d 6 in.
h 38 cm, w 28 cm, d 15.3 cm

Feminist issues are part of the art of **Judy Moonelis** and **Kukuli Velarde**, but neither does so with overtly literal messages, at least not politically so. Moonelis' angst-ridden work of the 1980s typified the style and alternative energies of the short-lived, but significant, East Village art movement in New York City. Velarde was born in Peru and her figures reflect a feminist viewpoint from a culture where the subjugation of women is more overt than in the USA or Europe. Her figures refer in their style, albeit subtly, to the work of the Peruvian pre-Columbian potters.

Above, left
Kukuli Velarde
Isichapuitu, 1998
Installation at the Clay Studio,
Philadelphia
Low-fire earthenware
21 pieces, h 20 in.–24 in. each
h 50.8 cm–61 cm each

Above, right
Judy Moonelis
Untitled, 1986
Ceramic
h 29 in., w 29 in.
h 73.6 cm, w 73.6 cm

155

In 1931 the psychiatrist Eugene Beuker coined the term 'Mnemismus' to explain a condition whereby generations carry unconscious memories of the history of previous generations in their genetic makeup. This is a concept that Hungarian artist **Laszlo Fekete** has explored in his work. His 'complex accretions of cultural detritus' reflect the turmoil of Hungarian society which has endured one regime after another, each of which has tried to destroy the material presence of the preceding regime. Many of Fekete's works are made up of seconds and broken figurines from the Hungarian Herend factory, a strong patron of his work.

Above
Laszlo Fekete
Supermen's Mortal Combat, 1999
Porcelain
h 15¹/₂ in.
h 39.4 cm

Opposite
Laszlo Fekete
Statue on the Cross Way, 1995–96
Stoneware with overglazes
h 25¹/₂ in.
h 64.7 cm

157

Brazilian artist **Marco Paulo Rolla** also uses the broken figurine as a focus of his work, both small scale and sometimes full life size, spreading out their fractured parts in an installation format. What touches the viewer in these works is that their shattering reveals inner skeletons for these figures, suggesting that they are not frozen, lifeless imitations of mankind, but have some kind of inner life.

Marco Paulo Rolla
Oracle, 1999
Porcelain on wood
h 5⁷/₈ in., w 23¹/₄ in.,
l 44⁷/₈ in.
h 15 cm, w 60 cm, l 114 cm

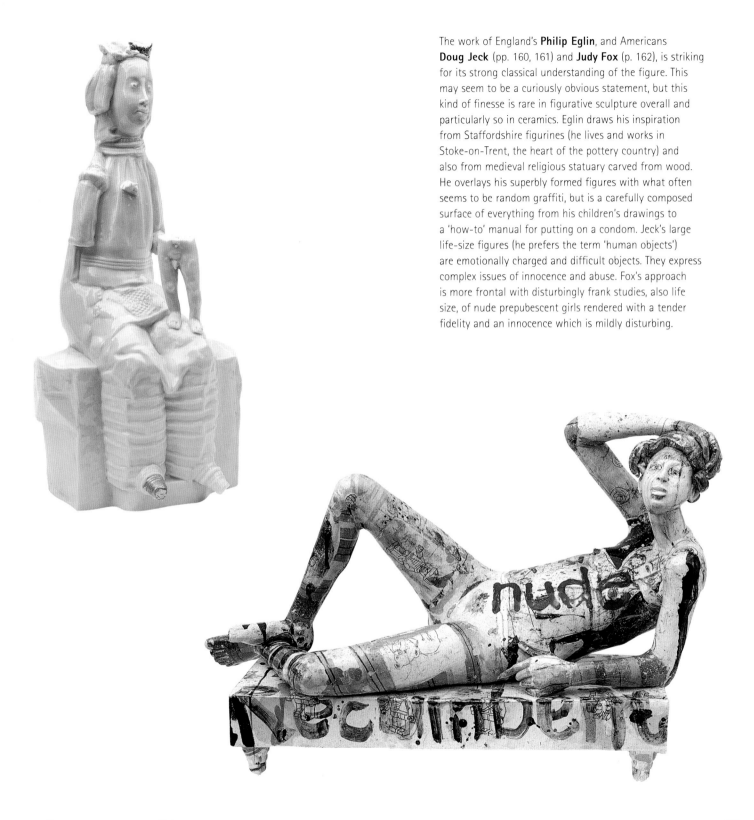

The work of England's **Philip Eglin**, and Americans **Doug Jeck** (pp. 160, 161) and **Judy Fox** (p. 162), is striking for its strong classical understanding of the figure. This may seem to be a curiously obvious statement, but this kind of finesse is rare in figurative sculpture overall and particularly so in ceramics. Eglin draws his inspiration from Staffordshire figurines (he lives and works in Stoke-on-Trent, the heart of the pottery country) and also from medieval religious statuary carved from wood. He overlays his superbly formed figures with what often seems to be random graffiti, but is a carefully composed surface of everything from his children's drawings to a 'how-to' manual for putting on a condom. Jeck's large life-size figures (he prefers the term 'human objects') are emotionally charged and difficult objects. They express complex issues of innocence and abuse. Fox's approach is more frontal with disturbingly frank studies, also life size, of nude prepubescent girls rendered with a tender fidelity and an innocence which is mildly disturbing.

Above
Philip Eglin
Caution, Irritant
Madonna, 2000
Porcelain
h 13¹/₂ in., w 6 in.
h 34.3 cm, w 15.3 cm

Right
Philip Eglin
Recumbent Nude, 1994
Whiteware
h 16¹/₂ in., w 24 in., d 10 in.
h 41.9 cm, w 61 cm, d 25.5 cm

Doug Jeck
*Study in Antique White
(Barricade)*, 2000
Ceramic and mixed media
h 54 in., w 60 in., d 28 in.
h 137.2 cm, w 152.4 cm,
d 71 cm

Doug Jeck
Heirloom, 2000
Ceramic and mixed media
h 73 in., w 17 in., d 21 in.
(with base)
h 185.4 cm, w 43 cm,
d 53.3 cm

Judy Fox
Rapunzel, 1999
Terracotta, casein
h 56¹/₂ in., w 26¹/₂ in.,
d 18 in.
h 143.5 cm, w 67.3 cm,
d 45.8 cm

French Canadian **Jean-Pierre Larocque** is best known for his painterly renderings of horses, but he also works with figures and his giant head and shoulder portraits are explosively powerful in their grotesque exaggeration. **Akio Takamori** changed direction in his career in 1995, moving from envelope vases with figurative drawing to individual figures, grouped and representing the 1950s inhabitants of a Japanese village. This direction holds personal memories of his hometown of Nobeoka where he grew up and the change in Japan since the Allied occupation. All forms of traditional peasant life are represented, from the fish salesman to the pot restorer. Later works have juxtaposed Takamori's villagers with classical paintings by Diego Velázquez, Michelangelo and others. Garth Clark writes in the catalog of Takamori's New York exhibition in 2000, 'The individual figures work as self standing sculptures. But their real sense of life emerges in groupings. They are, after all, about daily social transactions. It is the combinations of figures that begin to speak or chatter with the hum of village life. It is in these assemblages that Takamori's human landscapes come into their own. Grouped in pairs or foursomes one can feel the bustle, the collective murmur, the interdependencies, the relationships of dominance and submission.'

Watching the development of figurative ceramic sculpture over the past two decades has been fascinating. It is one of the areas of postmodern ceramics which has steadily increased in quality and depth of content. In the early part of the movement, there was an unfortunate tendency to produce figurative work that was predicated on banal humor and whimsy without the edge of Arneson's seditious joking. This was decorative art in the worst sense of the world. Much of this work had no more artistic validity than the most vacuous factory figurines. Also, many ceramic artists had been poorly schooled in the figure and their ineptness disfigured their art. By the mid-1990s it was apparent that there was newfound competence, strength, maturity, and profundity in the ceramic figure. The exciting part of this is that one feels a momentum that is, as yet, nowhere near its peak and so its brightest moments lie in the future.

Above, left
Jean-Pierre Larocque
Untitled, 1998
Stoneware
h 41 in.
h 104.1 cm

Above, right
Akio Takamori
Village People, 2000
Stoneware
h 20–36 in. each
h 50.8–91.4 cm each

Chapter 11
Sculpture: Abstraction

Abstract sculpture in clay today brings some associations from ceramic history, notably organic abstraction in the vessel tradition. The material itself, so plastic and malleable, places another distinctive stamp on the work. But by and large the motivations of the sculptors who work in this style are little different from those of colleagues working in the same language in other materials. These 'Orga-morphic' pieces, as writer Bob Ellison classifies them, are the result of a long lineage of twentieth-century exploration of the biomorphic and there is not a piece in this chapter that has not been touched by either the work of Constantin Brancusi, Max Ernst, Jean Arp, Isamu Noguchi, or Joan Miró.

Miró is of particular consequence to the ceramic world because of his significant body of work in clay—nearly five hundred sculptures, vessels, and gigantic tile murals—which has exerted a strong influence on ceramists since the 1950s. The influence of Salvador Dalí's paintings of melting forms also struck a chord amongst potters, connecting as it does with the nightmare vision many ceramists have had of opening the kiln after it has been over-fired and finding their work slumped, pooled, and puddled like a Surrealist dreamscape.

Ken Price is one of the masters of postmodern ceramics. He started making brightly painted work (often using automotive lacquer instead of glazes) in the early 1960s and ever since has created colorful abstractions of modernist inspiration, from his architectural cups of the early 1970s to his later pots with pornographic imagery. In the late 1980s and 1990s, Price explored the free form of his 'blobs'. The latest series is the most plastic and biomorphic of his career, reminiscent of similar forms made by Miró in the 1950s, but with a shimmering, flecked, and painted surface that has a new-age glamor and lustrous glow.

Barbara Nanning's (pp. 168, 169) approach to color is similar to that of Price. Her large public sculptures are first created as computer images and then carefully scaled up in Henk Trumpie's workshop, Struktuur 68, in the Hague, Netherlands. Her surface texture is seemingly rough with rich and saturated colors of yellow and blue. In superficial ways, **Bean Finneran's** (p. 169) sculpture has a similar quality to that of Nanning's. Both deliberately use color that is 'unnatural' so that they can play with natural form without mimicking it. Finneran works in San Francisco in a studio on a boardwalk over a salt-water marsh. The marsh grass is her strongest influence—it is constantly being shifted by tides and wind as the changing light also shapes and reshapes this vista. Finneran has been dealing for five years with a single element form, a curve, 'as a meditation upon multiplicity in nature. The many thousands of individual elements in each piece are not physically connected as another reflection of the natural process.'

Opposite, above
Ken Price
Green Glow, 1996
Ceramic, acrylic
h 14 in., w 14 in., d 10 in.
h 35.5 cm, w 35.5 cm,
d 25.5 cm

Opposite, below
Ken Price
Whisper, 1997
Ceramic, acrylic
h 15³/₄ in., w 18¹/₂ in.,
d 14 in.
h 40 cm, w 47 cm, d 35.5 cm

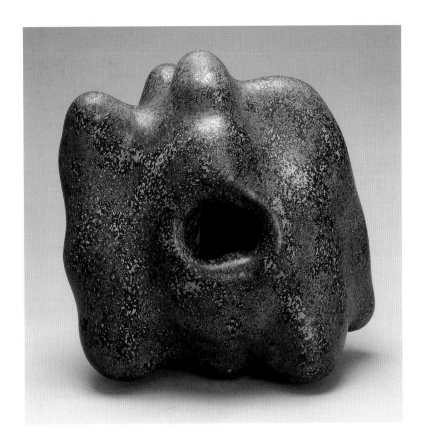

Top
Barbara Nanning
Botanica Series: Reclining Flower, 1997
Computer composition drawing; paper and ink

Above, right
Barbara Nanning
Botanica Series: Reclining Flower, 1997
Ceramic
h 110 in., w 87 in., d 87 in.
h 2.79 m, w 2.21 m, d 2.21 m

Opposite, above
Barbara Nanning
Botanica Series: Reclining Flower, 1997
Construction process

Right
Bean Finneran
Turquoise Ring, 2000
Low-fire clay, acrylic
paint, ceramic stain
h 24 in., diam. 96 in.
h 61 cm, diam. 244 cm

Yo Akiyama is one of the most impressive contemporary Japanese sculptors, whether in ceramics or any other material. His massive works can be over twenty feet (6 meters) in length and weigh several tons. The scale is important, even though he also works in smaller table-top sizes as well. In the larger works his surfaces take on drama. Using a blowtorch, he scorches the surfaces until they crack and split like a dried-up riverbed during a particularly fierce drought. At once harsh and beautiful, the surfaces curl and blister around long columns which have been placed on the ground in a gentle arc. Walking into a museum or gallery and confronting one of these works is awe inspiring, suggesting that they have been extruded from a volcano. **Pekka Tapio Paikkari** hails from Finland and so the break-up of surface does not come from the concept of heat, but one of cold as the title *Breaking Up of Ice* explains.

Above
Yo Akiyama
Oscillation II, 1995
Ceramic
h 37³/₄ in., l 251³/₄ in.,
d 42¹/₂ in.
h 95.9 cm, l 6.39 m,
d 1.08 m

Opposite, top
Pekka Tapio Paikkari
Breaking Up of Ice, 1992
Ceramic, silicon carbide,
aluminium oxide
w 78⁵/₈ in., d 78⁵/₈ in.
w 200 cm, d 200 cm

Opposite, middle, left
Alexander Lichtveld
Untitled, 1993
Stoneware
h 6¹/₂ in., w 14 in.
h 16.5 cm, w 35.5 cm

Opposite, middle, right
Frank Louis
Untitled, 1998
Stoneware, lacquer
h 25¹/₂ in., w 40⁷/₈ in.,
d 38¹/₂ in.
h 65 cm, w 104 cm, d 98 cm

Architecture is the starting point for German artist **Frank Louis**, Frenchman **Jacques Kaufmann**, and Dutchman **Alexander Lichtveld**. Lichtveld works both in the public arena with large floor-tile installations and, as shown here, small compact sculptural forms which are refined and architectonic in appearance. Louis creates portals that at the same time suggest shrines or temples, using raw stoneware edges which draw the form in three dimensions. Kaufmann works with bricks, making solid square columns which appear to have been plucked from a larger structure of some kind.

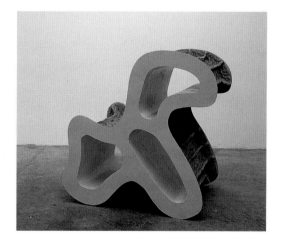

Right
Jacques Kaufmann
Eroded Blocks, 1996
Bricks and concrete
h 19⁵/₈, 19⁵/₈, 17⁵/₈ in.
h 50, 50, 45 cm

Sculpture: Abstraction   **Inge Pederson**
Blue Tradition, 1998
Stoneware
70³/₄ in.
180 cm

Walls are the focus of Norwegian sculptors **Inge Pederson** and **Søren Ubisch**. Pederson builds massive walls from extruded and shaped modules (extruding is pressing clay through a template, something like sausage making). Although it is not immediately obvious, Pederson has created the modules from the shape of a handled cup, presenting an old object in a new context. Ubisch, whose work graces many public buildings in Norway, created this wall with four thousand tile tubes to give a feeling of weightlessness and transparency. The latter is enhanced by the bright white glaze which amplifies the light as it passes through the wall.

Søren Ubisch
Construction, 1998
Earthenware with tin glaze
h 177 in., w 196¹/₂ in., d 4³/₄ in.
h 450 cm, w 500 cm, d 12 cm

Above, left
Raymon Elozua
*Stil1/Tob/Kra2/New4/Klin8>
2:Sc*, 1998
Digital print on paper

Above, right
Raymon Elozua
Stil1/Tob/Kra2/New4/Klin8>2:Sc,
1998
Terracotta, glaze, steel
h 12 in., w 31 in., d 36 in.
h 30.5 cm, w 78.7 cm, d 91.4 cm

Raymon Elozua has created his latest abstract sculpture with the help of a computer and the canvases of the New York School painters. Firstly, he analyses various canvases by digitally separating them into seven layers of color. He then plays with this visual data, looking for three-dimensional elements within the separations, building physically separate planes in clay and wire for each element. He then takes, say, the green of a Lee Krasner, the orange from a Hans Hoffmann, and the black from a Franz Kline, to create a hybrid composite which is translated into three dimensions. The codes are reflected in the title. For instance, *Stil1/Tob/Kra2/New4/Klin8>2:Sc* represents a layering of Clyfford Still, Mark Tobey, Lee Krasner, Barnett Newman, and Franz Kline.

Arnold Zimmerman is a master of massive ceramic sculpture. His huge works are built and fired in a mammoth studio in Brooklyn, New York, fitted with ceiling cranes and containing forklift trucks. His sculptures are often of gigantic scale such as his group of eight foot ($2^1/_2$ meters) high vessel forms that stand outside the Everson Museum of Art in Syracuse, New York. Even his small objects, weighing several hundred pounds, have an unruly energy and biomorphic urgency that takes over and dominates the space they occupy.

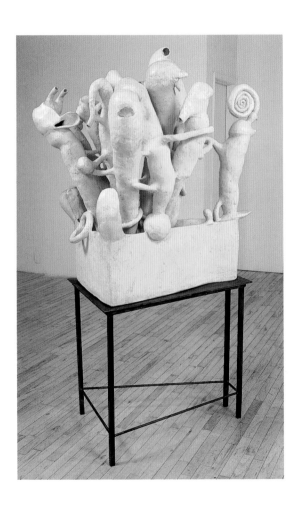

Arnold Zimmerman
Voyage to the Afterlife,
1996
Stoneware
h 49 in., w 45 in., d 32 in.
h 124.5 cm, w 114.3 cm, d 81.3 cm

A similar vision to that of Elozua, perhaps less dark, is apparent in **Dan Anderson's** work. His remarkable polychrome wood-fired vessels, in this case a teapot, are evocations of the small, corrugated processing plants for industrial products that one finds scattered across the American mid-Western plains, most often abandoned. Anderson has a deep affection for these metal buildings and enjoys their compositional abstraction and eroded texture. At the same time, these pieces document the dying years of small family farms in the USA and the inexorable takeover of this industry by huge corporate farming monoliths.

Dan Anderson
Chicago Water Tower
Teapot, 1993
Stoneware
h 6³/₄ in., w 12¹/₂ in.
h 17.1 cm, w 31.8 cm

Steven Montgomery, who was born and raised in Henry Ford's Detroit, the USA's automobile center, works on the edge where the man-made devolves back into nature. He also uses scale to create drama and his giant sculptural forms, mechanical structures of unspecific purpose, begin to melt and erode. In part this is a portrait of the rotting, post-industrial Brooklyn landscape where he has his studio, the site of dozens of abandoned factories, metal gardens of rusting pipes, and antiquated machines which decay while they await removal by the gentrification of the buildings as artist's lofts or headquarters for dot-com companies.

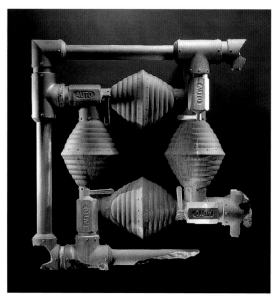

Above, left
Steven Montgomery
Quadrus, 1996
Painted ceramic
h 40 in., w 40 in., d 16 in.
h 101.6 cm, w 101.6 cm,
d 40.6 cm

Above, right
Steven Montgomery
Thermal Decline, 1999
Painted ceramic
h 9$^1/_2$ in., w 10$^1/_2$ in., d 7 in.
h 24 cm, w 26.8 cm, d 17.8 cm

The plumbing and machine imagery continues with **Steve Welch** and **Kevin Waller** who create pottery which is drawn from metal vessels. The raw seams they leave on view suggest sheets of metal roughly cut and soldered together. Pipes and other hardware extend this metaphor with a decrepit industrial edge. As Welch states in *Ceramics Monthly* magazine, November 2000, 'These forms, based on creative survival, touch me on an intuitive level.'

While much of this work has a darker context, technology's limitations rather than its promise, a kind of clay-based 'Blade Runner' vision, others view machinery with a gleeful optimism.

Above
Steve Welch
Port 16 and Port 17, 2000
Earthenware
h 24 in. to 36 in.
h 61 cm to 91.4 cm

Right
Kevin Waller
Double Silo, 2000
Stoneware
h 17 in., w 9^1/$_2$ in., d 4^1/$_2$ in.
h 43 cm, w 24 cm, d 11.4 cm

The complex ceramic machines of Japanese sculptor **Hideo Matsumoto** do not suggest the end of an era. Rather they seem ready to do whatever it is they do at the flick of a switch. Arms extend with counterbalances, while metal components join ceramic pieces. It has all the energy and purpose of a production line running ten to fifteen feet (3–4½ meters) in length. However, the purpose of this machine is, of course, obscure and each viewer brings to it their own imagined purpose.

Eric Van Eimeren and **Keiko Fukazawa** also approach industry as a kind of hybrid which is tied to nature. Fukazawa frequently combines industrial bric-à-brac which, like Astbury's early sculpture, is either emerging from or disappearing into rock-like forms, an extension of this Japanese artist's rock-garden heritage. Van Eimeren has a sci-fi look to his work. Carousel condiment servers look both like machines on their movable bearings and at the same time resemble mechanical insects. His surfaces often mimic reptile skin or other organic textures that project a fantasy view of tomorrow in which machine and organic life forms are merged in mutant utopia.

Above, left
Hideo Matsumoto
*Kakomitotte Mederu XII
(Episode 5)*, 2000
Ceramic
h 39³/₈ in., w 39³/₈ in.,
l 212 in.
h 1 m, w 1 m, l 5.4 m

Above, right
Keiko Fukazawa
Teaset, 1991
Whiteware
Teapot: h 5 in., w 7³/₄ in.
h 12.7 cm, w 19.7 cm

Opposite, below, left
Eric Van Eimeren
*Condiment Drawers with
Spoons*, 1999
Whiteware
h 24 in., w 7¹/₂ in.
h 61 cm, w 19 cm

Opposite, above, right
Eric Van Eimeren
*Carnival Server with
Spoons*, 1998
Whiteware
h 14 in., w 19 in.
h 35.5 cm, w 48.3 cm

187

Margaretha Daepp
Archaeology of the Future, 1993
Industrial shelves, terracotta,
glass
h 82$\frac{1}{4}$ in., w 78$\frac{5}{8}$ in.,
d 23$\frac{1}{4}$ in.
h 210 cm, w 200 cm, d 60 cm

The work of **Barbara Schmidt, Margaretha Daepp,** and **Marek Cecula** has none of the sense of erosion and disintegration that one sees in that of the other artists. Their vision of industry is almost frighteningly pure, almost slick. Daepp presents a small museum of industrial artifacts in her piece, *Archaeology of the Future* (1993). The organization of the molded, terracotta elements, with their clean lines and seeming objectivity, deliberately conveys the sense of the storage room of a museum or an archive, suggesting that there is a purposeful and revealing relationship between all the industrial elements on display. The overall irony of the work is the feeling of the high-tech shelving and the low-tech ceramics, unglazed terracotta being known as the lowest grade of peasant pottery, while the forms themselves suggest a highly sophisticated and informed design sense.

Schmidt is at her most avant-garde when working with components. The refinement of the small objects she uses has the clarity and purpose of computer chips or some other small, but miraculous, device from the advanced ceramics labs. Like Cecula, her work's designerly quality is not merely an affectation, but is informed by her design work. Schmidt has worked for KAHLA/Thüringen Porzellan GmbH since 1991 and has garnered numerous design awards in Germany, the USA, and Japan. Schmidt has retained the cleanness of industrial design in her art and when she begins to link her small objects together, as in *Cruciferae* (1995), the work crosses a line between ceramics and weaving, linking over eighty objects with wire, the thin sharp spikes splay out over the edges of the piece.

Cecula has spent decades designing successfully for industry and he, too, retains this experience in his art. He molds his pieces in porcelain and glazes them with a transparent glaze. The elegant, flowing forms look purposeful, as though they have a specific function and yet they are finally abstractions. Occasionally, he will place decals on the side of the works which suggest a quasi-corporate logo with impressive sounding names such as IMMUNEX, all of which are pure invention, provoking the viewer into imagining what activity these objects might support. They almost all deal with the idea of pouring, draining, or containing fluids. Even the metal bases on some pieces have draining holes anticipating a flow of liquid. They resemble laboratory hospital ware (although hospitals long ago replaced porcelain with plastic) and as a result, speak uncomfortably of mortality. In the age of AIDS, body fluids now convey a greater sense of threat than they did in the modernist era. With his spartan lines, elegance, and fine handling of materials, Cecula also manages to give his work a real formal beauty even while they remain containers of human anxiety.

Writing in 'Hygiene', Cecula's 1996 exhibition in New York, critic Gabi DeWald comments, 'Not the object, then, but rather the act of performing is now at the center of Cecula's works. We are no longer in the aseptic silence of the treatment and operating rooms but in the washing and defecating facilities. And we are no longer on our own; the objects stand in a row, they are to be used by several people at a time. We are in an institution. Here, one vomits, spits, urinates and masturbates in groups. There is no intimacy here: everything is public, uniform, washable, hygienic. Cecula fabricates the suggestion that these are mass-produced sanitary objects which have been alienated from their profane context for the purpose of art.'

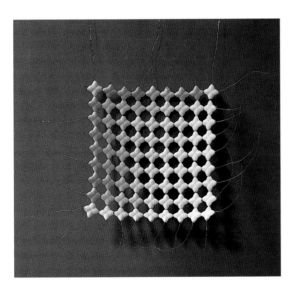

Barbara Schmidt
Cruciferae, 1995
Porcelain and wire
h 12 in., w 12 in., d 4 in.
h 30.5 cm, w 30.5 cm,
d 10 cm

189

Herbert Muschamp, the design and architecture critic of the *New York Times*, wrote about the growing love affair amongst the young with technology in 'The Happy Scary New Day for Design' (Sunday, October 15, 2000), noting that, 'It is scary to be living at a time when a particular creative field grips the public imagination as powerfully as [industrial] design has in recent years. I can't recall anything like it since the late 60s and early 70s when movies and pop music exercised a magnetic hold on the minds of baby boomers. Today the vigor pulses through fashion, furniture, art direction, graphics and product and image design with similarly captivating verve.' Muschamp also sees a hidden spirit of idealism returning, a cautious belief in technology noting that, 'As expressions of The New, these products have inherited the myth of progress, modernity's defining legend.' So when ceramic art captures both the aesthetic mood of our information age and the industrial past that gave birth to it, it is touching a deep wellspring in the minds of the under fifty audiences, giving a new definition to Phillip Johnson's 1934 concept of Machine Art.

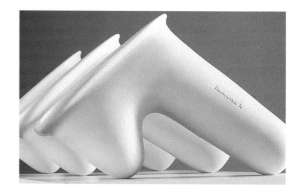

190   Post-Industrialism

Above, left; and above, right (detail)
Marek Cecula
Hygiene Series—Untitled IV, 1995
Vitreous china, wood, and steel
h 46 in., w 31 in., d 17 in. each
h 117 cm, w 78.7 cm, d 43 cm each

Opposite, above; and opposite, below (detail)
Marek Cecula
Hygiene Series—Untitled V, 1996
Vitreous china, wood, and steel
h 32 in., w 38 in., d 50 in. each
h 81.3 cm, w 96.5 cm, d 127 cm each

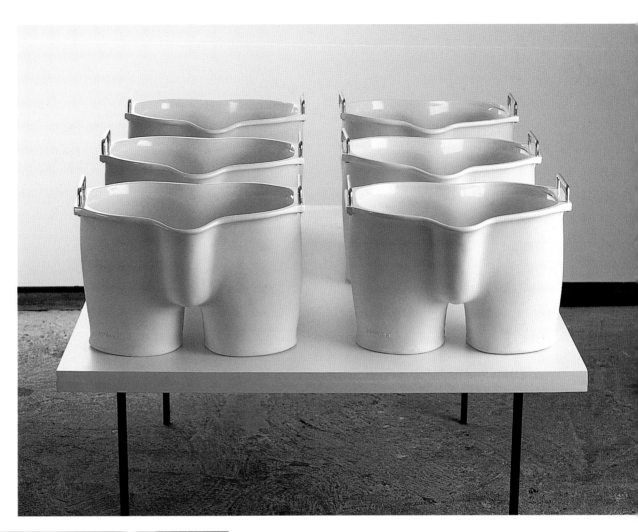

Yo Akiyama B. Shimonoseki, Japan, 1953. Akiyama is a third generation artist, working in the Kyoto area, a place regarded as the focus of avant-garde ceramics in Japan. He teaches at the Kyoto City University of Arts. In the mid-1970s Akiyama studied under Yagi Kazuo at the same university, where he became masterful at black-firing techniques. Kazuo (1918–79) was a founding member of the Sodeisha group in Kyoto and developed the black-firing method in the early 1960s. His sculptures are often huge, stretching twenty feet (6 meters) in length, with a surface that shows the impact of intense heat, crackled and disintegrating like a sun-dried mud-bed. In an article published by the Victorian Ceramic Group (Australia) Akiyama's work is described as follows, 'His cracked expanses of carbon impregnated clay relate to the geology and metaphysical beauty of the earth.' See Tomio Sugaya, *Metamorphosis of Contemporary Ceramics* (Shigaraki, Japan: The Museum of Contemporary Ceramic Art, 1991).

Dan Anderson B. St. Paul, MN, USA, 1945. Anderson received his B.S. from the University of Wisconsin, River Falls, WI, in 1968 and his M.F.A. from Cranbrook Academy of Art, Bloomfield Hills, MI, in 1970. Since 1970, Anderson has been Professor and Head of Ceramics at Southern Illinois University, Edwardsville, IL. He has received a record number of Illinois Arts Council Fellowships (1975, 1979, 1981, 1984, 1985, 1987, 1988, 1989, 1991, 1996, and 1999), a Ford Foundation Grant (1979) and an Individual Art Fellowship for the National Education Association (NEA) (1990). Anderson's pots, often grouped together in ways that re-create farm buildings in their landscape setting, are also utilitarian tea sets with the various structures becoming the sugar basin or cup, while the main building is the teapot. The effect of wood firing on his often brightly glazed pots mutes and subdues their tonality, and makes them approximate the weathered surface of actual farm buildings. Since 1968 he has had over forty one-person exhibitions, as well as participating in hundreds of group shows. Recent exhibitions include shows at Garth Clark Gallery, New York, NY; Gallery WDO, Chicago, IL; The Works Gallery, Philadelphia, PA; and SOFA, Chicago,

IL. Anderson's work is in the collections of Philadelphia Museum of Art, Philadelphia, PA; Charles A. Wustum Museum of Fine Arts, Racine, WI; Everson Museum of Art, Syracuse, NY; Mint Museum of Craft and Design, Charlotte, NC; and Carnegie Museum of Art, Pittsburgh, PA. See Tony Merino, 'Midwestern Clay: Anatomy and Architecture,' *Ceramics: Art and Perception* (No. 12, 1993); and Garth Clark, *The Artful Teapot* (New York: Watson-Guptill, and London: Thames & Hudson, 2001).

Paul Astbury B. Cheshire, England, 1944. Astbury studied, from 1960 to 1968 at the Stoke-on-Trent College of Art and from 1968 to 1971 at the Royal College of Art, London. He has exhibited actively since 1971 in seminal surveys such as 'New Directions in Ceramics,' Oxford Gallery, Oxford, 1972; 'State of Clay,' Sunderland Arts Centre, 1978 (toured Britain, Sweden, and Norway); and 'The Raw and the Cooked,' Museum of Modern Art, Oxford, 1993 (toured Britain, Japan, and France). In 1965 he presented 'Background,' a complex exhibition of raw clay works sealed in large white vitrines that was shown at the Diorama Gallery, London. Astbury has remained one of the most consistently avant-garde forces in ceramic art, or 'clay art' as he prefers to term it, always pushing the edge of both aesthetic and commercial values. See Emmanuel Cooper, 'Fired Earth—The Art of Paul Astbury,' *Ceramics: Art and Perception* (No. 21, 1995); Garth Clark, *The Potter's Art: A Complete History of Pottery in Britain* (London: Phaidon, 1995); and Paul Astbury, Emmanuel Cooper, and Julia Davis, *Document* (London: Blue Sky One, 1999).

Ralph Bacerra B. Garden Grove, CA, USA, 1938. Bacerra received his B.F.A.

from the Chouinard Art Institute, Los Angeles, CA, in 1961 and after two years of military service returned to head the ceramic department at Chouinard until 1972. He later joined the ceramics department at the Otis College of Art and Design, Los Angeles, CA, where he taught until 1998 when the department was closed. Best known to his students as 'Mr. Perfection,' Bacerra has an ability to create a highly complicated surface treatment, in keeping with the tradition of Japanese Imari works, but with his own contemporary spin on surface treatment. Bacerra received the Outstanding Achievement Award from the National Council on the Education of Ceramic Art in 1998 and is a fellow of the American Crafts Council. His work is in the collections of the Cooper-Hewitt National Design Museum, New York, NY; John Michael Kohler Arts Center, Sheboygan, WI; Long Beach Museum of Art, Long Beach, CA; Museum of Contemporary Ceramic Art in the Shigaraki Ceramic Cultural Park, Shigaraki, Japan; American Craft Museum, New York, NY; Los Angeles County Museum of Art, Los Angeles, CA; National Museum of American Art of the Smithsonian Institution, Washington, DC; and Victoria and Albert Museum, London. See Garth Clark, *American Ceramics* (New York: Abbeville Press, 1987); Jo Lauria, *Color and Fire* (Los Angeles: Los Angeles County Museum of Art, and New York: Rizzoli, 2000); Garth Clark and Oliver Watson, *American Potters Today* (London: Victoria and Albert Museum, 1985); and a recent monograph, Garth Clark, *Ralph Bacerra: A Survey* (New York: Garth Clark Gallery, 1999).

Anthony Bennett B. Evesham, Worcestershire, England, 1949. Bennett received a Diploma in Art and Design in 1971 from the Wolverhampton Polytechnic and an M.A. in 1974 from the Royal College of Art, London. Bennett was strongly influenced by American Funk ceramics—Wolverhampton Polytechnic was one of the first schools to acknowledge American Funk ceramics outside the USA. He evolved a style of carefully drawn, cartoon-like surreal images. An exceptional modeler,

Compiled by Garth Clark, Mark Del Vecchio, and John Pagliaro

Biographies

he has been commissioned by the Natural History Museum, London, to create Neanderthal figures for dioramas. Bennett has exhibited internationally, in both solo and group exhibitions, at Garth Clark Gallery, New York, NY, and Los Angeles, CA; Dolphin Gallery, Kansas City, MO; Los Angeles County Museum of Art, Los Angeles, CA; Rye Art Gallery, England; and Museum of Contemporary Ceramic Art in the Shigaraki Ceramic Cultural Park, Shigaraki, Japan. His work is in the collections of Auckland Museum, Auckland, New Zealand; Hastings Museum, England; Melbourne Museum, Australia; Museum of Contemporary Ceramic Art in the Shigaraki Ceramic Cultural Park, Shigaraki, Japan; Los Angeles County Museum of Art, Los Angeles, CA; and Ulster Museum, Belfast, Northern Ireland. See Garth Clark, *The Eccentric Teapot* (New York: Abbeville Press, 1989); Jo Lauria, *Color and Fire* (Los Angeles: Los Angeles County Museum of Art, and New York: Rizzoli, 2000); and Garth Clark, *The Artful Teapot* (New York: Watson-Guptill, and London: Thames & Hudson, 2001).

Claude Bouchard B. Quebec, Canada, 1957. Bouchard studied interior architecture at Collège François-Xavier Garneau, Quebec, Canada. He also studied architecture at the Université de Montreal. Bouchard has lived and worked in France since 1990. He taught at Columbia University, New York, NY, between 1991 and 1998, and was a Professor of Architecture for their New York/Paris program. Bouchard has acted as assistant to Serge Lutens, Artistic Director at Shiseido International, and has worked more specifically overseeing the project of an edition of vases for Artcodif, Paris, 2000. He has also worked extensively on design and layout for installations of shows at various museums—'Tea and Coffee Piazza' and '50 Years of Luminaire' at Musée des Arts Décoratifs, Montreal, Canada; 'The Space of a Time' at Musée McCord d'Histoire Canadienne, Montreal, Canada; and has produced multi-media projects for the Musée des Arts Décoratifs, Paris, helping them to develop ideas for interactive visitor stations. He has shown his work in solo shows at Anne Shelton Gallery, Paris; Ville de Chambery, France; Xanadou, Paris; and Galerie Jean Blanchaert, Milan and Faenza, Italy.

Hilbert Boxem B. Almaar, the Netherlands, 1939. Boxem studied at the Gerrit Rietveld Academy, Amsterdam (1957–61) and has been Professor of Ceramics and Sculpture at the Akademie Minerva in Groningen, the Netherlands, since 1971. Boxem's approach to the vessel is represented by large shard shapes with clear references to Greek and Roman vessels—baroque, Art Nouveau and Memphis ceramics with a concern for historical recognition. Boxem has exhibited extensively throughout Europe. His work is included in the collections of Stedelijk Museum, Amsterdam; Museum Boijmans van Beuningen, Rotterdam; Groninger Museum, Groningen; and Museum het Princesshof, Leeuwarden, all in the Netherlands. See Mieke G. Spruit-Ledeboer, *Nederlandse Keramiek 1975/1985* (Amsterdam: Allert de Lange b.v., 1985); and Liesbeth Cromelin, *Ceramics in the Stedelijk Museum* (Amsterdam: Stedelijk Museum of Modern Art, 1998).

Alison Britton B. Harrow, Middlesex, England, 1948. Britton was attracted to clay and its potential when she was twelve. In 1966 she attended the Leeds College of Art and Design and then continued her studies at the Central St. Martins School of Art and Design, London, from 1967 to 1970. She received her M.A. at the Royal College of Art, London. One of her tutors there was Hans Coper, who, along with Lucie Rie, was not bound to the brown pot aesthetic espoused by Bernard Leach and others. Encouraged by Coper, Britton, and classmates Jill Crowley, Elizabeth Fritsch, and Jacqueline Poncelet, felt free to move toward a more ornamented and architectonic style. Her personal clay art deals with the inherent inner and outer dichotomies found in the vessel form. She deliberately eschews the centrality implied in wheel-thrown pots, preferring to make asymmetrically constructed vessels. Like many of her generation, her influences come from both fine and decorative art. Britton's surfaces have as much to do with the traditions of pattern as they have to do with the free form of Jackson Pollock's paintings. Britton teaches at the Royal College of Art, London, and is a curator and critic of ceramics and has been awarded an OBE for her service to the crafts. Together with Martina Margetts, she curated the exhibition 'The Raw and the Cooked,' an influential survey of British ceramics that was organized in 1993 by the Museum of Modern Art, Oxford, and toured internationally. Britton's work has been exhibited extensively and is in the collections of numerous museums in Britain, Europe, Japan, and the USA. Her work was surveyed in the monograph by Peter Dormer and David Cripps, *Alison Britton, A View* (*In Studio* series) (London: Bellew Publishing, 1985); and more recently in Linda Sandino, *Alison Britton* (London: Barrett/Marsden Gallery, 2000); and Edward Lucie-Smith, 'Sources of Inspiration: Alison Britton,' *Crafts* (Nov/Dec 2000).

Toby Buonagurio B. Bronx, New York, USA, 1947. Buonagurio received her B.A. in Fine Arts in 1969 and her M.A. in 1971, both from the City College of New York. She is presently Professor of Art at the State University of New York at Stony Brook and Art Department Director of Undergraduate Studies. Buonagurio received an Art Medal of Honor from the Everson Museum of Art, Syracuse, NY (1990) and an Excellence in Arts Award from the Bronx Council of the Arts (1996). Since the 1970s, Buonagurio has championed the possibilities of surface treatments using low-fire gold glazes, acrylic paints, and flocking on her fantastic robots and racing-shoe sculptures. Buonagurio has exhibited extensively throughout the USA, and had numerous one-person exhibitions at the Monique Knowlton Gallery, New York, NY, and Bernice Steinbaum Gallery, New York, NY. Her work is included in many public collections, including Mint Museum of Craft and Design, Charlotte, NC; Everson Museum of Art, Syracuse, NY; and American Craft Museum, New York, NY. See Susan Wechsler, *Ceramics Today* (Geneva: Olizane, 1984); Garth Clark, *American Ceramics: the Collection of the Everson Museum of Art* (New York: Rizzoli, 1989); and Judith Schwartz, *Confrontational Clay: The Artist as Social Critic* (New York: Exhibits USA, 2000).

Mark Burns B. Springfield, OH, USA, 1950. Burns received his B.F.A. in 1972 from the College of the Dayton Art Institute, OH, with a major in ceramics. He received his M.F.A. in 1974 at the University of Washington, Seattle, WA, under Howard Kottler and Patti Warashina. He has taught at the College of the Dayton Art Institute, OH; University of Washington, WA; Factory of Visual Arts, Seattle, WA; State University of New York at Oswego, NY; University of the Arts, Philadelphia, PA; and California State University, Chico, CA. Since 1991 he has been Professor and Head of the Ceramics Department at the University of Nevada, Las Vegas, NV. Burns employs bizarre, exotic, and sadomasochistic imagery in his immaculately crafted works. In 1977 he held his first of numerous one-man exhibitions at the Helen Drutt Gallery, Philadelphia, PA; and subsequently in New York as well. In 1984 he was commissioned by the Pennsylvania Academy of the Fine Arts to create an installation as a homage to the architect Frank Furness. The Society for Art in Crafts, Verona, PA, organized a mid-career survey of his work in 1986 entitled *Mark Burns—Decade in Philadelphia*. Burns' sculptures are in the public collections of the Everson Museum of Art, Syracuse, NY; Philadelphia Museum of Art, Philadelphia, PA; Stedelijk Museum, Amsterdam, the Netherlands; and Musée des Arts Décoratifs, Montreal, Canada. His work is discussed by art theorist Dave Hickey in 'Mark Burns Venetian America,' *American Craft* (June/July 1998).

Kathy Butterly B. Amityville, NY, USA, 1963. Butterly received her B.F.A. in 1986 from the Moore College of Art and Design, Philadelphia, PA, and an M.F.A. from the University of California, Davis, CA, in 1990. Butterly was the recipient of an Empire State Craft Alliance Grant in 1995 and a New York Foundation for the Arts Grant in 1999. Working in colored porcelains, Butterly's work is comprised of small-scale sculptural cup forms with folded walls, rich color, and multi-fired surface applications. She has exhibited regularly in New York at the Franklin Parrasch Gallery. Butterly's work is in the collections of the Museum het Kruithuis, 's-Hertogenbosch, the Netherlands; M. H. De Young Memorial Museum, San Francisco, CA; and Mint Museum of Craft and Design, Charlotte, NC. See Arthur C. Danto and Janet Koplos, *Choice of America* ('s-Hertogenbosch: Museum het Kruithuis, 1999); Timothy H. Burgard, *The Art of Craft* (San Francisco: M. H. De Young Memorial Museum, 1999); Gretchen Adkins, 'The Pots of Kathy Butterly,' *Ceramics: Art and Perception* (No. 23, 1996); and April Kingsley, 'Kathy

Butterly: Miniature Monuments,' *American Ceramics* (Vol. 13, 2000).

Lidya Buzio B. Montevideo, Uruguay, 1948. She studied painting and drawing with Horacio Torres, José Luis Montes, and Guillermo Fernandez from 1964 to 1966, and ceramics with José Collell in 1967. In 1967 she moved to the USA and set up a studio in New York. She found herself drifting toward cityscapes after her move to New York, creating slab-built burnished pots with roof-top images. Her work is in numerous public collections including the Brooklyn Museum of Art, New York, NY; Los Angeles County Museum of Art, Los Angeles, CA; Nelson-Atkins Museum of Art in Kansas City, MO; and Victoria and Albert Museum, London. From 1983 she exhibited her work at the Garth Clark Gallery in New York and Los Angeles. She has recently ended her career in ceramics, and is currently working in wood, but still within her speciality of urban architecture. See John Beardsley, Jane Livingston, and Octavio Paz, *Hispanic Art in the United States: Thirty Contemporary Painters and Sculptors* (Houston: Museum of Fine Arts, and New York: Abbeville Press, 1987); Garth Clark, *Ceramic Echoes: Historical References in Contemporary Ceramics* (Kansas City: Contemporary Art Society, 1983); Garth Clark and Oliver Watson, *American Potters Today* (London: Victoria and Albert Museum, 1985).

Claudi Casanovas B. Barcelona, Spain, 1956. Casanovas' work is distinctive

because of its dramatic scale and his ferocious use of rough, craggy volcanic-like forms. Part of his creativity is expressed in the unique workshop equipment that allows him to shape, move, and fire his enormous four-hundred pound plates, giant bowls and five foot (1.35 m) high amphorae. Exhibitions of his work have included solo shows at Garth Clark Gallery, New York, NY; Galerie Besson, London; Galeria Rosa Pous, Girona, Spain; Galeria Lluis Heras, Palafrugell, Spain; Galeria Joan Gaspar, Barcelona, Spain; Museu de Ceramica, Barcelona, Spain; Musée d'Art Contemporain, Dunkerque, France; Keramikmuseet Grimmerhus, Middelfart, Denmark; Museu d'Argentona, Barcelona, Spain; and Museum Boijmans van Beuningen, Rotterdam, the Netherlands. His work is in the collections of Museu de Ceramica, Barcelona, Spain; Hetjens Museum, Düsseldorf, Germany; Museo Internazionale delle Ceramiche, Faenza, Italy; Museu d'Art Modern, Girona, Spain; Museum Boijmans van Beuningen, Rotterdam, the Netherlands; Museum of Contemporary Ceramic Art in the Shigaraki Ceramic Cultural Park, Shigaraki, Japan; and Musée de la Céramique, Vallauris, France. See J. Corredor-Matheos, *Claudi Casanovas: Cercles* (Barcelona: Galeria Joan Gaspar, 1994); and Maria Lluisa Borras, *Claudi Casanovas: Pedra Foguera* (Düsseldorf: Hetjens Museum, 1996).

Marek Cecula B. Kielce, Poland, 1944. Cecula studied and was apprenticed in Israel. Since 1977 he has worked in New York City. He is the Head and Coordinator of the Ceramics Department of the Parsons School of Design, New York. Cecula was known primarily as a ceramics designer both for industry and for his own low-volume production unit. His breakthrough came after working on new ideas at the European Ceramic Work Center in 's-Hertogenbosch, the Netherlands, in 1994. The work from this experimental period was shown for the first time at the Garth Clark Gallery in New York under the title 'Scatology.' Subsequently, he has produced one groundbreaking body of work after the other, 'Hygiene' in 1996 and 'Violations' in 1998. His work is in the collections of the Los Angeles County Museum of Art, Los Angeles, CA; Mint Museum of Craft and Design, Charlotte, NC; Museum of Fine Arts, Boston, MA; and Cooper-Hewitt National Design Museum, New York, NY. See Lydia Tugendrajch, *Marek Cecula: Scatology Series* (New York: Garth Clark Gallery; and Rotterdam: Galerie Maas, 1994); Gabi Dewald, *Marek Cecula: Hygiene* (New York: Garth Clark Gallery, and San Francisco: Modernism, 1996); Jozef A. Mrozek, *Marek Cecula*

(Warsaw: Centre for Contemporary Art, 1999); and Garth Clark, *The Artful Teapot* (New York: Watson-Guptill, and London: Thames & Hudson, 2001).

Michael Cleff B. Bochum, Germany, 1961. Cleff began his ceramic career on a student exchange program in Chicago, IL, from 1977 to 1978, and was an apprentice to a potter at Garmisch-Partenkirchen, Germany, from 1980 to 1982. He has had his own studio since 1987 and studied fine arts at the Academy of Art, Düsseldorf, Germany, with Fritz Schwegler from 1990 to 1996. His late 1990s work comprises geometric stoneware forms which have a strong architectonic presence, with various openings glazed with a warm shino glaze and thin blue lines drawn to take the viewer's eye both in and around the object. In *Ceramic Art Notes* (April 7–May 2, 1998), Garth Clark writes that, 'Cleff's work is intriguing because it meshes two unlikely worlds. His pottery looks like the love child between a 17th century Japanese shino potter and the minimalist painter Agnes Martin.' This work is warmed by a rich shino glaze with very crisp edges. He is the winner of numerous prizes, namely the Richard Bampi Preis, Germany (1990), the first prize of the 1997 Competition held by the Savings Bank of Nassau, Germany, and the winner of the Grand Prix at the 50th Concorso Internazionale della Ceramica d'Arte, Faenza, Italy, in 1997. Cleff's work can be found in the collections of the Richard Bampi Society, Germany; Museum of Ceramics in Westerwald, Germany; American Craft Museum, New York, NY; Museo Internazionale delle Ceramiche, Faenza, Italy; Los Angeles County Museum of Art, Los Angeles, CA; and Charles A. Wustum Museum of Fine Arts, Racine, WI. See Barbara Christin, 'Michael Cleff: In a Vibrant Order,' *Ceramics: Art and Perception* (No. 34, 1998).

Margaretha Daepp B. Oppligen, Switzerland, 1959. Daepp studied at the Ecole des Arts Décoratifs, Geneva (1982–84) and the Academy of Arts in Berlin (1989–92). In 1993 she received a grant from the Aeschlimann-Corti-Foundation and a residency at the European Ceramic Work Center in 's-Hertogenbosch, the Netherlands. Working with commercial earthenware, Daepp's seemingly industrial forms are hand cast and assembled. She has exhibited at Galerie Michele Zeller, Bern, Switzerland; the Tabula Rasa, Biel, Switzerland; and Goldrausch IV, Berlinische Galerie in Martin-Gropius-Bau, Germany. See Walo van Fellenberg, *Die Teile und das ze* (Bern: Berner Kunstmitteilungen, Sept/Oct 1994).

Wouter Dam B. Utrecht, the Netherlands, 1957. Dam was educated at the Gerrit Rietveld Academy, Amsterdam (1975–80) and has worked from his studio in Amsterdam since 1982. He received a Major Grant for the Arts from the Fonds B.K.V.B. in 1992 and a Grant State Fund for the Arts, Fonds B.K.V.B. in 1994. Dam's irregular and sensual bottomless vessels sit on their sides, allowing the viewer to look through the forms with their soft matte surfaces. He has exhibited regularly throughout the USA and Europe, with one-person exhibitions at the Carla Koch Gallery, Amsterdam; Barrett/Marsden Gallery, London; and Frank Lloyd Gallery in Los Angeles, CA. His work is included in the collections of Stedelijk Museum, Amsterdam, the Netherlands; Musée des Arts Décoratifs, Paris; and Detroit Institute of Arts, Detroit, MI. See Thomas Piche, Jr., 'Wouter Dam,' *American Ceramics* (Vol. 11, 1999); and Thomas Piche, Jr., 'Wouter Dam's See-through Smoothies,' *Ceramic Review* (Jan/Feb 2001).

Robert Dawson B. New York, NY, USA, 1953. Dawson lives and works in London. He studied ceramics and fine art at the Camberwell College of Arts, London, receiving a B.A. in 1993 and an M.A. at the Royal College of Art, London, in 1999. Dawson's use of the eternal dinnerware classic 'Willow Pattern' has been turned on its head with stunning originality since his one-person exhibition 'Appropriating the Willows' at the Studio Pottery Gallery, Exeter, in 1997. He has exhibited extensively throughout England, including 'Hot Off the Press' at the Tullie House Museum and Art Gallery, Carlisle, and 'The Plate Show' organized by the Collins Gallery, Glasgow, which toured the world. See Paul Scott and Terry Bennett, *Hot Off the Press* (London: Bellew Publishing, 1996); Paul Scott and Laura Hamilton, *The Plate Show* (Glasgow: Collins Gallery, 1998); and Sally Howard, 'Robert Dawson and the Willow Pattern Plate,' *Ceramics: Art and Perception* (No. 27, 1997).

John deFazio B. Reading, PA, USA, 1959. DeFazio earned a B.F.A. in ceramics at Philadelphia College of Art (1981) and took an M.F.A. in sculpture, San Francisco Art Institute, CA, in 1984. He has been a visiting artist and lecturer at the University of Nevada, Las Vegas, NV, and the University of Washington, Seattle, WA (both 1998). DeFazio's awards include an NEA Visual Art Fellowship (1986) and a New York Foundation for the Arts Fellowship (1991). DeFazio works with molded readymades, mostly items considered to be kitsch, transforming them with irony and humor. He has undertaken many commissions, including a massive ceramic and glass table for the boardroom of MTV in New York. His work has been widely exhibited with, amongst others, shows at Harrison Gallery, Philadelphia, PA; Garth Clark Gallery, New York, NY; Dolphin Gallery, Kansas City, MO; American Craft Museum, New York, NY; Baltimore Clayworks, Baltimore, MD; San Angelo Museum of Fine Arts, San Angelo, TX; and Museum of Contemporary Ceramic Art in the Shigaraki Ceramic Cultural Park, Shigaraki, Japan. DeFazio's work appears in the collections of Honolulu Museum of Contemporary Art, Honolulu, HI; Museum of Contemporary Ceramic Art in the Shigaraki Ceramic Cultural Park, Shigaraki, Japan; Mint Museum of Craft and Design, Charlotte, NC, and others. See Dave Hickey, *Stardumb*, Illustrated by John DeFazio (San Francisco: Artspace, 1999); and Garth Clark, *The Artful Teapot* (New York: Watson-Guptill, and London: Thames & Hudson, 2001).

Roseline Delisle B. Rimouski, Quebec, Canada, 1952. Delisle received her Diplôme d'Etudes Professionnelles in 1973 from the Institute of Applied Arts, Montreal, Quebec, and in 1978 set up a studio in Venice, CA. Her work, always done with meticulously thrown porcelain forms, is colored in either black or cobalt slip, creating horizontal stripes applied by hand, but with an industrial precision. In 1985 she received a commission from the J. Paul Getty Center for the History of Art and Humanities in Santa Monica, CA, to create vessels for their entrance area. She has exhibited in Japan, Canada, and the USA, with regular solo shows at the Gallery Koyanagi, Tokyo; Frank Lloyd Gallery, Santa Monica, CA; and John Berggruen Gallery in San Francisco, CA. Her work is included in the collections of Tokyo National Museum, Japan; Musée du Quebec, Canada; Los Angeles County Museum of Art, Los Angeles, CA; and The Metropolitan Museum of Art, New York, NY. See Martina Margetts, *International Crafts* (London: Thames & Hudson, 1991); Craig R. Miller, *Modern Design, 1890–1990* (New York: The Metropolitan Museum of Art, 1990); Garth Clark, *American Ceramics* (New York: Abbeville Press, 1987); and Kristine McKenna, *Roseline Delisle* (Santa Monica: Frank Lloyd Gallery, 1999).

Stefano Della Porta B. Rome, Italy, 1958. Della Porta has exhibited extensively throughout Italy, beginning in 1983 with the show 'Monocromie Tra Le Nature Morte' at the Galleria Studio del Canova, Rome. Further exhibitions have been held at Galleria Il Patio, Ravenna (1994); Circolo degli Artisti, Faenza (1996); Galleria Marco Rossi Lecce, Rome (1997); and Galleria Erica Fiorentini, Rome (1999). His work was included in the Concorso Internazionale della Ceramica d'Arte at the Museo Internazionale delle Ceramiche, Faenza, Italy, in 1997. His large, oversized, super-realistic sculptures often reflect the neurosis of contemporary life. See Gian Carlo Bojani and Dirma Dal Prato, *50 Premio Faenza: Concorso Internazionale della Ceramica d'Arte* (Faenza: Studio 88, 1997).

Kim Dickey B. White Plains, NY, USA, 1964. Dickey received a B.F.A. in

ceramics, Rhode Island School of Design, Providence, RI, in 1986, and an M.F.A. from New York State College of Ceramics at Alfred University, New York, NY (1988). Dickey currently holds an Assistant Professorship at the University of Colorado, Boulder, CO, where she has taught since 1999. She has been a visiting artist at nearly twenty colleges and universities over the past decade, and held visiting professorships at six institutions during this time. Dickey's work has been widely exhibited, including at Garth Clark Gallery; Thomas Healy Gallery; Jack Tilton Gallery; Jane Hartsook Gallery; and Bronwyn Keenan Gallery, all New York; Rule Modern and Contemporary Gallery, Denver, CO; Museum of Contemporary Art, Denver, CO; and Everson Museum of Art, Syracuse, NY. Her work is in the public collections of Museum of Contemporary Art, Honolulu, HI; and Everson Museum of Art, Syracuse, NY. See Garth Clark, *The Eccentric Teapot* (New York: Abbeville Press, 1989); and Garth Clark, *The Artful Teapot* (New York: Watson-Guptill, and London: Thames & Hudson, 2001).

Rick Dillingham B. Lake Forest, IL, USA, 1952; D. Sante Fe, NM, USA, 1994. Dillingham studied at the California College of Arts and Crafts, Oakland, CA, and received his B.F.A. from the University of New Mexico; Albuquerque, NM, in 1974. In 1979 he completed his M.F.A. at California's Claremont Graduate University. Dillingham received Visual Artist's Fellowships from the NEA in 1977 and 1982. Apart from his work as an artist, Dillingham was involved in a broad range of activities. He was a dealer in historic Native American pottery and curated a number of exhibitions. Dillingham's pottery reflected his knowledge of, and interest in, Native American prehistoric pottery. He became intrigued by the notion of the vessel as an assembly of shards when he was restoring pots at the Museum of New Mexico, Laboratory of Anthropology, in Santa Fe, NM. He created what Garth Clark calls 'a symphony of shards,' breaking the pots into pieces and carefully reassembling them and painting the individual pieces with color, or pattern, or gilding them with gold leaf. See Jan Adelman, Garth Clark, Tom Collins, and Malin Wilson, *Rick Dillingham* (Santa Fe: Rotary Club, 1993); and Joseph Traugott, *Rick Dillingham 1952–1994: A Retrospective Exhibition* (Albuquerque: University of New Mexico Art Museum, 1994).

Gary DiPasquale B. Sayerville, NJ, USA, 1953. DiPasquale studied at Ocean County College, NJ (1972–73), the School of the Museum of Fine Arts, Boston, MA (1973–74) and the Massachusetts College of Art, Boston,

MA (1975–78). He maintains a studio in New York, working almost exclusively with slab-constructed geometric forms. DiPasquale makes one-off works, as well as hand-made production pottery. He has exhibited extensively since 1980, including solo shows at the Works Gallery in Philadelphia, PA; and Alianza Gallery, Boston, MA.

Paul Dresang B. Appleton, WI, USA, 1948. Dresang earned a B.A. in art, University of Wisconsin, Oshkosh, WI (1970). He took his M.F.A. at University of Minnesota, Minneapolis, MN (1974). He has guest lectured and given workshops at colleges and universities across the USA. Dresang received an NEA Visual Artist's Fellowship Grant (1988) and the Illinois Art Council Fellowship Finalist Grant (1999). Recently his work has involved variations on the teapot form, concealed, but suggested, beneath trompe-l'oeil leather, replete with zippers and clasps, whose numbers and placement draw a mood of fetish about these objects. Dresang has exhibited his work in many venues, including the Nancy Margolis Gallery, New York, NY; Ferrin Gallery, Northampton, MA; The Clay Studio, Philadelphia, PA; American Craft Museum, New York, NY; Frederick F. Weisman Art Museum, Minneapolis, MN; and Los Angeles County Museum of Art, Los Angeles, CA. His work is in the permanent collections of Los Angeles County Museum of Art, Los Angeles, CA; Renwick Gallery of the Smithsonian American Art Museum, Washington, DC; and The Mint Museum of Craft and Design, Charlotte, NC. See Leslie Ferrin, *Teapots Transformed: Exploration of an Object* (Madison: Guild Books, 2000).

Michael Duvall B. Grand Rapids, MI, USA, 1950. Duvall was a ceramics major from 1972 to 1974 at the Wayne State University, Detroit, MI. He has operated his studio full time since 1975. His broad exhibition record includes shows at Joy Horwich Gallery, Chicago, IL; Garth Clark Gallery, New York, NY and Los Angeles, CA; The Works Gallery, Philadelphia, PA; Ferrin Gallery, Northampton, MA; Craft Alliance, St. Louis, MO; American Craft Museum, New York, NY; Museum het Kruithuis, 's-Hertogenbosch, the Netherlands; Victoria and Albert Museum, London; and Columbus Museum of Art, Columbus, OH. Duvall's work appears in the collections of Newark Museum, Newark, NJ; Museum het Kruithuis, 's-Hertogenbosch, the Netherlands; and Victoria and Albert Museum, London. See Mark Del Vecchio, 'Michael Duvall,' *Functional Glamour* ('s-Hertogenbosch: Museum het Kruithuis, 1989).

Ken Eastman B. Watford, Hertfordshire, England, 1960. Eastman studied at the Edinburgh College of Art, Scotland, receiving a B.A. Hons in 1983, and at the Royal College of Art, London, receiving an M.A. in ceramics in 1987. His work has been shown in numerous solo and group exhibitions; he currently exhibits with Barrett/Marsden Gallery, London; and Gallery de Witte Voet, Amsterdam. His work is in the collections of the Norwich City Art Gallery, England; Museum Boijmans van Beuningen, Rotterdam, the Netherlands; Museum of Contemporary Ceramic Art in the Shigaraki Ceramic Cultural Park, Shigaraki, Japan; Württembergisches Landesmuseum, Stuttgart, Germany; Victoria and Albert Museum, London; and Museo Internazionale delle Ceramiche, Faenza, Italy. He has received numerous awards, including the Grand Prix of the Concorso Internazionale della Ceramica d'Arte, Faenza, Italy. See Alison Britton, *Ken Eastman* (Nottingham: Angel Row Gallery, 1998); and Tanya Harrod and Martin Bodilsen Kaldahl, *British Ceramics.2000.dk* (Middelfart, Denmark: Keramikmuseet Grimmerhus, 2000).

Edward Eberle B. Tarentum, PA, USA, 1944. Eberle received a B.S. from Edinboro State College, PA, in 1971, and his M.F.A. from New York State College of Ceramics at Alfred University, New York, NY, 1976. The artist's voluminous, lidded porcelain vessels draw vague allusions to houses and architecture. His elaborate sgraffito imagery narrates, with lively parades of people, the interior life of his 'houses.' Eberle's imagery fluctuates deftly between tonal representation of bodies in space, and graphic surface pattern that serves to reinforce the pot's formal structure. Many influences can be found in his work, from black-and-white Mimbres pottery to painting and decoration on early Greek vases. Eberle directs the eye between lavish, lyrical narrative imagery, and the 2D line of the form they move around. His accolades include a Visual Artist's Fellowship from the NEA in 1987. Eberle has exhibited his work widely, in both solo and group shows, at Garth Clark Gallery, New York, NY; Perimeter Gallery, Chicago, IL; Temple Gallery, Philadelphia, PA; Joanne Rapp Gallery, Scottsdale, AZ; Northern Clay Center, Minneapolis, MN; and Carnegie Museum of Art, Pittsburgh, PA, amongst others. His work is in the collections of Carnegie Museum of Art, Pittsburgh, PA; Charles A. Wustum Museum of Fine Arts, Racine, WI; and Detroit Institute of Arts, Detroit, MI. See Janet Koplos, 'Edward Eberle at Garth Clark,' *Art in America* (May 1996); and Garth Clark, *The Artful Teapot* (New York: Watson-Guptill, and London: Thames & Hudson, 2001).

Philip Eglin B. Gibraltar, 1959. Eglin studied in England at the Harlow Technical College (1977–79), the Staffordshire Polytechnic (1979–82), and received an M.A. in ceramics from the Royal College of Art, London, in 1986. He teaches at Staffordshire University in the historical seat of English ceramics, Stoke-on-Trent. He keeps a studio in nearby Newcastle-under-Lyme. His work champions the figure, referring to classical, medieval, and contemporary postures. Venus and Madonna figures are often covered in graffiti-like images or left pristine in a rich, glossy glaze. His work is in the collections of Stedelijk Museum, Amsterdam, the Netherlands; Victoria and Albert Museum, London; Los Angeles County Museum of Art, Los Angeles, CA; and Mint Museum of Craft and Design, Charlotte, NC. He won the prestigious Jerwood Prize for Ceramics in 1996 as the most promising young ceramic sculptor in Britain. In 2001 the Victoria and Albert Museum in London plans a one-man exhibition. His work is published in a catalog of the international touring exhibition 'The Raw and The Cooked,' organized in 1993 by the Museum of Modern Art, Oxford, as well as 'Philip Eglin—A Staffordshire Tradition,' The South Bank Centre, London 1991; and numerous articles in *Ceramic Review*, *Crafts*, *Ceramics: Art and Perception*, and other publications. See Alison Britton and Oliver Watson, *Philip Eglin* (Edinburgh: The Scottish Gallery, 1997).

Raymon Elozua B. Germany, 1947. Elozua studied at the University of Chicago and has been a visiting lecturer at colleges and universities throughout the USA since 1979. He has taught ceramic sculpture at New York University, NY (1982–86); Rhode Island School of Design, Providence, RI (1983); California College of Arts and Crafts, Oakland, CA (1983); and Pratt Institute School of Art and Design, Brooklyn, NY (1984–85). He has been the recipient of NEA Fellowships in painting and sculpture (1980, 1981 and 1987), as well as a New York Foundation for the Arts Fellowship in Ceramics (1988). His solo exhibitions include shows at Pfizer Gallery, New York, NY; Garth Clark Gallery, New York, NY; Habatat-Shaw Gallery, Detroit, MI; Braunstein Gallery, San Francisco, CA; O.K. Harris Gallery, New York, NY; and Carlo Lamagna Gallery, New York, NY. Elozua's work is in the collections of American Craft Museum, New York, NY; Everson Museum of Art, Syracuse, NY; Los Angeles County Museum of Art, Los Angeles, CA; Mint Museum of Craft and Design, Charlotte, NC; and Charles A. Wustum Museum of Fine Arts, Racine, WI. See Garth Clark, *American Ceramics* (New York: Abbeville Press, 1987); Garth Clark, Mary F. Douglas, Carol E. Mayer, Barbara Perry, Todd D. Smith, and E. Michael Whittington, *Selections from Allan Chasanoff Ceramic Collection* (Charlotte, NC: The Mint Museum of Craft and Design, 2000); and Jo Lauria, *Color and Fire* (Los Angeles: Los Angeles County Museum of Art, and New York: Rizzoli, 2000).

Zhou Ding Fang B. Yixing, China, 1965. Ding Fang is one of two students of Xu Xiu Tang, a 'national craft master' of China. She has earned the rank of 'craft master'. She works within the established traditions of Yixing ware: teapots, small sculpture, and literati objects known for trompe-l'oeil effects and their general degree of exacting detail. Her work has been reproduced in publications in China, Hong Kong, Taiwan, and Singapore. The artist's work has appeared as an image adorning a series of Chinese postage stamps featuring famous Yixing pots. Ding Fang has shown at Garth Clark Gallery, New York, NY. Her work is in the collections of the British Museum, London; Asian Art Museum, San Francisco, CA; Mint Museum of Craft and Design, Charlotte, NC; and Beijing Art Capital Museum, Beijing, China. See Lee Jingduan, ed., *Charm of Dark-Red Pottery Teapots* (Nanjing: Yilin Press, 1992); and Garth Clark, *The Artful Teapot* (New York: Watson-Guptill, and London: Thames & Hudson, 2001).

Laszlo Fekete B. Budapest, Hungary, 1949. Fekete studied at the Academy of Applied Arts, Budapest, from 1969 to 1974. As was the tradition amongst artists during the communist era, Fekete focused mainly on international juried exhibitions, winning a string of medals, prizes, and diplomas for his work from the Hungarian Cultural Ministry, the French Cultural Ministry, the Mino Triennial, and the Academy of International Ceramics. Since 1994 he has exhibited with the Garth Clark

Gallery, New York, NY. Fekete's work takes on a grand theme, the layered cultural detritus of over five hundred years of successive regimes in Hungary, each of which has attempted to wipe out the traces of the previous power. In some of his work he collaborates with the Herend Porcelain factory in Hungary, using their seconds to assemble sardonic commentaries on taste and culture. His work is in the collections of Mint Museum of Craft and Design, Charlotte, NC; Museum of Applied Arts, Budapest, Hungary; and Mino Triennial, Mino, Japan. See Garth Clark and Laszlo Fekete, *Laszlo Fekete* (New York: Garth Clark Gallery, 1997); Garth Clark, Mary F. Douglas, Carol E. Mayer, Barbara Perry, Todd D. Smith, and E. Michael Whittington, *Selections from Allan Chasanoff Ceramic Collection* (Charlotte, NC: Mint Museum of Craft and Design, 2000); and Garth Clark, *The Artful Teapot* (New York: Watson-Guptill, and London: Thames & Hudson, 2001).

Bean Finneran B. Cleveland, OH, USA, 1947. Finneran studied at the University of Michigan Museum School and the Massachusetts College of Art and has been an Associate Artistic Director, designer and performer at the SOON 3 Theatre Company in San Francisco, CA, since 1972. She has exhibited in the 'Ceramics for the 21st Century' at LEF in St. Helena, CA; 'Landscapes and Memory' at the Haines Gallery and the Braunstein/Quay Gallery, both in San Francisco, CA. Finneran's organic sculptures use universal geometry by placing thousands of small porcelain parts, stacked and arranged as nature would have created them through the ebb and flow of ocean tides. Her work is in the collection of Microsoft, Seattle, WA.

Jean-François Fouilhoux B. Corbeil-Essonnes, France, 1947. Fouilhoux studied at the Ecole Nationale Supérieure des Arts Appliqués, Paris. He is the recipient of the Max Laeuger Preis (1995); the Fletcher Challenge Ceramics Award (1998); and the Internationale Handwerkmesse, München (1999). Fouilhoux works in porcelain, creating jagged carved sculptural bowls with mysterious and unique celadon glazes.

Extensively exhibiting throughout Europe, he has had regular solo shows with galerie b 15 in Munich, Germany. His work is in the collections of the Musée National de Céramique de Sèvres, Paris; Musée Ariana, Geneva, Switzerland; Fletcher Collection, New Zealand; and Los Angeles County Museum of Art, Los Angeles, CA. See Robert Deblander, 'Le Retour de Celadon,' *La Revue de la céramique et du verre* (Nov/Dec 1993); Hans Peter Jakobson, 'Dritter Max Laeuger Preis der Stadt Lorrach,' *Neue Keramik* (Nov/Dec 1995); Ariane Grenon, 'Jean-François Fouilhoux, Celadons,' *Courrier des Métiers d'Arts* (Jan/Feb 1996); and Hubert Treuille, 'Fouilhoux's Search for the Perfect Celadon,' *Ceramics: Art and Perception* (No. 29, 1997).

Léopold Foulem B. Bathurst, New Brunswick, Canada, 1945. He received his B.A. from the Alberta College of Art and Design, Calgary, Alberta, Canada, and an M.A. from the Indiana State University, IN, in 1988. Foulem works with ceramics from a decidedly conceptual point of view and has been the inspiration for a group of Canadian artists—Richard Milette, Jeannot Blackburn, and Paul Mathieu—with a similar bent, known loosely as 'Quebecois Clay'. Foulem writes and lectures extensively on ceramics, as well as being an active exhibitor. He has had numerous solo exhibitions since 1969, most recently with Prime Gallery in Toronto and Garth Clark Gallery in New York, NY. He has shown at forty-two museums and has been in 180 group exhibitions. His work is in many collections, including Los Angeles County Museum of Art, Los Angeles, CA. In 1999 he received one of Canada's top accolades, the Jean A. Chalmers National Crafts Award. See Paul Bourassa, *Phantasmes et Soucoupes: Ceramics by Leopold L. Foulem* (Saint-Laurent: Musée d'Art Saint-Laurent, 2000).

Judy Fox B. Elizabeth, NJ, USA, 1957. Fox received her B.A. in 1978 from Yale University, New Haven, CT, and her M.A. at the Institute of Fine Arts, New York University, NY, in 1983. She has been a regular visiting artist and lecturer throughout the USA, most recently at the Rhode Island School of Design, Providence, RI, and Bennington College, New York, NY. Fox has received a Jonathon Edwards Arts Award (1978); an Individual Artist's Grant from the NEA (1988 and 1994); and residency at the MacDowell Colony, Peterborough, NH. Fox works in white earthenware, creating her child sculptures with uncomfortable exactness, using an acrylic surface. She has had numerous one-person exhibitions at P.P.O.W. in New

York and was included in the 'Ceramic National 2000' at the Everson Museum of Art, Syracuse, NY. See *My Little Pretty: Images of Girls in Contemporary Women Artists* (Chicago: Museum of Contemporary Art, 1997); Carol Diehl, 'Figures in Limbo,' *Art in America* (Nov 2000); and Bill Arning, 'Judy Fox's Strange Beings,' *American Ceramics* (Vol. 13, 2000).

Viola Frey B. Lodi, CA, USA, 1933. Frey received her B.F.A. in 1956 from the California College of Arts and Crafts, Oakland, CA, and in 1958 received her M.F.A. from Tulane University, New Orleans, LA. In 1965 she became a part-time member of the CCAC faculty and in 1970 the full-time head of the ceramics department. Frey's larger-than-life sized figures achieve an impressive level of whimsy, given their imposing scale. They are menacing and playful at the same time. While they are often stiff in their gesture and expression, Frey's figures, with loose painterly and boisterously colorful surfaces, remain accessible, and akin to naive or folk art, though her sense of unrefined form and figuration is clearly deliberate. Often her richly colored surfaces serve to underscore the stiffness of her figures, by way of bold black outlines filled in by outrageous coloring that makes her sculptures simultaneously two dimensional and three dimensional; they are paintings and sculptures all at once. Her vast exhibition record includes solo shows at Rena Bransten Gallery, San Francisco, CA; Frank Lloyd Gallery, Santa Monica, CA; Riva Yares Gallery, Scottsdale, AZ and Santa Fe, NM; Nancy Hoffman Gallery, New York, NY; Norton Gallery of Art, West Palm Beach, FL; Asher/Faure Gallery, Los Angeles, CA; Wichita Center for the Arts, Wichita, KS; Fresno Museum of Art, Fresno, CA; Oakland Museum of California, Oakland, CA; and Seattle Art Museum, Seattle, WA. Frey's work is in the collections of American Craft Museum, New York, NY; Contemporary Arts Center, Honolulu, HI; Detroit Institute of Arts, Detroit, MI; Everson Museum of Art, Syracuse, NY; Los Angeles County Museum of Art, Los Angeles, CA; The Metropolitan Museum of Art, New York, NY; Museum of Contemporary Art, Los Angeles, CA; Philadelphia Museum of Art, Philadelphia, PA; Museum of Contemporary Ceramic Art in the Shigaraki Ceramic Cultural Park, Shigaraki, Japan; and Whitney Museum of American Art, New York, NY. See Garth Clark, *Viola Frey: Retrospective* (Sacramento: Crocker Art Museum, 1981); Garth Clark and Patterson Simms, *It's All Part of the Clay: Viola Frey* (Philadelphia: Moore College of Art and Design, 1984); and Reena Jana, 'Viola Frey: Survey 1969–1981,' *Ceramics: Art and Perception* (No. 41, 2000).

Elizabeth Fritsch B. Wales, 1940. Fritsch studied at the Birmingham School of Music and Royal Academy of Music, London (1958–64). She took her M.A. in ceramics in 1970 at the Royal College of Art, London. Fritsch's unique approach to ceramics has been extremely influential. She was one of the first to begin to play with the vessel as an image using drawing techniques (foreshortening, for instance) to create the illusion of fully three-dimensional pots that were actually flattened and compressed. Her touring exhibition 'Pots About Music,' organized in 1978 by the Leeds City Art Galleries, was one of the most influential exhibitions of the 1970s. Fritsch was also the 1970 recipient of the Herbert Read Memorial Prize, and of the Silver Medal for Ceramics through the Royal College of Art, London. Her vast exhibition record includes solo shows throughout England at Northern Centre for Contemporary Art, Sunderland; Pilschuer Fine Art, London; Galerie Besson, London; Leeds City Art Galleries, Leeds; Victoria and Albert Museum, London; Royal College of Art, London; Royal Museum, Edinburgh, Scotland; and Hetjens Museum, Düsseldorf, Germany. Her work is in the collections of Crafts Council, London; Victoria and Albert Museum, London; Dansk Kunstindustrie, Copenhagen, Denmark; Museum Boijmans van Beuningen, Rotterdam, the Netherlands; and The Metropolitan Museum of Art, New York, NY. See Peter Dormer and David Cripps, *Elizabeth Fritsch* (*In Studio* series) (London: Bellew Publishing, 1986); Edward Lucie-Smith, *The World of the Makers* (London: Paddington, 1975); and Edward Lucie-Smith, *Elizabeth Fritsch: Vessels from Another World, Metaphysical Pots in Painted Stoneware* (London: Bellew Publishing, 1993).

Sueharu Fukami B. Kyoto, Japan, 1947. Sueharu graduated in 1963 from the Kyoto Ceramics Training School and in 1965 from the Kyoto Arts and Crafts Training Center. Sueharu received the Grand Prize at the Kyoto Arts and Crafts Exhibition twice (1974 and 1978), and was awarded the Grand Prize at the Concorso Internazionale della Ceramica, Faenza, Italy, in 1985. He is considered the leading master in the use of celadon glaze in a sculptural context. His searing, sharp porcelain 'blades' are amongst the best minimalism in Japanese art. Both molded and cast, his sculptural pieces are finished with his signature *seihakuji* (pale blue) glaze. His exhibition record includes shows at Gallery Third Floor, Kyoto; Gallery Takashimaya, Tokyo, Yokohama, Osaka, and Kyoto; the Japan Society, New York, NY; and National Museum of Modern Art, Tokyo, Japan. His work is in the collections of National Museum of Modern Art, Tokyo, Japan; Museo Internazionale delle Ceramiche, Faenza, Italy; Victoria and Albert Museum, London; British Museum, London; Everson Museum of Art, Syracuse, NY; and Brooklyn Museum of Art, New York, NY. See Kenji Kaneko, 'Sueharu Fukami: Formative Logic by Slip Casting,' *Kerameiki Techni* (August 2000).

Keiko Fukazawa B. Tokyo, Japan, 1955. Fukazawa earned her B.F.A. at Musashino Art University, Tokyo, Japan, in 1979 and her M.F.A. in ceramics is from Otis College of Art and Design, Los Angeles, CA (1986), where she was taught by Ralph Bacerra. In the interim between taking these degrees Fukazawa was a student in Shigaraki, Japan, and independently studied other regional pottery styles and techniques throughout Japan. Since 2000, Fukazawa has taught at Loyola Marymount University, Los Angeles, CA, and in the California State Prison system for more than eight years, and perhaps her dedication to this work has shaped her personal work more than any other one force. Fukazawa describes the act of literally breaking her vessels as her way of escaping traditional limitations of form and process. While using this same exercise with her student wards, she has become an ultimate assimilator of imagery. Fukazawa's almost flagrantly juxtaposed cultural pastiche is born from a sense of spontaneity and graphic irreverence. A collage of student graffiti, commercial pop images (Japanese, American, and otherwise), and historical reproductions are 'cut and pasted' onto a 'scrapbook' surface. The bright palette of her plates and pots augments their bold graphic terms, and heightens our view of their cultural kaleidoscope. Her many exhibitions include six one-person shows at Garth Clark Gallery, Los Angeles, CA, Kansas City, MO, and New York, NY. Her group shows include exhibitions at Los Angeles County Museum of Art, Los Angeles, CA; California African-American Museum, Los Angeles, CA; American Craft Museum, New York, NY; Forum for Contemporary Art, St. Louis, MO; and Dorothy Weiss Gallery, San Francisco, CA. Her work is in the permanent collections of National Museum of History, Taipei, Taiwan, Republic of China; Los Angeles County Museum of Art, Los Angeles, CA; and Charles A. Wustum Museum of Fine Arts, Racine, WI. See Susan Peterson, *Contemporary Ceramics* (New York: Watson-Guptill, 2000).

Micheline Gingras B. Quebec, Canada, 1947. Gingras studied at the Ecole des Beaux-Arts de Quebec, receiving her M.F.A. in 1969. She is presently a member of the faculty of Saint Ann's School, Brooklyn, NY, and maintains a studio in New York. In 1976 Gingras received an Arts Visual Grant from the Ministry of Cultural Affairs, Quebec, and a residency at the Watershed Center for the Ceramic Arts, Portland, ME, in 1989. While Gingras studied as a painter and works in a variety of sculptural materials, she also collaborated with Raymon Elozua on his ageing sculptures of 'Water Towers' and abandoned 'Drive-In Movie Screens.' She has exhibited extensively in Canada and the USA, including 'New Art Forms' at the Nancy Margolis Gallery, New York, NY (1990); 'Time Capsule' at Paula Cooper Gallery, New York, NY (1995); and the traveling exhibition 'Confrontational Clay: the Artist as Social Critic' (2000–2001). Gingras' work is included in the collections of the Canadian Art Bank, Ottawa, Canada; Musée du Quebec, Canada; and the Quebec House in New York, NY. See Leo Rosshandler, *La Nouvelle Figuration Québécoise Face A l'Environment Urbain* (Montreal: La Main Mécanique, 1979); and Judith Schwartz, *Confrontational Clay: The Artist as Social Critic* (New York: Exhibits USA, 2000).

Linda Gunn-Russell B. London, England, 1953. Gunn-Russell attended the Camberwell School of Art and Crafts, London, from 1971 to 1975. Her approach to ceramics was influenced by teachers Glenys Barton, John Forde, Ian Godfrey, Colin Pearson, and Janice Tchalenko. She was also affected by the works of British ceramist Clarice Cliff, the American painter and sculptor Roy Lichtenstein, and the French painter Henri Matisse, as well as by the patterns found in Japanese kimonos and Islamic miniatures. Gunn-Russell's work elaborates on

visual tricks of perspective. In these she combines humor and an anthropomorphic sensibility with functionally based objects. Her method is first to draw shapes and then to slab build them, allowing her to maintain a graphic sensibility that provides a contrast with the three-dimensional aspects of her pieces. Her work is in the collections of the Los Angeles County Museum of Art, Los Angeles, CA, and other public institutions. See Abigail Frost, 'Exhibition Review,' *Crafts* (Jan/Feb 1985).

Chris Gustin B. Chicago, IL, USA, 1952. Gustin earned a B.F.A. in ceramics at Kansas City Art Institute, Kansas City, MO, in 1975. His M.F.A. is from New York State College of Ceramics at Alfred University, New York, NY (1977). Gustin is Professor Emeritus, University of Massachusetts, Dartmouth, MA, and has taught at numerous schools since 1978. He has given workshops and lectures at over fifty colleges, schools, and art centers throughout the USA. Gustin's accolades include, amongst others, two Visual Artist's Fellowships from the NEA (1978 and 1986). His sculptures are both formal and sensual, composites of seductively fused volumes. While his vessels make vague allusions to function, they primarily evoke the figure. His tactile, glazed surfaces enhance the pieces' sensuous line and form. Clearly conceived in the round, Gustin's sculptures defy frontal orientation, and transform themselves continually as the viewer moves around them. Gustin's broad exhibition history includes group and solo shows at Judy Ann Goldman Fine Art, Boston, MA; The Works Gallery, Philadelphia, PA; John Elder Gallery, New York, NY; Garth Clark Gallery, Los Angeles, CA, New York, NY, and Kansas City, MO; Objects Gallery, Chicago, IL; Los Angeles County Museum of Art, Los Angeles, CA; SOFA, New York, NY (Ferrin Gallery); Renwick Gallery of the Smithsonian American Art Museum, Washington, DC; Museum of Contemporary Ceramic Art in the Shigaraki Ceramic Cultural Park, Shigaraki, Japan; and American Craft Museum, New York, NY. His work appears in the collections of Everson Museum of Art, Syracuse, NY; Detroit

Institute of Arts, Detroit, MI; Los Angeles County Museum of Art, Los Angeles, CA; Mint Museum of Craft and Design, Charlotte, NC; and Victoria and Albert Museum, London. See Garth Clark, *American Ceramics* (New York: Abbeville Press, 1987); and Susan Peterson, *The Craft and Art of Clay* (New Jersey: Prentice Hall, 1991).

Babs Haenen B. Amsterdam, the Netherlands, 1948. After working as a dancer, Haenen began her visual art studies at the Gerrit Rietveld Academy, Amsterdam (1974–79) and the Shinnersbridge Pottery, with Marianne de Trey, in Dartington, England (1977–78). Haenen's technique is working with colored porcelain slabs she mixes herself and builds into organic, colorful vessels. Lately her work has gone from typical vertical vessel forms to more complex works that incorporate two or more separate pieces, creating colorful tabletop landscapes. Haenen was the recipient of the 1987 Werbeurs Stichting Fonds voor Beeldende Kunsten, Vormgeving en Bouwkunst, the 1990 Werbeurs Ministrie van VVVC and the 1991 Inax Design Prize for Europe from Japan. Her works can be found in the Museum Boijmans van Beuningen, Rotterdam, the Netherlands; Carnegie Museum of Art, Pittsburgh, PA; Frans Halsmuseum, Haarlem, the Netherlands; Hetjens Museum, Düsseldorf, Germany; Museum of Contemporary Ceramic Art in the Shigaraki Ceramic Cultural Park, Shigaraki, Japan; Cooper-Hewitt National Design Museum, New York, NY; Mint Museum of Craft and Design, Charlotte, NC; and Charles A. Wustum Museum of Fine Arts, Racine, WI. See

Garth Clark and Ineke Werkman, *Babs Haenen* (Leeuwarden: Museum het Princesshof, 1991); and Marjan Boot, *The Turbulent Vessel, Babs Haenen: A Decade of Work 1991–1998* (Amsterdam: The Stedelijk Museum, 1998).

Emil Heger B. Konstanz, Germany, 1961. Heger studied at the Institut für Kunstlerische Keramik, Höhr-Grenzhausen (1990–93) and has been a teacher there since 1999. He is a founding member of the Keramikgruppe Grenzhausen, a collaborative workshop created in 1992. In 1992 and 1995, Heger was the recipient of the Westerwaldpreis for salt glazed ceramics and was awarded a medal from the President of the Senate of the Republic at the 50th Concorso Internazionale della Ceramica d'Arte, Faenza, Italy, in 1997. Heger's tightly thrown and extenuated vessels are presented in groupings suggesting multiple figures in monochromatic glazes. He has exhibited in numerous exhibitions throughout Europe. See Gian Carlo Bojani and Dirma Dal Prato, *50 Premio Faenza: Concorso Internazionale della Ceramica d'Arte* (Faenza: Studio 88, 1997).

Steve Heinemann B. Toronto, Ontario, Canada, 1957. Heinemann holds an Honors Diploma (1979) from Sheridan College School of Craft and Design, Mississauga, Ontario, Canada. His B.F.A. in ceramics (1981) was taken at Kansas City Art Institute, Kansas City, MO. Heinemann received his M.F.A. (1983) from New York State College of Ceramics at Alfred University, New York, NY. He has been an instructor at both Sheridan College School of Craft and Design, Mississauga, Ontario and at Ontario College of Art and Design, Toronto, Ontario, Canada. Heinemann was the 1996 recipient of the Saidye Bronfman Award for Excellence in Canadian Craft and has received Le Prix D'Excellence, National Biennial of Ceramics twice (1988 and 1994). He has given workshops and lectures at schools and universities in Canada, Japan, Korea, the USA, and England. His broad exhibition record includes solo shows at Prime Gallery, Toronto, Ontario, Canada; Nancy Margolis Gallery, New York, NY; Galerie Elena Lee, Montreal, Canada; and Ontario Crafts Council, Toronto, Ontario, Canada. His work is in the collections of Auckland Museum, Auckland, New Zealand; Victoria and Albert Museum, London; Museum het Kruithuis, 's-Hertogenbosch, the Netherlands; Canadian Museum of Civilization, Ottawa, Canada; National Museum of History, Taipei, Taiwan, Republic of China; and Museum of Fine Arts, Boston, MA. See Margaret Cannon, 'Thinking in Clay', *Ontario Craft* (July/Aug 1996); and Earl Miller, 'Ideas in Containers', *Ceramics: Art and Perception* (No. 32, 1998).

Jan Holcomb B. Washington, DC, USA, 1945. Holcomb received a B.A. in 1968 and a B.F.A. in 1974, both from the University of Michigan, Ann Arbor, MI, and received his M.A. in ceramics at California State University, Sacramento, CA, in 1977. He is currently instructor of ceramics at the Rhode Island School of Design, Providence, RI. Holcomb has received two NEA Grants (1979 and 1988). He works with thematic sculptural wall works and freestanding sculptures that express frailties and faults in the human condition. Holcomb has been exhibiting in the USA since 1977, and his work has been included in the survey exhibitions 'Poetry of the Physical', American Craft Museum, New York, NY (1986–88) and 'The George and Dorothy Saxe Collection', Toledo Museum of Art, Toledo, OH; Newport Harbor Art Museum, CA; Renwick Gallery of the Smithsonian American Art Museum, Washington, DC; and St. Louis Art Museum, St. Louis, MO (1993–95). See Garth Clark, *American Ceramics* (New York: Abbeville Press, 1987).

Nicholas Homoky B. Sarvar, Hungary, 1950. Homoky's family emigrated to England in 1956. He attended Bristol Polytechnic, England, from 1970 to 1973, and the Royal College of Art, London, from 1973 to 1976. He studied painting, sculpture, graphics, and draughtsmanship. All of these are evident as elements in his subsequent work in ceramics. Homoky comments that he, 'finally chose to work with clay because it seemed to be the only medium capable of being as purely expressive as it was functional.' The artist is fascinated with opposites: black versus white, line versus form, and the appearance of function versus the lack of. His work has been included in numerous exhibitions worldwide and is in the collections of the Los Angeles County Museum of Art, Los Angeles, CA; Victoria and Albert Museum, London; and Museum Boijmans van Beuningen, Rotterdam, the Netherlands. See John Fowles and Nicholas Homoky, *Nicholas Homoky* (Yoevil: Marston House, 1997).

Sergei Isupov B. Stavrapole, Russia, 1963. Isupov studied at the Ukrainian State Art School, Kiev, Ukraine, 1982. He took both his B.A. and M.F.A. (1990) in ceramics at the Art Institute of Tallinn, Estonia. In 1993, Isupov emigrated from Estonia to the USA, and has since made Kentucky his home and workplace. His pieces are complex unions of articulated figuration, conjoined with less resolute forms, that contort to meet their resting surface. They are animated, and upright, while still appearing painfully subjected to some oblique, diffuse gravity. All of his formal convolutions are reinforced by a stark, surreal surface, in both image and color. Man becomes beast, body becomes face, and the artist's ability to express human (animal) sexual appetite, and its complex social component, leaves us with saturated narratives that are essentially deep questions, despite their level of visual completeness. Isupov's gymnastic imagery melds two-dimensional narrative onto his hyper-gestural narrative figures, and these pictorial surfaces alternately recede into, and then overwhelm, his refined forms. Isupov has given workshops and lectured widely since 1990 at, amongst others, the Rhode Island School of Design, Providence, RI, and Penland School of Crafts, Penland, NC (both 2000). He has received the Smithsonian Craft Show Top Award for Excellence (1996). Isupov's work has been widely exhibited, including shows at SOFA, Chicago, IL, New York, NY, and Miami, FL (Ferrin Gallery); Connell Gallery, Atlanta, GA; Dorothy Weiss Gallery, San Francisco, CA; Los Angeles County Museum of Art, Los Angeles, CA; Mint Museum of Craft and Design, Charlotte, NC; and Charles A. Wustum Museum of Fine Arts, Racine, WI. His work appears in the collections of Tallinn Museum of Applied Art, Estonia; Museum of Applied Art, Tuman, Russia; Museum of Contemporary Ceramics, Summe, Ukraine; Oslo Museum of Applied Art, Oslo, Norway; Mint Museum of Craft and Design, Charlotte, NC; and Los Angeles County Museum of Art, Los Angeles, CA. See Leon Nigrosh, 'Erotica in Ceramic Art, Sexual, Sensual and Suggestive', *Ceramics: Art and Perception* (No. 38,

1999); Leslie Ferrin, *Teapots Transformed: Exploration of an Object* (Madison: Guild Books, 2000); and Garth Clark, *The Artful Teapot* (New York: Watson-Guptill, and London: Thames & Hudson, 2001).

Doug Jeck B. Jersey City, NJ, USA, 1963. Jeck received his B.F.A. at the Appalachian Center for Arts and Crafts, Smithville, TN, in 1986 and his M.F.A. at the School of the Art Institute of Chicago, IL, in 1989. He is currently Professor of Ceramics at the University of Washington, Seattle, WA. In 1989 Jeck received a Fellowship Exhibition Award at the School of Art, Chicago, IL; a Visual Artist's Fellowship Grant from the NEA (1990) and twice won the Virginia A. Groot Foundation Grant (1997 and 1998). Jeck creates figurative sculpture he refers to as 'human objects' expressing, in exact detail, human forms with appendages removed and fetishistic hair additions. His work is in the collections of Los Angeles County Museum of Art, Los Angeles, CA; Johnson Wax Collection, Racine, WI; and the Schein-Joseph International Museum of Ceramic Art, Alfred, NY. See Peter Selz, 'Doug Jeck at Dorothy Weiss,' *Art in America* (Sept 1997); and Eric Fredericksen, 'The Body Made Strange, Familiar Monsters,' *The Stranger* (May 1998).

Barbara Kaas B. Wadern, Germany, 1963. Kaas studied at the Ecole des Arts et Metiers, Luxembourg (1983-85) and at the Institut für Kunstlerische Keramik, Höhr-Grenzhausen (1990-93). She has been a part of the Keramikgruppe Grenzhausen since 1999. In 1989 Kaas received the Prize for Young Ceramists, Foerderpreis für das Kunsthandwerk, Rheinland-Pfalz, and she has participated in numerous exhibitions in Europe since 1991.

Martin Bodilsen Kaldahl B. Randers, Denmark, 1954. Kaldahl received an M.A. in ceramics and glass at the Royal College of Art, London, in 1990, and maintains a studio in Copenhagen, Denmark, where he teaches at the Denmark Design School. In 1989 he received a Travel Scholarship from the Royal College of Art, London, and in 1996 an award from the Danish Contemporary Art Foundation. Kaldahl's works are large minimal and abstract forms suggesting a possible function that he surfaces in textured matte finishes. He has exhibited extensively in Europe, with solo exhibitions at Barrett/Marsden Gallery, London; Gallery Norby, Copenhagen; and Clara Scremini Gallery, Paris. His work is in the collections of the Contemporary Art Society, England; Keramikmuseet Grimmerhus, Middelfart, Denmark; and Rohsska Museet, Sweden.

Jacques Kaufmann B. Casablanca, Morocco, 1954. Kaufmann studied between 1974 and 1977 at the Ecole des Arts Décoratifs, Geneva, Switzerland and between 1984 and 1986 he served as Head of the Project for Action Ceramique, Rwanda. Kaufmann was director of the Center of Applied Arts of Geneva (1994-95), and was a Professor of Applied Arts at Vevey, Switzerland, in 1995. His work often deals with the modularity of the brick as a starting point for powerful, yet simple, architectural elements. His broad exhibition record includes solo shows at Galerie La Proue, Lucerne, Switzerland; Galerie Heimatwerk, Zürich, Switzerland; Galerie Blas and Knoda, Stockholm, Sweden; Galerie Baezner-Zufferey, Geneva, Switzerland; Galerie Ipso Facto, Lucerne, Switzerland; Galerie Marianne Brand, Geneva, Switzerland; and Galerie Kunst and Keramik, Deventer, the Netherlands. His work is in the collections of Musée Ariana, Geneva, Switzerland; Kunsthandwerkmuseum, Berlin, Germany; Musée des Arts Décoratifs, Lucerne, Switzerland; Musée Bellerive, Zürich, Switzerland; Everson Museum of Art, Syracuse, NY; Musée Historique et des Porcelaines, Nyon, France; Auckland Museum of Applied Art, Auckland, New Zealand; and Total Museum for Contemporary Arts, Seoul, South Korea. See *Kerameiki Techni* (21, 1995); and *Ceramics: Art and Perception* (No. 20, 1995).

Junko Kitamura B. Kyoto, Japan, 1956. Kitamura completed her graduate course in ceramics at the Kyoto City University of Art in 1987 and maintains a studio in Tokyo. She has won prizes for her work from the Siga Prefecture Art

Exhibition (1983), twice from the Kyoto Art and Crafts Exhibition (1984 and 1985), and the World Triennial Exhibition of Small Ceramics, Zagreb, Croatia (1997). Kitamura's thrown vessels are made of black stoneware. While still damp, she will sharpen a piece of bamboo and meticulously penetrate freehand geometric patterns throughout the walls of her works and fill the indentations with white slip, creating a unique version of inlay. Kitamura has exhibited widely throughout Japan and the USA, with solo shows at Gallery Koyanagi, Tokyo, Japan; and Garth Clark Gallery, New York, NY; and her artwork is included in the collections of the British Museum, London; National Museum of Modern Art, Tokyo, Japan; Brooklyn Museum of Art, New York, NY; and Freer Gallery of Art and Arthur M. Sackler Gallery, Smithsonian Institution, Washington, DC.

Cindy Kolodziejski B. Augsburg, Germany, 1962. Kolodziejski received her B.F.A. from Otis College of Art and Design, Los Angeles, CA, where she studied under Ralph Bacerra, and her M.F.A. from California State University, Long Beach, CA, under Tony Marsh. She uses her highly refined painter's skill to create irreverent and intimate images on her cast vessel forms. Whether drawn from her own personal experience or from art history, the artworks tell stories that are startling and provocative. Lately, a mirrored distortion has crept into the scenes. Faux metal bases and handles add to the overall impression of consummate skill in the work of this up-and-coming artist. She has exhibited in solo and group exhibitions since 1988 and her work is in the public collections of American Craft Museum, New York, NY; Los Angeles County Museum of Art, Los Angeles, CA; Mint Museum of Craft and Design, Charlotte, NC; and National Museum of History, Taipei, Taiwan, Republic of China; and Museum of Contemporary Ceramic Art in the Shigaraki Ceramic Cultural Park, Shigaraki, Japan. See Jo Lauria,

'Pluperfect—The Painted Narrative Vessels of Cindy Kolodziejski,' *Ceramics: Art and Perception* (No. 19, 1995); Stephen Luecking, *Cindy Kolodziejski* (New York: Garth Clark Gallery, and Los Angeles: Frank Lloyd Gallery, 1999).

Howard Kottler B. Cleveland, OH, USA, 1930; D. Seattle, WA, USA, 1989. Kottler studied at Ohio State University, receiving his B.F.A. in 1952, an M.F.A. in 1956, and a Ph.D in 1964. He also received an M.F.A. from the Cranbrook Academy of Art, Bloomfield Hills, MI, in 1957. He taught at Ohio State University from 1961 to 1964, and then from 1964 till his death at the University of Washington, Seattle, WA. He was one of the most influential teachers in the ceramic-sculpture movement. He was arguably, with Michael Frimkess, the first of the true postmodernists working in ceramics and his series of plates in the late 1960s, using commercially available decals of Leonardo da Vinci's *The Last Supper* and *Mona Lisa*, Thomas Gainsborough's *The Blue Boy*, and Grant Wood's *American Gothic*, are early classics of his dinner plate genre. A generation of successful artists has emerged from his teaching: Jacqueline Rice, Michael Lucero, Mark Burns, and many others. He received a Fullbright Grant in 1957 and an NEA fellowship in 1975. Kottler exhibited extensively and by 1978 he had been included in over 250 one-man exhibitions in the USA, but he tended to show mainly at smaller venues and avoided the more influential mainstream galleries. In the years from 1981 to 1987 he withdrew from the exhibition circuit. He returned with one of his first major exhibitions in nearly ten years, organized by the Bellevue Art Museum, WA. LeMar Harrington wrote of an exhibition of his work that it was, 'filled with garish subtleties. It was like walking into Kottler's private cache of ceremonial vessels—vessels for rites of the gods of humor, of satire, of energy,

of joy, of sex, of life, of another universe.' His work is in the public collections of The Metropolitan Museum of Art, New York, NY; American Craft Museum, New York, NY; Los Angeles County Museum of Art, Los Angeles, CA; Mint Museum of Craft and Design, Charlotte, NC; and the Everson Museum of Art, Syracuse, NY. See Patricia Failing, *Howard Kottler: Face to Face* (Seattle: University of Washington Press, 1995).

Joyce Kozloff B. Somerville, NJ, USA, 1942. Kozloff earned a B.F.A. at Carnegie Institute of Technology, Pittsburgh, PA (1964). She took her M.F.A. at Columbia University, New York, NY (1967). Kozloff was the 1999–2000 recipient of the Jules Guerin Fellowship, Rome Prize, American Academy in Rome, Italy. She has been awarded two NEA Grants, one in painting (1977) and the other in drawing, prints, and artists' books (1985). Kozloff has taught at universities and schools across the USA, as well as participating in the International Art Workshop, Teschemakers, New Zealand. Since 1998 she has served on the board of governors of Skowhegan School of Painting and Sculpture, Skowhegan, ME. Kozloff was one of the members of the Pattern and Decoration movement (P+D) in the late 1970s and early 1980s with artists such as painter Robert Kushner, and ceramist Betty Woodman (with whom she collaborated in 1980 on a series of ceramic vessels). Kozloff has focused mainly on public art, incorporating her activist position on women's art. Her exhibition record, spanning more than three decades, includes solo shows at DC Moore Gallery, New York, NY; Midtown Payson Galleries, New York, NY; Tile Guild, Los Angeles, CA; Lorence-Monk Gallery, New York, NY; Nina Freudenheim Gallery, Buffalo, NY; Robert Berman Gallery, Los Angeles, CA; Nancy Drysdale Gallery, Washington, DC; Allrich Gallery, San Francisco, CA; Barbara Gladstone Gallery, New York, NY; National Museum of Women in the Arts, Washington, DC. Kozloff's work is in the collections of Brooklyn Museum of Art, New York, NY; The Metropolitan Museum of Art, New York, NY; Mint Museum of Craft and Design, Charlotte, NC; Museum of Modern Art, New York, NY; Renwick Gallery of the Smithsonian American Art Museum, Washington, DC; National Museum of Women in the Arts, Washington, DC; and Whitney Museum of American Art, New York, NY. See Patricia Johnston, Hayden Herrera, and Thalia Gouma-Peterson, *Joyce Kozloff: Visionary Ornament* (Boston: Boston University Art Gallery, 1986); and Akkiko Busch, 'Accessories of Destination: The Recent Work of Joyce Kozloff,' *American Ceramics* (Vol. 12, No. 1, 1995).

Charles Krafft B. Seattle, WA, USA, 1947. Krafft is an emphatically self-taught artist. Though much of his prominent ceramic work exploits a facile mastery of Delft porcelain tradition, their content makes them sharply political and unquestionably contemporary. Krafft deeply skews our expectations by revising wartime histories (with a de-glamorizing bias) within a tradition that has customarily built its content *out of* its form and surface. Krafft portrays such startling events of human mortality as the sinking of the Titanic in classic Delft blue and white. He has subverted traditional souvenir plates, with versions that depict horrific events, including Dresden plates picturing planes over the city during the Second World War, complete with inscriptions welcoming the British bombers. Adorned with standard Delft decorative motifs, Krafft renders replicas of the weapons used by secret police in historic wartime theaters. Krafft has received grants from ArtsLink/CEC International Partners, New York (1995 and 1997). He has exhibited his work widely for more than three decades, including shows at Aaron Packer Gallery, Chicago, IL; Garth Clark Gallery, New York, NY; Villa Delirium Delftworks, Seattle, WA; Davidson Gallery, Seattle, WA; Contemporary Art Center, Cincinnati, OH; Seattle Art Museum, Seattle, WA; Spode Museum, Stoke-On-Trent, UK; and The Art Kitchen, Amsterdam, the Netherlands. Krafft has work in the collections of Whatcom Museum of History and Art, Bellingham, WA; and the Museum of Northwest Art, La Conner, WA. See Paul Scott and Terry Bennett, *Hot Off the Press* (London: Bellew Publishing, 1996); Paul Scott and Laura Hamilton, *The Plate Show* (Glasgow: Collins Gallery, 1998); Charles Krafft, 'Disasterware,' *American Ceramics* (Vol. 10, 1993); and Charles Krafft, 'Villa Delirium Delft Works,' *Ceramics Monthly* (Sept 1998).

Anne Kraus B. Short Hills, NJ, USA, 1956. After receiving a B.A. in painting from the University of Pennsylvania, PA, Kraus received a B.F.A. from Alfred University, New York, NY, in 1982. She continues her love of painting today, creating narrative scenes on vessels. On a single artwork there are many different images with meticulously printed text. Together they explore stories that depict man's tenuous balance between reality and the unknown, a psychological state Kraus mines in all her work. A recent development in her work are large, wall-hung tile pictures drenched in color. She keeps an active dream journal as an idea source. Her work is included in numerous public collections, including Los Angeles County

Museum of Art, Los Angeles, CA; Museum of Fine Arts, Houston, TX; Newark Museum, Newark, NJ; Carnegie Museum of Art, Pittsburgh, PA; Everson Museum of Art, Syracuse, NY; Museum of Contemporary Ceramic Art in the Shigaraki Ceramic Cultural Park, Shigaraki, Japan; and Victoria and Albert Museum, London. See Jo Lauria, *Color and Fire* (Los Angeles: Los Angeles County Museum of Art, and New York: Rizzoli, 2000); and Garth Clark, *Anne Kraus: A Survey* (New York: Garth Clark Gallery, 1998).

Daniel Kruger B. Cape Town, South Africa. Kruger studied from 1971 to 1972 at the University of Stellenbosch, Stellenbosch and from 1973 to 1974 at Michaelis School of Fine Art in Cape Town. In 1974 he moved to Germany, studying with Hermann Junger at the Akademie der Bildenden Künste in Munich. He is an active teacher and has been a visiting tutor at the Royal College of Art, London; Rhode Island School of Design, Providence, RI; and the Mizuno College of Jewelry in Tokyo. In the 1990s he began to work more actively in ceramics as well as in metal. Kruger has exhibited extensively throughout Europe since 1980. See Justin Hoffman, et al., *Daniel Kruger Keramiek* (Munich: Museum für Völkerkunde, 1993).

Geert Lap B. Venlo, the Netherlands, 1951. Lap studied in the Netherlands at the Koninklijke Akademie voor Kunst en Vormgeving in 's-Hertogenbosch from 1974 to 1976 and the Gerrit Rietveld Academy, Amsterdam from 1976 to 1979. Lap's postminimalist vessels have been widely exhibited since 1980 and he has been represented by the Garth Clark Gallery, New York, NY, since 1987. In addition to his art pieces, Lap has also produced some memorable designs for the Cor Unum factory, 's-Hertogenbosch. His work is in the collections of the Museum Boijmans van Beuningen, Rotterdam; Frans Halsmuseum, Haarlem; Stedelijk Museum, Amsterdam, all in the Netherlands; Museum für Kunst und Gewerbe, Hamburg; and Kunstgewerbe Museum, Berlin, both in Germany; The Metropolitan Museum of Art, New York, NY; Cooper-Hewitt

National Design Museum, New York, NY; Los Angeles County Museum of Art, Los Angeles, CA; and Musée des Arts Décoratifs, Montreal, Canada. See Garth Clark and Erik Beenker, *Geert Lap—The Thrown Form* (Rotterdam: Museum Boijmans van Beuningen, 1989); and Allaard Hidding, *Geert Lap—99 Variations* (Leeuwarden: Museum het Princesshof, 1993).

Jean-Pierre Larocque B. Montreal, Quebec, Canada, 1953. Larocque studied at Concordia University, Montreal, receiving a B.F.A. in 1986 and an M.F.A. in 1988 at the New York State College of Ceramics at Alfred University, New York, NY. He taught at various schools between 1988 and 1995 when he joined the California State University, Long Beach, CA, remaining there until 1997. He now lives and works in Montreal. He has shown in numerous group exhibitions and has had solo exhibitions with Revolution: A Gallery Project, Ferndale, Michigan; Dorothy Weiss Gallery, San Francisco, CA; and Garth Clark Gallery, New York, NY. He works sculpturally, mainly on huge human heads and smaller scaled, but equally powerful, horses. His work is in the collections of the Mint Museum of Craft and Design, Charlotte, NC; Arkansas Arts Center, Little Rock, AR; and Schein-Joseph International Museum of Ceramic Art, Alfred, NY. See George Melrod, 'Dynamic Disarray,' *American Ceramics* (Vol. 12, No. 2, 1996); and Karen L. Kleinfelder, *Jean-Pierre Larocque: Palimpsest* (Ferndale: Revolution, 1996).

James Lawton B. Fairborn, OH, USA, 1954. Lawton received a B.S.

in constructive design (ceramics and enamels) at Florida State University, Tallahassee, FL, in 1976 and an M.F.A. in ceramics at Louisiana State University, Baton Rouge, LA, in 1980. Lawton has held various teaching posts since 1986, in Chicago, IL; Alfred University, NY; and Baton Rouge, LA. He is currently Associate Professor of Ceramics, CVPA University of Massachusetts, Dartmouth, MA. Amongst his numerous awards are two Visual Arts Fellowships (1984 and 1986) from the NEA. Since 1979 Lawton has given over forty workshops throughout the USA and Europe. His keen sense of design and balance is always evident within the formal lyricism of his pots. There are elements within his pieces that ground them squarely in the realm of potterly traditions, their flawless craftsmanship and fluid construction not least amongst these. While his surface motifs are often strongly graphic, their subtle hue and halos melt pattern into the clay surface, and confound our sense that the graphicness exists separately from the pot's 'skin.' Lawton's broad exhibition record includes shows at Clay Works Gallery, Philadelphia, PA; Mobilia Gallery, Cambridge, MA; Gallery 1021, Chicago, IL; Garth Clark Gallery, Los Angeles, CA, New York, NY, and Kansas City, MO; Everson Museum of Art, Syracuse, NY; Northern Clay Center, Minneapolis, MN; and Museum of Contemporary Ceramic Art in the Shigaraki Ceramic Cultural Park, Shigaraki, Japan. His work is in the permanent collections of Los Angeles County Museum of Art, Los Angeles, CA; Victoria and Albert Museum, London; Mint Museum of Craft and Design, Charlotte, NC; and Georgia Museum of Art, Athens, GA. See Jo Lauria, *Color and Fire* (Los Angeles: Los Angeles County Museum of Art, and New York: Rizzoli, 2000); and Susan Peterson, *Contemporary Ceramics* (New York: Watson-Guptill, 2000).

Ah Leon B. Taiwan, Republic of China, 1953. Ah Leon chose not to continue the family tradition of farming and instead attended the Taiwan National College of Art, graduating in 1976.

From 1978 to 1982 he apprenticed with master potters throughout Taiwan. Inspired first by the five-hundred-year old Chinese Yixing tradition and then encouraged to innovate by the work of American ceramist, Richard Notkin, Ah Leon brought a new ambition to the field, increasing scale dramatically and using his knowledge as a Bonsai master to create some of the most convincing and seductive trompe-l'oeil surfaces of his time, culminating with his 1997 touring exhibition of the sixty-foot (18-meter) long *Bridge* organized by the Arthur M. Sackler Gallery/Freer Gallery of Art, Smithsonian Institution, Washington, DC. He has shown his work extensively in Amsterdam, Taipei, and New York at the Garth Clark Gallery. His work is in the public collections of the Arthur M. Sackler Gallery, Smithsonian Institution, Washington, DC; The Metropolitan Museum of Art, New York, NY; Mint Museum of Craft and Design, Charlotte, NC; National Museum of History, Taipei, Taiwan, Republic of China; and National Palace Museum, Taipei, Taiwan, Republic of China. Ah Leon is an instructor in the tea ceremony and a consulting editor to *Purple Sands Magazine* and *Tea Pot World*, both published in Taiwan. See Ah Leon, '14 Principles of a Good Teapot,' *Ceramics Monthly* (June–August 1991); and Claudia Brown, Garth Clark, David Wible, and Jan Stuart, *Beyond Yixing: The Ceramic Art of Ah Leon* (Taipei: Purple Sands Publishers, 1998).

Marilyn Levine B. Medicine Hat, Alberta, Canada, 1935. Levine first studied chemistry at the University of Alberta, Edmonton, receiving a B.S. in 1957, and an M.S. in 1959. Thereafter she studied at the School of Art, University of Regina, Saskatchewan, Canada. In 1970 she received her M.A. from the University of California, Berkeley, CA, and the following year her M.F.A. in sculpture. Since graduating she has taught in both Canada and the USA and has exhibited extensively. She has had numerous solo exhibitions with, amongst others, O.K. Harris Gallery, New York, NY; Rena Bransten Gallery, San Francisco, CA; and Asher/Faure Gallery, Los Angeles, CA. Levine's work employs a material transformation, giving clay the appearance of leather and she produces various satchels, suitcases, and other objects. This has identified her art with the Super-Realism movement and she was included in what is considered to be one of the defining exhibitions for this genre, 'Sharp Focus Realism' at the Sidney Janis Gallery, New York, NY, in 1972. In 1999 the MacKenzie Art Gallery in Regina organized a major retrospective of her work. See Sidney Janis, *Sharp Focus Realism* (New York: Sidney Janis Gallery, 1972); and Maija

Bismanis, *Marilyn Levine* (Regina: MacKenzie Art Gallery, 1998).

Alexander Lichtveld B. Amsterdam, the Netherlands, 1953. Lichtveld studied ceramics at the Gerrit Rietveld Academy, Amsterdam (1973–78) and has his studio in Amsterdam. He works in various scales, from tabletop sculptures to exterior installations, while always keeping to an architectural theme. He has exhibited in Europe, the USA, and Japan where he created an entrance at the Osaka Golf Course (1991). His solo exhibitions have been with Galerie Maria Chailloux, Amsterdam; Nishida Gallery, Japan; and Garth Clark Gallery, New York, NY. His work is in the collections of the Stedelijk Museum, Amsterdam, the Netherlands; Walker Art Center, Korea; and Everson Museum of Art, Syracuse, NY. See Karin Gaillard, *Contemporary Dutch Ceramics* (The Hague, 1988); *Opening Project*, European Ceramic Work Center (EKWC) Foundation ('s-Hertogenbosch: EKWC, 1991); Sabrina Kamstra, *As Far As Japan* ('s-Hertogenbosch: KW 14, 1996); and Geert Staal, *By-Lingual Sculpture* (Nara, Japan: Nishida Gallery, 1986).

Andrew Lord B. Rochdale, England, 1950. Lord studied at the Rochdale School of Art from 1966 to 1968 and ceramics at the Central St. Martins School of Art and Design in London until 1971. After leaving school, he moved to Rotterdam and later Amsterdam, where he exhibited at Art and Project, a highly respected and innovative gallery. In 1981 Lord had his first exhibition in the USA, at the BlumHelman Gallery in New York, NY, and has since shown with Anthony d'Offay Gallery, London; Galerie Bruno Bischofberger, Zürich, Switzerland; and Andre Emmerich Gallery, New York, NY. His work has been included in numerous group and solo exhibitions and in 1995 he was one of the artists selected for the Biennial at the Whitney Museum of American Art, New York. He is currently represented by Gagosian Gallery, New York, NY. He resides and keeps his studio in New York City and has a second home in Carson, NM. His work plays with sophisticated notions of geometry, of still life, and of appropriation from

modern painters, ranging from Cézanne to Picasso and Braque. His work is in various public collections, including The Stedelijk Museum, Amsterdam, the Netherlands; Museum Boijmans van Beuningen, Rotterdam, the Netherlands; Los Angeles County Museum of Art, Los Angeles, CA; and Victoria and Albert Museum, London. See Christopher Knight, *Andrew Lord* (New York: BlumHelman, 1984); and James Schuyler, *Poems: Andrew Lord, Sculptures* (Zürich: Edition Bruno Bischofberger, 1992).

Frank Louis B. Hannover, Germany, 1966. Louis studied at the Fachhochschule Niederrhein in Krefeld (1988–93) and at the Hochschule für Bildende Künste in Braunschweig (1996–2000) and maintains a studio in Solingen. He received the 2nd prize at the Concorso Internazionale della Ceramica d'Arte in Faenza, Italy (1995) and the Richard Bampi Preis (1996). Louis' sculptures are organic in content and are constructed of double walls of supple waves, often applying non-ceramic materials to his fired clay. He has exhibited continuously since 1993, and was included in Bienal Europea de Ceramica at the Museu de Céramica de Manises, Valencia, Spain (1995); Bewegung-Europaische Keramik at Keramion, Germany (1996); and had a solo exhibition at the Hetjens Museum, Düsseldorf, Germany (2000). See Sally Schoene, 'Frank Louis: Playing with Contrasts,' *Kerameiki Techni* (Aug 2000); and Antje Soleau, 'Frank Louis: From Ceramist to Sculptor,' *Neue Keramik* (Jan/Feb 2001).

Michael Lucero B. Tracy, CA, USA, 1953. Lucero received his B.A. in 1975 from Humboldt State University, Arcata, CA, and his M.F.A. in 1978 from the University of Washington, Seattle, WA. Lucero moved to New York City after receiving his M.F.A., and recently set up his studio in Weschester County, NY, and currently has a studio in Italy as well. He has exhibited extensively since 1977, with over one hundred group and solo exhibitions. He has had numerous one-person exhibitions in New York—first with Charles Cowles Gallery and currently with David Beitzel Gallery, as well as shows with Dorothy Weiss Gallery, San Francisco, CA; and Garth Clark Gallery in Los Angeles, CA. He has received Ford Foundation Grants (1977–78), fellowships from the NEA (1979, 1981, and 1984), and Creative Artists' Public Service Program (1980). In 1976 he received the Young American Award from the Museum of Contemporary Crafts in New York, NY, and in 1993, the Richard Koopman Distinguished Chair in the Visual Arts, University of Hartford, CT. His work is in the collections of the High Museum of Art, Atlanta, GA; Hirshhorn Museum and Sculpture Garden, Washington, DC; The Metropolitan Museum of Art, New York, NY; Mint Museum of Craft and Design, Charlotte, NC; New Museum of Contemporary Art, New York, NY; Seattle Art Museum, Seattle, WA; and Toledo Museum of Art, Toledo, OH. In 1996 the Mint Museum of Craft and Design, Charlotte, NC, organized a large retrospective exhibition of his work which toured the USA. See Mark R. Leach and Barbara Bloemink, *Michael Lucero: Sculpture* 1976–1995 (New York: Hudson Hills Press, 1996).

Marilyn Lysohir B. Sharon, PA, USA, 1950. Lysohir studied at the Centro Internazionale di Studi, Verona, Italy (1970–71). She received her B.A. from Ohio Northern University, Ada, OH, in 1972 and her M.F.A. from Washington State University, Pullman, WA, in 1979. She has lectured at colleges and universities throughout the USA, as well as in Canada, Australia, Denmark, and Africa. Among many awards, Lysohir was the recipient of a WESTAF/NEA Regional Fellowship for Visual Art (1989), two Sudden Opportunity Grants, Idaho Commission on the Arts (1993 and 1995), and an Idaho Artist Fellowship (1996). She makes extremely large-scale ceramic sculpture. The Los Angeles critic Suzanne Muchnic stated that her work has strange vectors and despite the 'clear position on the infiltration of military aggression [Lysohir] walks a precarious line between decoration and politics.' She has exhibited her work widely, including solo shows at Asher/Faure Gallery, Los Angeles, CA; Garth Clark Gallery, Kansas City, MO; Linda Hodges Gallery and Foster/White Gallery, both Seattle, WA; Denis Ochi Fine Arts, Ketchum, ID; Elzay Gallery, Wilson Art Center, Ada, OH; Boise Art Museum, Boise, ID; and Art Gallery of Hamilton, Hamilton, Ontario, Canada. Her group shows include those at

American Craft Museum, New York, NY; San Angelo Museum of Fine Arts, San Angelo, TX; Sybaris Gallery, Royal Oak, MI; William Traver Gallery, Seattle, WA; Byron C. Cohen Gallery, Kansas City, MO; Herning Museum, Herning, Denmark; Bellevue Art Museum, WA; and Tacoma Art Museum, Tacoma, WA. See Garth Clark, *American Ceramics* (New York: Abbeville Press, 1987).

Phillip Maberry B. Stanford, TX, USA, 1951. Maberry studied at East Texas State University in Commerce, TX, receiving his B.A. in 1975. He did graduate work at Wesleyan University, Middletown, CT, from 1975 to 1976, and later worked at the Brooklyn Museum of Art School, NY, and the Fabric Workshop in Philadelphia, PA. Maberry uses ceramics as well as paint, fabric, thrift-store finds, and assembled objects to create highly decorated interiors. In his early ceramic work he focused on slip-cast porcelain pieces with organic or geometric surface decorations. His present output adapts the abstract forms used in the decorative arts of the 1950s. In 1981 he created a gallery-sized installation for the Biennial of the Whitney Museum of American Art, New York, NY, and ever since has worked extensively on public and private tile installations, murals, bathrooms, kitchens, and recently a complex 25,000 square ft environment of walls and floors and an entire indoor swimming pool for a private home in Massachusetts. Maberry has taken part in dozens of major exhibitions and has had regular solo exhibitions, in the early 1980s with Hadler/Rodriguez, New York, NY, and later with the Garth Clark Gallery, Los Angeles, LA, Kansas City, MO, and New York, NY. His work is in the public collections of Los Angeles County Museum of Art, Los Angeles, CA; and Victoria and Albert Museum, London. See Garth Clark, *The Artful*

Teapot (New York: Watson-Guptill, and London: Thames & Hudson, 2001).

James Makins B. Johnstown, PA, USA, 1946. Makins took his B.F.A. at Philadelphia College of Art, PA, 1968. His M.F.A. (1973) is from Cranbrook Academy of Art, Bloomfield Hills, MI. He currently teaches at Philadelphia College of Art and Design, University of the Arts, PA. His broad teaching history includes positions at Parsons School of Design (1979–82) and New School for Social Research (1970–90), both in New York. Makins has also instructed at numerous other colleges, schools, universities, and potteries in New York and elsewhere. He has lectured throughout the USA, Europe, and Asia. Among the awards he has received are several NEA Fellowship Awards (1976, 1980, and 1990), Japanese International Cooperation Agency (JICA) International Ceramic Fellowship, Korea (1997); and a Silver Medal, 49th Concorso Internazionale della Ceramica d'Arte, Faenza, Italy (1998–99). Working primarily in porcelain, Makins creates works with distinctive throwing lines on functional and non-functional works. His broad exhibition record dating back to 1969 includes shows at Dorothy Weiss Gallery, San Francisco, CA; Dai Ichi Arts Ltd., New York; Zacheta Gallery, Warsaw, Poland; Hangnam Gallery, Seoul, South Korea; Galerie du Midi, Lausanne, Switzerland; Musée des Arts Décoratifs, Paris; Mint Museum of Craft and Design, Charlotte, NC; American Craft Museum, New York, NY; and Dowse Art Museum, Aotearoa, New Zealand. His work is in the collections of the American Craft Museum, New York, NY; Everson Museum of Art, Syracuse, NY; Philadelphia Museum of Art, Philadelphia, PA; Museum of Contemporary Ceramic Art in the Shigaraki Ceramic Cultural Park, Shigaraki, Japan; and Renwick Gallery of the Smithsonian American Art Museum, Washington, DC. See Bert Carpenter, 'James Makins,' *American Ceramics* (Vol. 10, No. 4, 1993).

Bodil Manz B. Copenhagen, Denmark, 1943. After studying at the School of Arts and Crafts, Copenhagen, from 1961 to 1965, she went on to study in Mexico at the Escuela de Diseno y Artesanias in 1966 and University of California, Berkeley, CA. Her contact with Peter Voulkos while in Berkeley was inspirational in freeing Manz from the traditional limitations and expectations of her education. Manz settled in her native Denmark to make pots of startling simplicity and modernism. She currently works in cast porcelain, using the translucency of the material to meld any pattern on the inner and outer skins of her cylinders. In 1984 she designed the dinner service 'Facet' for Bing and Grøndahl. Manz has won the Danish State Art Foundation award several times, First Prize in the Japanese Mino Competition and the Grand Prix in the World Triennial of Small Ceramics. She was one of ten artists chosen by Janet Mansfield, editor of *Ceramics: Art and Perception*, as one of the major ceramic artists of the late 20th century for an exhibition at the Museo Internazionale delle Ceramiche, Faenza, Italy. Her work is in the Nationalmuseum, Stockholm, Sweden; Tai Pei Fine Arts Museum, Taiwan; Museum of Decorative Art, Helsinki, Finland; Museum het Princesshof, Leeuwarden, the Netherlands; Bewegung-Europaische Keramik at Keramion, Germany; Los Angeles County Museum of Art, Los Angeles, CA; and Carnegie Museum of Art, Pittsburgh, PA. Her work is illustrated in numerous catalogs and books. See Doris Kuyken-Schneider, 'Bodil Manz's Cylinders,' *Ceramics: Art and Perception* (No. 27, 1997); David Revere McFadden and Ursula Ilse-Neuman, *Defining Craft 1—Collecting for the New Millennium* (New York: American Craft Museum, 2000); and Le Ministère Danois des Affaires Culturelles, *Bodil et Richard Manz* (Paris: Le Fonds National pour l'Art Danois, 1986).

Tony Marsh B. New York, NY, USA, 1953. Marsh holds a B.F.A. from California State University, Long Beach, CA (1978). Between 1978 and 1981 he was assistant to Mr. Shimaoka in Mashiko, Japan. Marsh's work combines bowl vessels and still-life elements in a decidedly contemporary vision. The objects that fill his bowls, and reference still-life compositions, are reductive volumes that are both austere and playful. These volumes teeter somewhere between building blocks and implements, clinical in their precision, but jovial in their form and interplay. Often Marsh's bowls and the forms they contain are compulsively pierced over their entire

surface with small holes, which heighten our sense that he has fashioned a still-life sculpturally. His surface treatment tends to unify and flatten the work the way a painting captures three-dimensional form (from 'life') and renders it in two dimensions (to 'stillness'). Marsh has exhibited his work widely since 1980, including shows at Garth Clark Gallery, New York, NY, and Los Angeles, CA; Frank Lloyd Gallery, Los Angeles, CA; Swidler Gallery, Detroit, MI; Takumi Gallery, Tokyo, Japan; and Pacific Grove Art Center, Pacific Grove, CA. His work appears in the public collections of Cranbrook Museum of Art, Cranbrook Academy of Art, Bloomfield Hills, MI; Los Angeles County Museum of Art, Los Angeles, CA; and Takumi Folk Art Gallery, Tokyo, Japan. See Susan Peterson, *Contemporary Ceramics* (New York: Watson-Guptill, 2000); Martha Drexler Lynn, *Clay Today: Contemporary Ceramists and their Work* (San Francisco: Chronicle Books, 1990); and Garth Clark, *The Artful Teapot* (New York: Watson-Guptill, and London: Thames & Hudson, 2001).

Paul Mathieu B. Bouchette, Quebec, Canada, 1954. Mathieu received his M.A. from San Francisco State University, CA, in 1984 and an M.F.A. from University of California, Los Angeles, CA, in 1987. The artist has studied at centers and colleges throughout the Canadian Provinces, and holds a Diploma in Printmaking (1982) from Université du Québec à Montréal (UQAM), Montreal. His awards include an 'A' Grant, Canada Arts Council (1996) and the Jean A. Chalmers National Crafts Award (2000). Mathieu currently holds a teaching position at Emily Carr Institute of Art and Design, Vancouver, BC. Since 1976 he has taught at locations in Canada, the USA, and Mexico. Mathieu has said of his own work, 'The seduction of the decorative aspects is challenged by the confrontational, political and potentially disturbing images. This combination of conventional, generic pottery forms with an overall decorative surface disrupted by highly charged images constitute at this point the core of my investigation.' The artist's work has been shown, group and solo, at Prime Gallery, Toronto, Canada; Stride Gallery, Calgary, Canada; Galerie Barbara Silverberg, Montreal, Canada; Nancy Margolis Gallery, New York, NY; Garth Clark Gallery, New York, NY and Los Angeles, CA; Burlington Art Centre, Ontario, Canada; Musée du Québec, Canada; Gardiner Museum of Ceramic Arts, Toronto, Canada; Museum of Contemporary Ceramic Art in the Shigaraki Ceramic Cultural Park, Shigaraki, Japan; and Everson Museum of Art, Syracuse, NY. Mathieu's work is in the collections of Victoria and Albert

Museum, London; Musée des Arts Décoratifs, Montreal, Canada; Museum of Contemporary Ceramic Art in the Shigaraki Ceramic Cultural Park, Shigaraki, Japan; Los Angeles County Museum of Art, Los Angeles, CA. See Garth Clark, *The Eccentric Teapot* (New York: Abbeville Press, 1989); Gloria Lesser, 'Getting to the Heart of the Matter,' *Ceramics: Art and Perception* (No. 28, 1997); and Paul Bourassa, *Foulem, Mathieu, Milette* (Quebec: Musée du Quebec, 1997).

Hideo Matsumoto B. Kyoto, Japan, 1951. Matsumoto received a B.F.A. in agriculture from the Tokyo University of Agriculture and Technology in 1975. He received an additional B.F.A. in ceramics from Kyoto City University of Art in 1980. His M.F.A. from the same institution was taken in 1982. Matsumoto also studied at the International Studio of Ceramics, Kecskemét, Hungary (1984) and at the Stuttgart Academy of Art, Germany (1985). He has been a full-time lecturer in ceramics at Kyoto Keika University (1989–96), as well as an Assistant Professor (1997–present). He has received, amongst other awards, a Bronze Award, and 2nd International Ceramic Festival, Mino, Japan (1989). Matsumoto incorporates clay elements as part of larger, composite mechanisms that reference industrial function. Through his elaborate constructions of steel cantilevers acting on clay forms, the sculptures depict some inscrutable industrial conveyor in stasis. While all of the interplay, tension, and balance allude to function, we remain unable to make sense of the mechanics that his pieces establish. Their strangeness comes from an overriding familiarity that persists within a realm of secrecy and other worldliness. Matsumoto has exhibited his work widely, in Japan and Europe, including shows at Gallery Nakamura, Kyoto, Japan; Meguro Ceramic Gallery, Yokkaichi, Japan; Gallery MORI, Tokyo; Saitouan-Loft Gallery, Hagi, Japan; Kecskemét City Culture Center, Kecskemét, Hungary; National Museum of Art, Osaka, Japan; Keramikmuseet Grimmerhus, Middelfart, Denmark; Museum van Bommel, van Dam, Holland;

and Walbrzych District Museum, Poland. His work appears in the collections of the Museum of Contemporary Ceramic Art in the Shigaraki Ceramic Cultural Park, Shigaraki, Japan; National Museum of Art, Osaka, Japan; Victoria and Albert Museum, London; and Keramion Museum, Germany. See Tomio Sugaya, 'Hideo Matsumoto,' *Ceramics: Art and Perception* (No. 24, 1996); and Tomio Sugaya, *Metamorphosis of Contemporary Ceramics* (Shigaraki, Japan: The Museum of Contemporary Ceramic Art, 1991).

Beverly Mayeri B. New York, NY, USA, 1940. Mayeri received her B.A. from the University of California, Berkeley, in 1967 and her M.A. from San Francisco State University in 1976. In 1982 and 1988 Mayeri received a Visual Artist's Fellowship from the NEA and in 1991 a Virginia A. Groot Foundation Recognition Grant. Mayeri works in an elongated sculptural format, stretching and slicing her figures. Her acrylic painted surfaces add a softness to the work which calms the impact of her surrealist vision. Mayeri has exhibited extensively in the USA with solo shows at the Dorothy Weiss Gallery, San Francisco, CA; Perimeter Gallery, Chicago, IL; and Robert Kidd Gallery, Birmingham, MI. She has been included in numerous survey exhibitions, including the *55th Scripps Ceramic Annual* in 1999 and the 'Color and Fire: Defining Moments in Studio Ceramics, 1950-2000' at the Los Angeles County Museum of Art, Los Angeles, CA, in 2000. See Jo Lauria, *Color and Fire* (Los Angeles: Los Angeles County Museum of Art, and New York: Rizzoli, 2000); Garth Clark, *American Ceramics* (New York: Abbeville Press, 1987); and Cheryl White, 'Beverly Mayeri,' *American Ceramics* (Vol. 12, No. 3, 1997).

Richard Milette B. l'Assomption, Quebec, Canada, 1960. Milette studied at Cégep du Vieux, Montreal, from 1978 to 1982, but earned his B.F.A. in 1983 at Nova Scotia College of Art and Design. He lives and works in Montreal. He has exhibited his work in solo shows at Nancy Margolis Gallery, New York, NY; Garth Clark Gallery, Los Angeles, CA; Prime Gallery, Toronto; and Galerie Barbara Silverberg, Montreal. His group shows have been at Galerie Lieu Ouest, Montreal; SOFA, Chicago, IL (Joanne Rapp Gallery); Musée Marsil, Saint-Lambert, Canada; Everson Museum of Art, Syracuse, NY; American Craft Museum, New York, NY; and Prime Gallery, Toronto. See Paul Bourassa, *Foulem, Mathieu, Milette* (Quebec: Musée du Quebec, 1997); and Leslie Ferrin, *Teapots Transformed: Exploration of an Object* (Madison: Guild Books, 2000).

Steven Montgomery B. Detroit, MI, USA, 1954. Montgomery earned his M.F.A. from Tyler School of Art, Temple University, PA, in 1978. He studied philosophy, and was awarded a B.A. in 1976 from Grand Valley State College, Allendale, MI. He has been a lecturer and visiting artist at Tyler School of Art and has more recently served as an adjunct faculty (lecturer) at New York University. Montgomery's ceramic objects exist in some temporal and physical suspension, between machine and artifact, vessel and tool. His slipcasting of metal surfaces provides trompe-l'oeil effects, and the corrosion that figures so heavily in his pieces suggests an inscrutable sense of the object's history. He is interested in clay for its transformational capacities, which enable him to invent his own technology. The formal paradox of his work is this rivalry between material and form; his vessels give the sense of industrial objects frozen, but strangely impermanent—of some peculiar brand of entropy caught in stasis. In 1990 the artist received an Artist's Fellowship from the New York Foundation for the Arts, and in 1999 a grant from the Pollock/Krasner Foundation, NY, which are rarely awarded in his field. Montgomery has exhibited widely in the USA and abroad, including shows at Dorothy Weiss Gallery, San Francisco, CA; O.K. Harris Gallery, New York, NY; Garth Clark Gallery, New York, NY; and Nancy Margolis Gallery, New York, NY. His works are included in the collections of The Metropolitan Museum of Art, New York, NY; Renwick Gallery of the Smithsonian American Art Museum, Washington, DC; Everson Museum of Art, Syracuse, NY; Mint Museum of Craft and Design, Charlotte, NC; and Museum of Contemporary Ceramic Art in the Shigaraki Ceramic Cultural Park, Shigaraki, Japan. See Garth Clark, *The Eccentric Teapot* (New York: Abbeville Press, 1989); Robert C. Morgan, *Steven Montgomery* (New York: O.K. Harris Gallery, and Syracuse: Everson Museum of Art, 1998); Garth Clark, *The Artful Teapot* (New York: Watson-Guptill, and London: Thames & Hudson, 2001); and Rita Reif in *New York Times: Art and Architecture* (December, 6 1998).

Judy Moonelis B. Jackson Heights, Queens, NY, USA, 1953. Moonelis holds a B.F.A. (cum laude) from Tyler School of Art, Temple University, PA (1975) and an M.F.A. from New York State College of Ceramics at Alfred University, New York, NY (1978). She was an important and innovative force in a new wave of raw, tough, expressionistic figurative art that came from New York's East Village in the 1980s. The East Village explosion was short lived, but much of this art found its way into the mainstream of new American art. Moonelis has twice received Individual Fellowships through the NEA (1980 and 1986) and was a recipient of the Virginia A. Groot Foundation Grant in 1991. She has also received two Individual Fellowships, New York Foundation for the Arts (1985 and 1989). Since 1999 Moonelis has been Artist in Residence, Fairleigh Dickinson University, NJ. She has served visiting professorships and has been a visiting artist at universities and colleges across the USA since the late 1970s. Her wide exhibition record includes solo shows at John Elder Gallery, New York, NY; The Clay Studio, Philadelphia, PA; Rena Bransten Gallery, San Francisco, CA; Helen Drutt Gallery, Philadelphia, PA; and Manchester Craftsmen's Guild, Pittsburgh, PA. Her work is in the collections of American Craft Museum, New York, NY; Cranbrook Museum of Art, Cranbrook Academy of Art, Bloomfield Hills, MI; Everson Museum of Art, Syracuse, NY; Pennsylvania Academy of the Fine Arts, Philadelphia, PA; and Renwick Gallery of the Smithsonian American Art Museum, Washington, DC. See Karen Chambers, 'Judy Moonelis,' *American Ceramics* (Vol. 13, No. 2, 1999).

Thomas Naethe B. Berlin, Germany, 1954. Naethe was apprenticed under Gisela Schliessler, Krosselbach, Germany from 1973 to 1976. He then studied at the State Technical School for Ceramic Design, Höhr-Grenzhausen, Germany (1978–81). In 1981 he earned a diploma for his Masters examination and Designer's examination. Between the years 1982 and 1988 he was involved jointly in a workshop/studio with Rita Ternes, Bippen, Germany, and since 1988 in a joint workshop in Utzerath/Eifel. He has been awarded the Westerwaldpreis, German Ceramics, Höhr-Grenzhausen twice (1982 and 1992). Naethe's reductive stoneware vessels are highly formal by design. They play on relationships between the strong convex and concave lines established in their profiles. The bases upon which his vessels often rest have strong sculptural harmony with the principal forms, and he says of his use of surface and color on the base rings in particular that '[They] separate and unite the individual parts simultaneously.' His pieces are often assembled from several thrown parts, once they come off the wheel. The surfaces, which heighten the sculptural thrust of his vessels, are achieved through use of colored slips, coloring salts, porcelain slip, oxides, and a white feldspar glaze. See Marlene Jochem, 'Thomas Naethe: Vessel Compositions,' Neue Keramik (Jan/Feb 2001).

Ron Nagle B. San Francisco, CA, USA, 1939. Nagle received his art education and B.A. from San Francisco State College, CA. Between 1961 and 1978, he taught sporadically at the San Francisco Art Institute, CA; University of California at Berkeley; California College of Arts and Crafts, Oakland, CA; and several other schools. In 1960 he connected with the so-called Abstract Expressionist Ceramics group around Peter Voulkos. He was particularly influenced by the work of two members of the group, Ken Price and Michael Frimkess. By 1963, having seen an exhibition of the work of Giorgio Morandi at the Ferus Gallery in Los Angeles, CA, he decided to adopt a narrow focus—the cup—and has worked almost exclusively with this domestic icon ever since. From 1990 to 1999 he received Faculty Research Grants from Mills College, Oakland, CA. His first exhibition was at the Dilexi Gallery, San Francisco, CA, in 1968. Since then he has exhibited at the Quay Gallery in San Francisco, CA; Charles Cowles Gallery, New York, NY; Rena Bransten Gallery, San Francisco, CA; and since 1995, the Garth Clark Gallery, New York. Nagle has had over thirty solo exhibitions and has been included in hundreds of group exhibitions. In 1993 the Art Gallery of Mills College, Oakland, CA, organized the touring exhibition 'Ron Nagle: A Survey Exhibition 1958–1993.' He has work in the public collections at Carnegie Museum of Art, Pittsburgh, PA; Mint Museum of Craft and Design, Charlotte,

NC; Philadelphia Museum of Art, Philadelphia, PA; Stedelijk Museum, Amsterdam, the Netherlands; Museum het Kruithuis, 's-Hertogenbosch, the Netherlands; Victoria and Albert Museum, London; and the San Francisco Museum of Modern Art, CA. Nagle has received numerous awards and fellowships, including the NEA (1974, 1979, and 1986), Mellon Grants (1981 and 1983) and Visual Arts Award of the Flintridge Foundation (1998). He currently teaches at Mills College in Oakland, CA. See Jane Adlin, Contemporary Ceramics: Selections from The Collection in the Metropolitan Museum of Art (New York: The Metropolitan Museum of Art, 1998); Garth Clark, American Potters: The Work of Twenty Modern Masters (New York: Watson-Guptill, 1981); John Coplans, Abstract Expressionist Ceramics (Irvine, CA: University of California, 1966); Michael McTwigan, Ron Nagle: A Survey Exhibition 1958–1993 (Oakland, CA: Mills College Art Gallery, 1963); and Jo Lauria, Color and Fire (Los Angeles: Los Angeles County Museum of Art, and New York: Rizzoli, 2000).

Kohei Nakamura B. Kanazawa, Japan, 1948. Nakamura holds a B.A. from Tama University of Fine Arts (1973). In 1979, Nakamura received a National Fellowship from the Agency for Cultural Affairs, and was selected as the first Domestic Researcher. He received the Grand Prix, Yagi-Kazuo Prize Competition of Contemporary Ceramics (1989). His work has been widely exhibited in Japan and the USA, including shows at Tamura Gallery, Tokyo, Japan; Ban Gallery, Osaka, Japan; Gallery Koyanagi, Tokyo, Japan; Garth Clark Gallery, New York, NY; Museum of Contemporary Ceramic Art in the Shigaraki Ceramic Cultural Park, Shigaraki, Japan; National Museum of Contemporary Art, Seoul, South Korea; Museum of Modern Art, Shiga, Japan; and National Museum of Modern Art,

Tokyo, Japan. His work is in the collections of Museum of Modern Art, Shiga, Japan; National Museum of Modern Art, Kyoto, and Tokyo, Japan; Yamaguchi Prefectural Museum of Art, Yamaguchi, Japan; Everson Museum of Art, Syracuse, NY; and The Metropolitan Museum of Art, New York, NY. See Alexandra Munroe, 'The Art of Kohei Nakamura,' American Ceramics (Vol. 12, No. 1, 1995); and Tomio Sugaya, Metamorphosis of Contemporary Ceramics (Shigaraki, Japan: Museum of Contemporary Ceramic Art, 1991).

Barbara Nanning B. the Hague, the Netherlands, 1957. Nanning has been a full-time lecturer at Gerrit Rietveld Academy, Amsterdam (1993) and Hoge School voor de Beeldende Kunsten, Amsterdam (1994–95). She received an award from the Fletcher Challenge, Auckland, New Zealand (1992). Nanning's work tends to be large, acrid-colored organic forms, often designed as public sculptures. She has exhibited her work for more than two decades, including shows at Galerie Dis, Maastricht, the Netherlands; Galerie 'L', Hamburg, Germany; Gallery Clara Scremini, Paris; Gallery Koyanagi, Tokyo; Nancy Margolis Gallery, New York, NY; Gallery Aspects, London; Gallery de Witte Voet, Amsterdam; and Gallery Maas, Rotterdam, the Netherlands. Her work appears in the collections of Stedelijk Museum, Amsterdam, the Netherlands; Museum Boijmans van Beuningen, Rotterdam, the Netherlands; Rijksmuseum Twenthe, Enschede, the Netherlands; Museum for Fine Arts, Boston, MA; Museum of Contemporary Ceramic Art in the Shigaraki Ceramic Cultural Park, Shigaraki, Japan; Musée des Arts Décoratifs, Paris; and Seoul Metropolitan Museum, Seoul, South Korea. See Tomio Sugaya, Metamorphosis of Contemporary Ceramics (Shigaraki, Japan: Museum of Contemporary Ceramic Art, 1991); Sabrina Kamstra, As Far As Japan ('s-Hertogenbosch: KW 14, 1996); and Liesbeth Cromelin, Travels in Time and Space (Amsterdam: Keramiek Atelier, 1988).

Art Nelson B. Denver, CO, USA, 1942; D. Oakland, CA, USA, 1994. Nelson studied at the University of Colorado, Boulder, CO, where he received his B.A. in 1964, and at the California College of Arts and Crafts (CCAC), Oakland, CA, receiving his M.F.A. in 1969. In the same year he began to teach at the CCAC, where he held the position of associate professor of art. In addition to maintaining an active program of exhibitions and teaching, Nelson was also one of several artists active in the art/industry program of exhibitions at Kohler Industries in Sheboygan, WI.

Nelson was a brilliant technician and could take on any process and within a matter of weeks achieve mastery of the technique. This allowed several radical shifts in the style of his work, from faux Super-Realist over-scaled works with strong sexual overtones that seemed to be made of chromed metal and leather to brightly colored nested vessels in the postmodernist style. See Garth Clark, *American Ceramics* (New York: Abbeville Press, 1987); and Charles Fiske 'Art Nelson,' *American Ceramics* (Vol. 2, No. 1, 1983).

Matt Nolen B. Key West, FL, USA, 1960. Nolen holds a B.A. from Auburn University, Auburn, AL (1983). Prior to this, he studied at the Gadsden Museum School, Gadsden Museum of Art, Gadsden, AL (1969–75). He maintains a studio in New York City. Nolen received an NEA Regional Fellowship (Mid-Atlantic Arts Foundation) in 1995, as well as two Empire State Craft Alliance Grants (1991 and 1995) and a Fellowship from the New York Foundation for the Arts (1995). Nolen's forms, which are based on the function of each piece, are very much like a 'traffic jam' with all the excesses and neurosis of contemporary life playing out loudly on the sides of his narrative vessels. His exhibition record includes shows at ARCHON, New York, NY; Garth Clark Gallery, New York, NY, and Los Angeles, CA; Nancy Margolis Gallery, New York, NY; Helen Drutt Gallery, Philadelphia, PA; Nancy Drysdale Gallery, Washington, DC; William Traver Gallery, Seattle, WA; Dolphin Gallery, Kansas City, MO; and Ferrin Gallery, Northampton, MA. His work appears in the collections of Banff Arts Centre, Banff, Alberta, Canada; Cooper-Hewitt National Design Museum, New York, NY; and Everson Museum of Art, Syracuse, NY. See Peter Dormer, *The New Ceramics: Trends & Traditions* (London: Thames & Hudson, 1995).

Richard Notkin B. Chicago, IL, USA, 1948. Notkin earned a B.F.A. in 1970 under Ken Ferguson at the Kansas City Art Institute, Kansas City, MO, and was one of Robert Arneson's students at TB9 at Davis, California, where he earned an M.F.A. in 1973. He currently maintains a studio in Helena, MT,

where is active on the board of the Archie Bray Foundation for the Ceramic Arts. Notkin has made several trips to China and has been deeply influenced by the centuries old tradition of Yixing pottery from which he has adopted precise working methods and a penchant for trompe-l'oeil. He uses his artwork as an extension of his conscience, believing art should be socially activist. For over ten years he used the teapot format to focus on military adventures and questionable foreign policy around the world with particular focus on nuclear weaponry and energy. 'Strong Tea' organized by Seattle Art Museum, Seattle, WA, in 1990 and 'Passages' in 1999 were two touring museum exhibitions devoted exclusively to Notkin's work. Notkin's work is in the collections of The Metropolitan Museum of Art, New York, NY; Cooper-Hewitt National Design Museum, New York, NY; Carnegie Museum of Art, Pittsburgh, PA; Charles A. Wustum Museum of Fine Arts, Racine, WI; Mint Museum of Craft and Design, Charlotte, NC; Musée des Arts Décoratifs, Montreal, Canada; Stedelijk Museum, Amsterdam, the Netherlands; Museum of Contemporary Ceramic Art in the Shigaraki Ceramic Cultural Park, Shigaraki, Japan; and Victoria and Albert Museum, London. See Vicki Halper, *Strong Tea* (Seattle: Seattle Art Museum, 1990); and Louana M. Lackey, 'Not Just Another Pretty Vase,' *Ceramics Monthly* (October 2000).

Magdalene Odundo B. Nairobi, Kenya, 1950. Odundo attended school in her homeland and in New Delhi, India. In 1971 she moved to England and studied at the Cambridge College of Art, Cambridge (1971–73), West Surrey School of Art and Design, Farnham (1973–76), and the Royal College of Art, London (1979–82). Her work reflects the influences of her native Kenya, building with coils and burnishing the surface. Her first solo exhibition was in 1977 at the Africa Center, London, and since she has shown extensively in Britain, Europe, and the USA. In 1995, 'Ceramic Gestures: New Vessels by Magdalene Odundo,' a major exhibition, toured the USA. Her work is in the collections of Los Angeles County Museum of Art, Los Angeles, CA; The Metropolitan Museum of Art, New York, NY; Victoria and Albert Museum, London; Museum het Kruithuis, 's-Hertogenbosch, the Netherlands; and many other museums. See Marla C. Berns, *Ceramic Gestures: New Vessels by Magdalene Odundo* (Santa Barbara: University Art Museum, University of California, 1995); and Yvonne Joris, John Picton and Geert Staal, *Magdalene Odundo* ('s-Hertogenbosch: Museum het Kruithuis, 1994).

Lawson Oyekan B. London, England, 1961. Oyekan holds a B.A. (with honors) in three-dimensional design and ceramics from Central St. Martins School of Art and Design, London (1988). His M.A. (ceramics and glass) was taken in 1990 at the School of Applied Arts, Royal College of Art, London. Oyekan was awarded membership of the Académie International de la Céramique, Geneva, Switzerland (2000). His work, done in both stoneware and porcelain, often includes penetration of the walls of his vessels, with both large and small openings, to allow the viewer to enter the pieces in various ways. Occasionally the work resembles the landscapes of Africa. Oyekan's exhibition record includes shows at Garth Clark Gallery, New York, NY; Canary Wharf/Barrett/ Marsden Gallery, London; Galerie Peter Herrmann, Stuttgart, Germany; Galerie Anderwereld, Groningen, the Netherlands; Bruton Gallery, Bath, England; Botier Gallery 12, Brussels, Belgium; and Leicester City Gallery, Leicester, England. His work appears in the collections of Los Angeles County Museum of Art, Los Angeles, CA; Oxford Science Park, Magdalen College, Oxford, England; Shipley Museum and Gallery, Gateshead, England; and Museum of Contemporary Ceramic Art in the Shigaraki Ceramic Cultural Park, Shigaraki, Japan. See Pamela Johnson, 'Dimensions of Light,' *Crafts* (Jan/Feb 1994); and Barry Schwabsky, 'Lawson Oyekan,' *American Craft* (Aug/Sept 2000).

Pekka Tapio Paikkari B. Somero, Finland, 1960. Paikkari studied at Kuopio Academy of Handicraft and Design, Finland. He has worked for Arabia Museum, Helsinki, Finland, since 1983. Paikkari has twice been the recipient of one-year grants from the Finnish State (1991 and 1998) and also received a working stipend from the Finnish State in 1997. His large, compelling artworks often reflect the dramatic forces in nature, deceptively controlled in his studio. His solo exhibitions include shows at Arabia-Nuutajarvi Shop, Helsinki, Finland; Gallery Bronda, Helsinki, Finland; Gallery Pinotheca, Jyvaskyla, Finland; Arabia Museum, Design Forum and Museum of Art and Design, both

Los Angeles, CA; San Francisco Museum of Modern Art, San Francisco, CA; Oakland Museum of California, Oakland, CA; Stedelijk Museum, Amsterdam, the Netherlands; National Museum of Modern Art, Tokyo, Japan; and Whitney Museum of American Art, New York, NY. See Suzanne Foley, *Robert Hudson/Richard Shaw: Work in Porcelain* (San Francisco: San Francisco Museum of Modern Art, 1973); Ruth Braunstein, *Richard Shaw: Illusionism in Clay 1971–1985* (San Francisco: Braunstein Gallery, 1985); and Jo Lauria, *Color and Fire* (Los Angeles: Los Angeles County Museum of Art, and New York: Rizzoli, 2000).

Michael Sherrill B. Providence, RI, USA, 1954. Sherrill is primarily self-taught and acknowledges influences from the artists of the Penland School of Crafts, NC, and the Arrowmont School of Arts and Crafts, TN. Exhibitions of his work include 'The Penland Connection: Contemporary Works in Clay,' The Society of Arts and Crafts, Boston, MA (1996); 'The White House Collection of American Crafts,' National Museum of American Art of the Smithsonian Institution, Washington, DC (1993–99, touring exhibition); 'Erotica in Ceramic Art,' Ferrin Gallery, Northampton, MA; and 'Color and Fire: Defining Moments in Studio Ceramics, 1950–2000,' Los Angeles County Museum of Art, Los Angeles, CA (2000). Sherrill's work is included in the collections of the Howard Hughes Foundation, Bethesda, MD; Mint Museum of Craft and Design, Charlotte, NC; and Renwick Gallery of the Smithsonian American Art Museum, Washington, DC. See Jo Lauria, *Color and Fire* (Los Angeles: Los Angeles County Museum of Art, and New York: Rizzoli, 2000); and Garth Clark, *The Artful Teapot* (New York: Watson-Guptill, and London: Thames & Hudson, 2001).

Peter Shire B. Los Angeles, CA, USA, 1947. Shire received his B.F.A. from the Chouinard Art Institute in Los Angeles, CA, in 1970 and was an early member of the Milan-based Memphis design group headed by Ettore Sottsass. Shire has had one-person shows at William Traver Gallery in Seattle, WA; Morgan Gallery in Kansas City, MI; Janus Gallery and Dan Saxon Gallery, both in Los Angeles, CA. He is represented by Frank Lloyd Gallery, Santa Monica, CA. In 1984 Shire received an award for his contribution to the XXIII Olympiad Los Angeles and 'The Esquire Register' in 1985 from *Esquire Magazine*. His work is in the collections of the Art Institute of Chicago, Chicago, IL; Everson Museum of Art, Syracuse, NY; Los Angeles County Museum of Art, Los Angeles, CA; San Francisco Museum of Modern Art, San Francisco, CA; and the Israel Museum, Jerusalem, Israel. See Peter Shire, *Tempest in a Teapot: The Ceramic Art of Peter Shire* (New York: Rizzoli, 1991); *Peter Shire, Tea Types: An Opera* (Los Angeles: Tea Garden Press, 1980); and Jo Lauria, *Color and Fire* (Los Angeles: Los Angeles County Museum of Art, and New York: Rizzoli, 2000).

Alev Ebüzziya Siesbye B. Istanbul, Turkey, 1938. Siesbye studied sculpture at the Academy of Fine Arts and from 1956 to 1958 worked at Fureya's Ceramic Workshop, both in Istanbul. For two years she worked as a production worker in ceramic factories in Höhr-Grenzhausen, Germany, and returned to Turkey to work for two more years at the Eczacibasi Ceramic Factories Art Workshop in Istanbul. But the years 1963 to 1968, while she was an artist at Royal Copenhagen, Denmark, left their strongest impression on her work. Made of stoneware, her work is coil built, but has the appearance of being 'thrown,' with her signature small foot on which the bowls are balanced. Siesbye received the Eckersberg Medal in 1983, the Sanat Kurumu Ceramics Prize in 1988, and the Prins Eugen Medal in Stockholm, Sweden, in 1995. Her work is in over thirty public and museum collections, amongst which are the Danish Museum of Decorative Art, Copenhagen, Denmark; Cooper-Hewitt National Design Museum, New York, NY; Los Angeles County Museum of Art, Los Angeles, CA; Musée Bellerive, Zürich, Switzerland; Museum of Decorative Arts, Gent, Belgium; Nationalmuseum in Stockholm, Sweden; and Ulster Museum, Belfast, Northern Ireland. See Garth Clark, *Alev Ebuzziya Siesbye* (Istanbul: Kaleseramik Sanat Yayinlari, 1999).

Bobby Silverman B. Port Jefferson, NY, USA, 1956. Silverman received a B.F.A. in 1981 from the Kansas City Art Institute, Kansas City, MO, and an M.F.A. from New York State College of Ceramics at Alfred University, New York, NY (1983). His one-person exhibitions have included those at the Jane Hartsook Gallery at Greenwich House Pottery in New York (1989); the European Ceramic Work Center in 's-Hertogenbosch, the Netherlands (1998); and Farrell/Pollack Fine Art, Brooklyn, NY (2000). Silverman has received three fellowships from the New York State Council of the Arts (1988), the NEA (1995) and the Louisiana State Council of the Arts (1999). His work is in the collections of American Craft Museum, New York, NY; Fred Marer Collection, Scripps College, Claremont, CA; and the Archie Bray Foundation for the Ceramic Arts, Helena, MT. See Bobby Silverman, 'Objects of Pure Perception,' *American Craft* (June/July 1999).

Richard Slee B. Carlisle, Cumbria, England, 1946. Slee studied at the Carlisle College of Art and Design from 1964 to 1965, at the Central St. Martins School of Art and Design, London, where he received his B.A. (ceramics) in 1970 and at the Royal College of Art, London, receiving an M.A. (design) in 1988. Since 1988 he has been a principal lecturer at Camberwell College of Arts, London, and since 1992 has been a professor at the London Institute.

Since 1970 he has had numerous solo exhibitions and participated in many group exhibitions and now exhibits with Barrett/Marsden Gallery, London. One of the most respected and innovative artists of his generation, his work has been a focus in most of the major surveys of British ceramics, including the controversial 'Fast Forward,' ICA, London (1985); the touring exhibition 'The Raw and the Cooked' organized in 1993 by the Museum of Modern Art, Oxford; and 'Contemporary British Ceramics' at the Keramikmuseet Grimmerhus, Middelfart, Denmark, in 2000. His work is in the collections of the Leicester City Museum, Leicester, England; Los Angeles County Museum of Art, Los Angeles, CA; National Museum of Modern Art, Kyoto, Japan; Nationalmuseum, Stockholm, Sweden; and Stedelijk Museum, Amsterdam, the Netherlands. See John Huston, *Richard Slee: Ceramics* (*In Studio series*) (London: Bellew Publishing, 1990); Oliver Watson, *Richard Slee: Grand Wizard of Studio Ceramics* (London: Barrett/Marsden Gallery, 1998); and Grayson Perry, *Richard Slee* (London: Barrett/Marsden Gallery, 2000).

Martin Smith B. Braintree, Essex, England, 1950. Martin Smith began his career at Ipswich School of Art (1970–71), received a B.A. at Bristol Polytechnic in 1971 and an M.A. at the Royal College of Art, London, where he studied from 1975 to 1977. He rates the ceramist Gordon Baldwin as the most significant single influence on his work. His vessels are made of earthenware and have a reductivist, postminimal edge. Smith has exhibited his work extensively since 1975 in his native England, all over Europe, and in the USA. He has had numerous solo exhibitions in the USA at the Garth Clark Gallery in Los Angeles, CA, Kansas City, MO, and New York, NY, and is currently represented in Europe by Barrett/Marsden Gallery, London. In 1996 the Museum Boijmans van Beuningen, Rotterdam, the Netherlands organized a retrospective of his work with the installation designed by the doyen of minimalist architects, John Pawson. His work is in numerous public collections, including the British Crafts Council in London; Stedelijk Museum, Amsterdam, the Netherlands; National Museum of Modern Art, Tokyo, Japan; Württembergisches Landesmuseum, Stuttgart, Germany; and The Metropolitan Museum of Art, New York, NY. He has taught at Brighton Polytechnic, the Camberwell College of Arts, London, and in 1989 joined the Royal College of Art, London, where he is currently Professor of Ceramics and Glass. See Alison Britton and Martina Margetts, *The Raw and The Cooked:*

New Work in Britain (Oxford: Museum of Modern Art, 1983); Jane Adlin, *Contemporary Ceramics: Selections from The Collection in the Metropolitan Museum of Art* (New York: The Metropolitan Museum of Art, 1998); Doris Kuyken-Schneider and Alison Britton, *Balance and Space, Martin Smith Ceramics 1976–96* (Rotterdam: Museum Boijmans van Beuningen, 1996); and Pamela Johnson, 'View from the Edge' *Crafts* (Nov/Dec 1992).

Frank Steyaert B. Dendermonde, Belgium, 1953. Steyaert studied architecture and ceramics at the Academie voor Schone Kunsten, Aalst, Belgium. He also studied jewelry and ceramics at the Academie voor Schone Kunsten, Antwerp, Belgium. Finally, Steyaert studied sculpture and ceramics at National Hoger Instituut, Antwerp, Belgium. He has been a Professor of Ceramics at the Academie voor Schone Kunsten, Deinze, Belgium, since 1975, and has held the same position at the Academie voor Schone Kunsten, Dendermonde, Belgium, since 1986. Stayaert has received both the Presidential Republic Prize (1982) and the Prize of the Italian Minister of Culture (1985), International Ceramic Conference, Faenza, Italy. For Steyaert himself his derelict ships are strongly symbolic. His works show bruised individuals with an inner life of their own, who evoke harrowing feelings of vulnerability, fear, and pain. The many rooms within his works represent their soul, calling forth many questions and are both tangible and deeply mysterious. His work has been exhibited at Nancy Margolis Gallery, New York, NY, as well as at various galleries in Belgium. His work is in the collections of Museum voor Sierkunst and Vormgeving, Gent, Belgium; Museo Internazionale delle Ceramiche, Faenza, Italy; Kestner Museum, Hannover, Germany; and Ulster Museum, Belfast, Northern Ireland. See Lieven Daenens, 'Frank Steyaert,' *Kerameiki Techni* (April 1999).

Piet Stockmans B. Leopoldsburg, Belgium, 1940. Stockmans was the designer at Royal Mosa, the Netherlands, from 1966 to 1989 where he created the coffee cup 'Sonja' which is the greatest selling cup design in the world, with over 32 million units (both legitimate and pirated). At the same time he followed a career of making one-off artworks and limited series in a distinctive, but limited, palette of poured porcelain slip and blue dip. He has received numerous awards for his work, including the 1988 Flemish Prize for Visual Art and the prestigious Henry van der Velde Prize from VIZO in 1999. In 1995 he was appointed the Cultural Ambassador of Flanders. Since 1969 he has been the professor of industrial design at the Katholieke Hogeschool Limburg in Gent, Belgium. Stockmans traffics in multiples, sometimes just a pair of cups in a box, while his installations have filled cathedrals and other public places with over 50,000 pieces in his distinctive palette of white slip-molded forms with blue slip. The modular approach is not unique in ceramics, but there are few other ceramic artists who match his vision, ambition, and industriousness. He is part wizard, part industrialist, part designer, part potter, part painter, part architect, and part conceptualist. All of these talents coalesce into one of the most original and compulsively productive contemporary ceramic artists today. His work has been extensively exhibited and is in numerous collections, including Los Angeles County Museum of Art, Los Angeles, CA; and Stedelijk Museum, Amsterdam, the Netherlands. See Jo Rombouts, ed., *Piet Stockmans* (Tielt, Belgium: Lannoo, 1996); and Garth Clark, Luc Verstraete, and Mimi Wilms, *Piet Stockmans* (Knokke-Heist: Cultureel Centrum, 2000).

Luis Miguel Suro B. Guadalajara, Mexico, 1972. Suro pursued Architectural Studies at I.T.E.S.O.A.C., Guadalajara, Mexico (1990–91). In 1989, he participated in a drawing and painting workshop at the Cultural Institute and Museum Cabanas, Guadalajara, Mexico. He worked from 1994–96 at Ceramic Project, Uriarte Talavera de Puebla, Mexico. With room-size installations, Suro's large-scale sculptures represent the tension of contemporary life; from indigestion to assassinations and suicides. His broad exhibition record includes solo shows at Leonora Vega Gallery, New York, NY; Landucci Gallery, Mexico City, Mexico; Modern Art Center, Guadalajara, Mexico; Pacifico Gallery, Puerto Vallarta, Mexico; El Buen Gobierno Gallery, Granada, Spain; El Almazen de la Nave Galeria, Madrid, Spain; and Arriba Gallery, Great Barrington, MA. See Anna Maria Fitch, 'En busca del lugar no conquistado,' *Art Vance Magazine* (June/July 1999).

Angus Suttie B. Tealing, Scotland, 1946; D. London, England, 1993. Suttie studied at the Camberwell School of Arts and Crafts, London (1976–79). This brilliant young artist had had only five solo exhibitions by the time his career was cut short by AIDS. His work was included in numerous group shows, including the defining exhibition 'The Raw and the Cooked,' organized by the Museum of Modern Art, Oxford, in 1993, which toured internationally. A widely respected artist, his work is in the public collections of the Crafts Council, London; Museum het Kruithuis, 's-Hertogenbosch, the Netherlands; Victoria and Albert Museum, London; National Museum of Modern Art, Kyoto, Japan; and others. In 1994 a memorial exhibition was held at Contemporary Applied Arts, London which traveled to the Scottish Gallery, Edinburgh; and Museum het Kruithuis, 's-Hertogenbosch, the Netherlands. See Alison Britton, et al., *Angus Suttie 1946–1993* (London: Contemporary Applied Arts, 1994); and Garth Clark, *The Potter's Art: A Complete History of Pottery in Britain* (London: Phaidon, 1995).

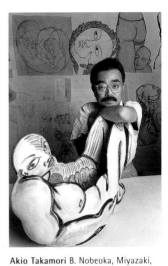

Akio Takamori B. Nobeoka, Miyazaki, Japan, 1950. Takamori studied at the Musashino Art University in Tokyo from 1969 to 1971. From 1972 to 1974 he was an apprentice with Oita, a master folk potter, working on traditional utilitarian pottery, Koishawara-ware, in Fukuoka. Takamori later studied with Ken Ferguson at the Kansas City Art Institute, Kansas City, MO, receiving his B.F.A. in 1976 and his M.F.A. from the New York State College of Ceramics at Alfred University, New York, NY, in 1978. His work was included in the 1977 'Young Americans: Clay' exhibition at the Museum of Contemporary Crafts, New York, NY, and he had his first solo exhibition in the USA at the Garth Clark Gallery, Los Angeles, CA, in 1983. Since then he has exhibited extensively in the USA, as well as in Europe and Japan. He maintains a studio in Seattle. Takamori worked sculpturally during his time at Kansas City and New York State College of Ceramics at Alfred University, New York, NY, but after leaving school returned to the vessel form and began to work innovatively with its structure, creating flat, envelope-shaped pots. In the mid 1990s a visit to the European Ceramic Work Center in 's-Hertogenbosch, the Netherlands, resulted in a decisive shift from vessels back to figures. The first exhibition of this work took place in 1997 at the Garth Clark Gallery, New York, on a T-shaped bridge carrying a throng of over forty figures, evoking the memories of growing up in the village of Nobeoka. Takamori's work can be found in the public collections of the Everson Museum of Art, Syracuse, NY; Mint Museum of Craft and Design, Charlotte, NC; Los Angeles County Museum of Art, Los Angeles, CA; Victoria and Albert Museum, London; Carnegie Museum of Art, Pittsburgh, PA; Kinsey Institute, Bloomington, IN; Museum het Kruithuis, 's-Hertogenbosch, the Netherlands; and

National Museum of History, Taipei, Taiwan, Republic of China. See Martha Drexler Lynn, 'Akio Takamori: Piquant Contemporary Observation, Time Honored Means,' *American Ceramics* (June/July 1993); Sarah Burns, et al., *The Art of Desire: Erotic Treasures from the Kinsey Institute* (Bloomington, Indiana: Kinsey Institute, School of Fine Arts Gallery, 1997); and Garth Clark, *Akio Takamori* (New York: Garth Clark Gallery, 2000).

Søren Ubisch B. Blaker, Norway, 1952. Ubisch holds a diploma from the National School of Arts, Oslo, Norway (1974). Through the Kyoto City University of Arts he did some elaborate field research and studied in Japan (1974–80). In 1984 this extensive project was accredited with a post doctoral scholarship through the Japan Foundation. He has, amongst many awards, been the recipient of a three-year National Scholarship for Artists, The Norwegian Culture Department (1993–95), as well as a study and travel grant through this same organization (1998). Ubisch works with large surfaces and small detail in a realm of spatial abstraction and, as walls, architectural reality. His broad exhibition record includes shows at RAM Gallery, Oslo, Norway; Kagawa Gallery, Takamatsu, Japan; and Tsuchihashi Gallery, Kyoto, Japan. His work is in the collections of Museum of Applied Arts, Bergen, Norway; Museum of Applied Arts, Trondheim, Norway; Museum of Applied Arts, Oslo, Norway; and the Norwegian Council for Cultural Affairs, Oslo. See Torbjorn Kvasbo and Jorunn Veiteberg, eds, *Norwegian Contemporary Ceramics* (Amsterdam: Arti et Amicitiae, 1999).

Hans van Bentem B. The Hague, the Netherlands, 1965. Van Bentem studied

at the Koninklijke Academie van Beeldende Kunsten den Haag, The Hague (1983–88). In 1990 he began a collaboration with Struktuur 68, a studio workshop founded by Henk Trumpie in the Hague that facilitates the design and execution of large-scale public-site work. Van Bentem was the 1998 recipient of the Bernadine de Neve Award, as well as many significant public commissions throughout the Netherlands. His current work is large-scale and figurative, making 7-ft high fantasy warriors and other mythic beings influenced somewhat by the Japanese tradition of Manga comic books. His exhibition record includes shows at Garth Clark Gallery, New York, NY; Loerakker Gallery, Amsterdam, the Netherlands; Dolphin Gallery, Kansas City, MO; Perimeter Gallery, Chicago, IL; MAEA Gallery, Paris; and Frans Halsmuseum, Haarlem, the Netherlands. See Geraart Westerink, 'Techno Buddha Meets Astro Boy' (*Glas en Keramiek I*, 1998); and Micha Ouwendijk, *Monumental Dutch Ceramics* (The Hague: Struktuur 68, 1990).

Eric Van Eimeren B. Long Beach, CA, 1965. Van Eimeren received a B.A. in applied design and ceramics from San Diego State University, CA, in 1987 and an M.F.A. in ceramics from the New York State College of Ceramics at Alfred University, New York, NY, in 1990. Among his many awards, he has received a WESTAF/NEA Regional Fellowship for Visual Artists (1993) and Merit Awards, National Teapot Show (1989 and 1996). The artist has maintained a permanent studio in Helena, MT, since 1993. Van Eimeren's exhibition record includes shows at Garth Clark Gallery, New York, NY, and Los Angeles, CA; Nancy Margolis Gallery, New York, NY; Joanne Rapp Gallery, Scottsdale, AZ; Crafts Alliance, St. Louis, MO; Northern Clay Center, Minneapolis, MN; and Helen Drutt Gallery, Philadelphia, PA. His work appears in the collections of the Mint Museum of Craft and Design, Charlotte, NC; and Charles A. Wustum Museum of Fine Arts, Racine, WI. See 'Portfolio,' *American Craft* (Aug/Sept 1994, p. 60); and Garth Clark, *The Artful Teapot* (New York: Watson-Guptill, and London: Thames & Hudson, 2001).

Kukuli Velarde B. Cusco, Peru, 1962. Velarde taught ceramic sculpture at Swarthmore College, Swarthmore, PA (2000). She was a recipient of the Evelyn Shapiro Foundation Fellowship, The Clay Studio, Philadelphia, PA (1997–99). Among many awards, she received the Leeway Foundation Window of Opportunity Award, Philadelphia, PA (1999) and the Anonymous was a Woman Grant, New York, NY (2000). Velarde has also been a panelist and lecturer at numerous universities in the USA and Peru. Her work expresses feminist themes, while at the same time invoking the style and format of pre-Columbian figural art. Her broad exhibition record includes solo shows at Galeria Pancho Fierro, Lima, Peru; El Puente Gallery, Lima, Peru; John Elder Gallery, New York, NY; Soho 20, New York, NY; The Clay Studio, Philadelphia, PA; and Santa Fe De Bogota Planetarium Gallery, Bogota, Columbia. See 'Portfolio,' *American Craft* (1999); Thomas Piche, Jr. and Justin Clemens, *Everson Museum of Art Ceramic National 2000* (Syracuse: Everson Museum of Art, 2000); and Kukuli Velarde, 'Isichapuitu,' *Ceramics Monthly* (Dec 1998).

Irene Vonck B. Dublin, Ireland, 1952. Vonck studied in England at Falmouth School of Art, Cornwall, in 1971. In 1972, she studied at Brighton Polytechnic, Sussex, and in the Netherlands at the Gerrit Rietveld Academy, Amsterdam, between 1973 and 1977. Her work has changed several times through her career, but first drew attention when she began to compose powerful vessel forms out of what seem to be larger-than-life brush strokes. Her exhibition record includes shows at Gallery de Witte Voet, Amsterdam, the Netherlands; Mostra Internazionale, Milan, Italy; Gallery Aspects, London; Anatol Orient Gallery, London; Marlborough Fine Art, London; Garth Clark Gallery, New York, NY; Helen Drutt Gallery, Philadelphia, PA; Westminster Gallery, Boston, MA; Museum Fodor, Amsterdam, the

Netherlands; International Ceramic Festival, Mino, Japan; Everson Museum of Art, Syracuse, NY; Crafts Council, London; Museum Boijmans van Beuningen, Rotterdam, the Netherlands; Kestner Museum, Hannover, Germany; Seasons/Ramakers Gallery, The Hague, the Netherlands; Stedelijk Museum, Amsterdam, the Netherlands; and Galerie DM Sarver, Paris. Her work is in the collections of the Stedelijk Museum, Amsterdam, the Netherlands; Museum Boijmans van Beuningen, Rotterdam, the Netherlands; Everson Museum of Art, Syracuse, NY; and Nordenfjeldske Kunstindustrimuseum, Trondheim, Norway. See Helly Oesterreicher, *Kuipers Oesterreicher, Vonck* ('s-Hertogenbosch: European Ceramic Work Center, 1995); and Liesbeth Cromelin, *Ceramics in the Stedelijk Museum* (Amsterdam: Stedelijk Museum of Modern Art, 1998).

Kevin Waller B. Los Angeles, CA, USA, 1961. Waller holds an A.A. (music and business accounting) from the Los Angeles Valley College, Los Angeles, CA. He studied music voice performance (1990) and ceramics at San Francisco State University, CA (1992); and ceramics at San Francisco City College, CA. He says about his work, 'The way [silos] jut from their surrounding catches my attention. I incorporate the atmosphere that surrounds these industrial monuments into my work.' His exhibition record includes shows at Dorothy Weiss Gallery, San Francisco, CA; SOFA, Chicago, IL; Mobilia Gallery, Cambridge, England; and Rivaga Art Gallery, Washington, DC. See 'Teapot Invitational,' *Kerameiki Techni* (April 1998).

Kurt Weiser B. Lansing, MI, USA, 1950. Weiser studied under Ken Ferguson at the Kansas City Art Institute, Kansas City, MO, and earned an M.A. from the University of Michigan, Ann Arbor, MI, in 1976. He was the director of the Archie Bray Foundation for the Ceramic Arts, Helena, MT, until 1988 when he began teaching at Arizona State University where he is now a Regents Professor. He casts biomorphically shaped porcelain vessels—lidded jars and teapots—loosely based on classical Asian forms on which he creates overabundant surfaces of luxuriant and overripe vegetation meticulously china-painted. Weiser has twice received a fellowship from the NEA. He has exhibited extensively since 1982 with the Garth Clark Gallery, New York, NY, Los Angeles, CA, and Kansas City, MO; and Frank Lloyd Gallery, Santa Monica, CA. His work is in the Victoria and Albert Museum, London; Los Angeles County Museum of Art, Los Angeles, CA; Carnegie Museum of Art, Pittsburgh, PA; Museum of Contemporary Ceramic

Art in the Shigaraki Ceramic Cultural Park, Shigaraki, Japan; Mint Museum of Craft and Design, Charlotte, NC; Charles A. Wustum Museum of Fine Arts, Racine, WI; and National Museum of History, Taipei, Taiwan, Republic of China. See Mark Leach, 'Kurt Weiser', *American Ceramics* (Vol. 11, No. 1, 1993); Ed Lebow, 'Glaze of Glory', *American Craft* (Dec/Jan 1995); and Garth Clark, *Kurt Weiser* (New York: Garth Clark Gallery, 1999).

Steve Welch B. Worthington, MN, USA, 1963. Welch holds a B.F.A. (magna cum laude) from Minnesota State University, Mankato, MN (1989). He took his M.F.A. (1992) at Louisiana State University, Baton Rouge, LA. Welch's broad teaching experience includes: Instructor of 2-D Design, University of Southern Maine (1999–2000); Instructor, Art Education, 2-D Design and Drawing, St. Joseph's College, Standish, ME (2000–01); and Instructor of Drawing, University of New England, Biddeford, ME (2001), amongst many other posts. His many awards include a Southern Arts Federation Visual Arts Fellowship, NEA (1993), as well as the 1994–95 Evelyn Shapiro Foundation Fellowship, The Clay Studio, Philadelphia, PA. Welch's vessels are often architectural in their most obvious reference, though sometimes they lean towards the figurative, in an abstract way. With assertively built surfaces, Welch incorporates process centrally, in his finished forms. The seams in his slab vessels are pronounced by dark colored slip, and help to delineate his 'patchwork' surface, where individual panels are boldly colored with abruptly contrasting, though often muted, tones. Color itself is the unit of construction in his vessel/buildings, and everywhere there is evidence of how his pieces are put together. Welch's exhibition record includes shows at Nancy Margolis Gallery, New York, NY; Gallery WDO, Charlotte, NC; Northern Clay Center, Minneapolis, MN; SOFA, Chicago, IL (The Works Gallery, Philadelphia); Perimeter Gallery,

Chicago, IL; and San Angelo Museum of Fine Arts, San Angelo, TX. His work is in the collection of the Everson Museum of Art, Syracuse, NY. See 'Portfolio', *American Craft* (Aug/Sept 1996, p. 59).

Betty Woodman B. Norwalk, CT, USA, 1930. Woodman studied at the School for American Craftsmen and then at Alfred University, New York, NY, from 1948 to 1950, majoring in pottery. As soon as she completed her studies, she set up her own studio on a production basis and has been self-supporting since then. From 1957 to 1973 she taught at and administered the City of Boulder, CO, Recreation Pottery Program, which has now evolved into a major ceramic center. As one of the oldest, largest, and most successful programs of its kind, the course has become something of a model, and Woodman has frequently consulted with directors of pottery programs in other cities. In 1976 she joined the Fine Arts Department of the University of Colorado, Boulder, CO, where she is now an associate professor. Woodman has received several awards, including Visual Artist's Fellowships from the NEA in 1980 and 1986 and selection as a visiting artist at the Manufacture Nationale de Sèvres in 1985. Since 1951, Woodman has lived and worked in Italy nearly every year for varying periods of time, ranging from two to twelve months. She maintains a summer studio in Antella, outside Florence. This constant cultural counterplay between the USA and Europe shows strongly in her work, particularly in that of the last ten years. In these works the forms and surface sensitivities, although explored with the dash and adventure associated with the more lively elements of

American ceramics, strongly reflect the Mediterranean ceramic tradition and ambience. In 1980 she established a studio in New York City and, through her collaborations with Joyce Kozloff (1981) and Cynthia Carlson (1982), she began to be identified with the Pattern and Decoration movement in American art. Woodman based her early reputation on being a production potter, a maker of utilitarian ware. Over the years function has become less of an issue in the literal sense, but it has remained a potent symbolic factor in her work. Although her work has expanded to include installations, monoprints, and other activities beyond the realm of the single vessel, the primary language of the pottery remains central to her art. 'Rather than trying to blur or obliterate the line between sculpture and pottery as many do', Woodman comments, 'I am concerned with producing pots that make a significant reference to the vernacular of pottery'.

An important aspect of her work is its play with history. Woodman appropriates (to use the patois of postmodernism) from many sources— Tang, Minoan, Oribe, Etruscan, Iznik, and even from the high-style porcelains of Sèvres. In his formal analysis of Woodman's aesthetic, Jeff Perrone examines this 'grafting' of history on her work. 'One must take another attitude toward the material of ceramics when describing Woodman's art. The material is history itself, a material body of shapes, forms, decoration—in a word, everything that signifies Style'. Her work has been exhibited extensively in numerous group exhibitions and solo exhibitions with the Garth Clark Gallery, Los Angeles, CA; Hadler Rodriguez Gallery and Max Protetch Gallery, New York since 1983. In 1996 the Stedelijk Museum, Amsterdam, the Netherlands, organized a touring exhibition of her work. Woodman's work is in the collections of the Cleveland Museum of Art, Cleveland, OH; Denver Art Museum, Denver, CO; Detroit Institute of Arts, Detroit, MI; Museum het Kruithuis, 's-Hertogenbosch, the Netherlands; The Metropolitan Museum of Art, New York, NY; Musée des Arts Décoratifs, Paris; St. Louis Art Museum, St. Louis, MO; Stedelijk Museum, Amsterdam, the Netherlands; and Victoria and Albert Museum, London. See Garth Clark, *American Potters: The Work of Twenty Modern Masters* (New York: Watson-Guptill, 1981); Jeff Perrone, 'Let them Eat Cake', *Village Voice* (February 5, 1985); Peter Schjeldahl and Geert Staal, *Opera Selecta: Betty Woodman* ('s-Hertogenbosch: Museum het Kruithuis, 1990); and Liesbeth Cromelin and Arthur C. Danto, *Betty Woodman* (Amsterdam: Stedelijk Museum of Modern Art, 1996).

Susan Shutt Wulfeck B. Augusta, GA, USA, 1951. Wulfeck holds a B.F.A. from the University of Illinois, Champaign-Urbana, IL (1981); and an M.F.A. from University of California, Los Angeles, CA (1984). Wulfeck also studied at the University of California, Santa Barbara, from 1969 to 1971. Wulfeck writes about her work that, 'Throughout the years, the source of my inspiration has been my appreciation and love of the pot and of the great traditions of pottery. The idea of still life also emerged naturally as a way for me to evoke a sense of context for the vessels. [My sculptural forms] have a front and a back, like a free-standing relief, enabling me to express my ideas both pictorially like a drawing or painting and 3-dimensionally like a sculpture.' Her exhibition record includes shows at Frank Lloyd Gallery, Santa Monica, CA; Garth Clark Gallery, New York, NY, and Los Angeles, CA; Los Angeles Craft and Folk Art Museum, Los Angeles, CA; Orange County Center for Contemporary Art, Santa Ana, CA; Frederick S. Wright Art Gallery, Los Angeles, CA; West End Gallery, Provincetown, MA; and Meyer Breier Weiss Gallery, San Francisco, CA. Her work is in the collections of Los Angeles County Museum of Art, Los Angeles, CA; and Mint Museum of Craft and Design, Charlotte, NC.

Lu Wen Xia B. Yixing, China, 1966. Xia is regarded for her innovation within her strongly Yixing process and style. A student of Xu Xiu Tang, she collaborates with artist Lu Jianxing (B. 1958) in their Sun and Rain workshop in Yixing. She has achieved the rank of 'Craft Master of China.' A repeated use of bamboo characterizes much of her work. It has been exhibited and published in China, Hong Kong, Taiwan, Singapore, and Malaysia, and shown at Garth Clark Gallery, New York, NY. Xia's work is in the Smithsonian Institution, Washington, DC; Asian Art Museum of San Francisco, CA; and Mint Museum of Craft and Design, Charlotte, NC. See Lee Jingduan, ed., *Charm of Dark-Red Pottery Teapots* (Nanjing: Yilin Press, 1992); and Garth Clark, *The Artful Teapot* (New York: Watson-Guptill, and London: Thames & Hudson, 2001).

Masamichi Yoshikawa B. Chigasaki City, Kanagawa, Prefecture Japan, 1946. Among a long list of awards, Yoshikawa received the Grand Prize, Izushi Porcelain Triennale Competition, Izushi, Japan, and twice received the Grand Prize, Asahi Contemporary Ceramics Competition, Nagoya (1981) and Osaka (1983), Japan. Yoshikawa takes the traditional celadon surface into a non-traditional format of bowl-like architectural structures that are assertively and sharply geometric. His broad exhibition record includes solo shows at Gallery TEN, Fukuoka; INAX Tile Museum, Tokoname; Akasaka Green Gallery, Tokyo; Gallery Hirawata, Shonan, all Japan; Galerie du Vieux-Bourg, Lausanne, Switzerland; galerie b 15, Munich, Germany; and Gallery Takashimaya, Tokyo, Japan. His work is in the collections of Japan Foundation, Tokyo, Japan; Victoria and Albert Museum, London; Kestner Museum, Hannover, Germany; Nyon Porcelain Museum, Nyon, Switzerland; Crafts Museum, Prague, Czech Republic; Tokoname City Museum, Tokoname, Japan; Brooklyn Museum of Art, New York, NY; and Landes Schleswig-Holstein Museum, Germany.

Arnold Zimmerman B. Poughkeepsie, NY, USA, 1954. Zimmerman holds a B.F.A. from Kansas City Art Institute, Kansas City, MO (1977). His M.F.A. (1979) was earned from New York State College of Ceramics at Alfred University, New York, NY. Zimmerman has held the post of Adjunct Professor, City College of New York, NY (1995 and 1996). He has held the same teaching position at New York University, New York, NY (1992) and Hunter College, New York, NY (1990) and has taught at Centro de Arte e Communicacao Visual (ARCO), Lisbon, Portugal (1993). The artist works with ceramics on a monumental scale and the fork lift truck is as much a part of his studio equipment as the kiln. He first began to attract attention for his huge eight-foot (2.4 meter) high vessels in the late 1980s and has now taken a more abstract turn, albeit with a strong anthropomorphic presence. Zimmerman was the 1999 recipient of a Sculpture Fellowship, New York Foundation for the Arts, and also received fellowships through the same organization in 1987 and 1991. He has received NEA Fellowships as well (1986 and 1990). Zimmerman has lectured extensively throughout the USA, Canada, and also in Portugal and Taiwan. His extensive exhibition record includes solo shows at John Elder Gallery, New York, NY; Nancy Margolis Gallery, New York, NY; Shaw/Guido Gallery, Pontiac, MI; Ratton Gallery, Lisbon, Portugal; Habitat-Shaw Gallery, Farmington Hills, MI; Garth Clark Gallery, New York, NY; Objects Gallery, Chicago, IL; and Helen Drutt Gallery, Philadelphia, PA. His work is in the collections of Brooklyn Museum of Art, New York, NY; Los Angeles County Museum of Art, Los Angeles, CA; Everson Museum of Art, Syracuse, NY; Mint Museum of Craft and Design, Charlotte, NC; Detroit Institute of Arts, Detroit, MI; and Nacional Museu do Azulejo, Lisbon, Portugal. See Garth Clark and Vicky A. Clark, *Keepers of the Flame: Ken Ferguson's Circle* (Kansas City: Kemper Museum of Contemporary Art, 1995); Garth Clark, Mary F. Douglas, Carol E. Mayer, Barbara Perry, Todd D. Smith, and E. Michael Whittington, *Selections from Allan Chasanoff Ceramic Collection* (Charlotte, NC: Mint Museum of Craft and Design, 2000); and Judy Clowes, 'Arnold Zimmerman Exhibition,' *American Ceramics* (Vol. 11, 1993).

Bibliography

The following is a selection of books and catalogs of general reference on ceramics, both modern and postmodern. Monographs and books on individual artists can be found listed in their biographies.

Adlin, Jane, *Contemporary Ceramics: Selections from the Collection in the Metropolitan Museum of Art*, Metropolitan Museum of Art, New York, 1996

Bennett, Dawn, Garth Clark and Mark Del Vecchio, eds., *Ceramic Millennium*, Ceramic Arts Foundation, New York, 2000

Britton, Alison, and Martina Margetts, *The Raw and the Cooked: New Work in Clay in Britain*, British Crafts Council, London, 1983

Clark, Garth, *American Ceramics: 1876 to the Present*, Abbeville Press, New York, rev. edn., 1987

Clark, Garth, *American Potters: The Work of Twenty Modern Masters*, Watson-Guptill, New York, 1981

Clark, Garth, *The Artful Teapot*, Watson-Guptill, New York, and Thames & Hudson, London, 2001

Clark, Garth, *The Book of Cups*, Abbeville Press, New York and London, 1990

Clark, Garth (Preface by Margie Hughto), *A Century of Ceramics in the United States, 1878–1978, A Study of Its Development*, E.P. Dutton, New York, 1979

Clark, Garth, ed., *Ceramic Art: Comment and Review, 1882–1977: An Anthology of Writings on Modern Ceramic Art*, E.P. Dutton, New York, 1978

Clark, Garth, *Ceramics and Modernism: The Response of the Artist, Designer, Craftsman and Architect*, Institute for Ceramic History, Los Angeles, 1982

Clark, Garth, *The Eccentric Teapot: Four Hundred Years of Invention*, Abbeville Press, New York, 1989

Clark, Garth, *The Potter's Art: A Complete History of Pottery in Britain*, Phaidon, London, 1995

Clark, Garth, *Production Lines: Art/Craft/Design*, Philadelphia College of Art, Philadelphia, 1982

Clark, Garth, et. al., *Who's Afraid of American Pottery*, Museum het Kruithuis, 's-Hertogenbosch, the Netherlands, 1983

Clark, Garth, and Oliver Watson, *American Potters Today: An Exhibition of American Studio Pottery*, Victoria and Albert Museum, London, 1985

Crommelin, Liesbeth, ed., *Ceramics in the Stedelijk*, Stedelijk Museum, Amsterdam, 1998

Dormer, Peter, *The New Ceramics: Trends and Traditions*, Thames & Hudson, New York and London, rev. edn., 1994

Dormer, Peter, ed., *Fast Forward: New Directions in British Ceramics*, Institute of Contemporary Art, London, 1985

Eijkelenboom-Vermeer, Margreet, and Doris Kuyken-Schneider, *Danish Ceramics*, Museum Boijmans van Beuningen, Rotterdam, 1995

Halper, Vicki, *Clay Revisions: Plate, Cup, Vase*, Seattle Art Museum, Seattle, 1987

Harrod, Tanya, *The Crafts in Britain in the 20th Century*, Yale University Press, New Haven, and the Bard Graduate Center for Studies in the Decorative Arts, New York, 1999

Klinge, Ekkart, *Keramik des 20. Jahrhunderts: Sammlung Welle*, Dumont, Cologne, 1996

Lauria, Jo, ed., *Color and Fire: Defining Moments in Studio Ceramics, 1950–2000: Selections from the Smits Collection and related works at the Los Angeles County Museum of Art*, Los Angeles County Museum of Art, Los Angeles in association with Rizzoli, New York, 2000

Levine, Elaine, *The History of American Ceramics from 1607 to the Present*, Abrams, New York, 1988

Lewenstein, Eileen, and Emmanuel Cooper, *New Ceramics*, Van Nostrand Reinhold, New York, and Studio Vista, London, 1974

Lynn, Martha Drexler, *Clay Today: Contemporary Ceramists and their Work: A Catalog of the Howard and Gwen Laurie Smits Collection at the Los Angeles County Museum of Art*, Chronicle Books, San Francisco, 1990

McCready, Karen, *Contemporary American Ceramics: Twenty Artists*, Newport Harbor Art Museum, Newport Beach, Calif., 1985

Nordness, Lee, *Objects USA*, Viking Press, New York, and Thames & Hudson, London, 1970

Préaud, Tamara, and Serge Gauthier, *Ceramics of the Twentieth Century*, Rizzoli, New York, and Phaidon, Oxford, 1982

Schnyder, Rudolf, et al., *Keramik Europas*, Keramikmuseum Westerwald, Höhr-Grenzhausen, 1994

Slivka, Rose, *The Object as Poet*, Smithsonian Institution Press, Washington D.C., 1977

Slivka, Rose, *West Coast Ceramics*, Stedelijk Museum, Amsterdam, 1979

Staal, Gert, Garth Clark, Mark Del Vecchio, et al., *Functional Glamour: Utility in American Ceramics*, Museum het Kruithuis, 's-Hertogenbosch, the Netherlands, 1987

Watson, Oliver, *Studio Pottery: Twentieth Century British Ceramics in the Victoria and Albert Museum Collection*, Phaidon, London in association with the Victoria and Albert Museum, London, 1993

Photo credits

The following abbreviations have been used: a above; b below; l left; m middle; r right

Terje Agnalt 172; Ole Akhoj 34l (Collection Seattle Art Museum, Seattle), 34r (Collection Lois Lunin and David Becker), 35 (Courtesy Garth Clark Gallery, New York); **Yo Akiyama** 170; **Noel Allum** 65 (Private collection), 78 (Private collection), 84a (Private collection), 84bl (Courtesy Garth Clark Gallery, New York), 87a (Courtesy Garth Clark Gallery, New York), 110 (Courtesy Garth Clark Gallery, New York), 111 (Courtesy Garth Clark Gallery, New York), 124 (Collection of the Mint Museum of Craft and Design, Charlotte), 153l (Courtesy Garth Clark Gallery, New York), 160 (Courtesy Garth Clark Gallery, New York), 161 (Collection of Vincent Lim and Bob Tooey), 184l (Collection of the Everson Museum of Art, Syracuse, NY), 184r; Artcodif 137al; **Arthur Aubry** 169b (Courtesy Eyre/Moore Gallery, Seattle); **Tim Barnwell** 136r (Courtesy Ferrin Gallery, Northampton); **David Beitzel Gallery, New York** 148bl, 149; **Anthony Bennett** 142al (Courtesy Garth Clark Gallery, New York); **Raymonde Bergeron** 117al, 117br (both Courtesy Garth Clark Gallery, New York); **John Bessler** 190al, 190br, 191ar, 191bl (all Courtesy Garth Clark Gallery, New York); **Hilbert Boxem** 109a; **Edgar Buonagurio** 153r (Collection of Joyce and Jay Cooper); **Mark Burns** 152br; **Gerry Cappel** 29a; **Christies Images** 23; **Garth Clark Gallery, New York** 12; **Dennis Cowley** 59l (Courtesy Max Protetch Gallery, New York); **David Cripps** 48a (Private collection), 85al (Courtesy Contemporary Applied Arts, London); **Cyan Crom** 83 (Courtesy Garth Clark Gallery, New York); **Anthony Cunha** 29b (Collection of Sonny and Gloria Kamm), 32a (Courtesy Frank Lloyd Gallery, Los Angeles), 32b (Courtesy Frank Lloyd Gallery, Los Angeles), 48b (Private collection), 61b (Private collection), 62b (Collection of the Los Angeles County Museum of Art, Los Angeles), 63r (Courtesy Frank Lloyd Gallery, Los Angeles), 66 (Courtesy Garth Clark Gallery, New York), 67r (Courtesy Garth Clark Gallery, New York), 88 (Private collection), 89 (Private collection), 102a (Courtesy Garth Clark Gallery, New York), 107a (Collection of Sonny and Gloria Kamm), 113b (Private collection), 115 (Private collection), 116a (Collection of Nanette Laitman), 116b (Collection of Nanette Laitman), 119l (Collection of Katharine and Anthony Del Vecchio), 121al, 121br, 126 (Private collection), 131b (Courtesy Garth Clark Gallery, New York), 137br (Collection of Sonny and Gloria Kamm), 141br (Private collection), 144 (Courtesy Frank Lloyd Gallery, Los Angeles), 150 (Collection of Sonny and Gloria Kamm), 151al (Collection of Sonny and Gloria Kamm), 151br (Collection of Sonny and Gloria Kamm), 171bl (Private collection), 186br (Private collection); **Margaretha Daepp** 188; **Wouter Dam** 43al (Courtesy Garth Clark Gallery, New York), 43br (Private collection); **Alf Georg Dannevig** 173; **James Dee** 85bl, 85br (both Courtesy Franklin Parrasch Gallery, New York), 155b (Collection of Pamela and Stephen Hootkin); **John deFazio** 152al; **Photo courtesy Laurent Delaye Gallery, London** 114l, 114r; **Stefano Della Porta** 97br; **Kim Dickey** 76al; **Paul Dresang** 95 (Collection of Laurie Britecoff and Greg Mancuso); **Michael Duvall** 30; **Guy Du Von** 145 (Courtesy Garth Clark Gallery, New York); **Edward Eberle** 128 (Courtesy Garth Clark Gallery, New York), 129l (Collection of the Los Angeles County Museum of Art, Los Angeles); eeva-inkeri 60 (Courtesy DC Moore Gallery, New York); **Philip Eglin** 159al, 159br (both Courtesy Garth Clark Gallery, New York); **Raymon Elozua** 174al, 174br, 182al, 182br; **M. L. Fatherree** 96 (Courtesy George Adams Gallery, New York), 97a (Courtesy George Adams Gallery, New York), 148l (Courtesy Rena Bransten Gallery, San Francisco); **Laszlo Fekete** 156 (Private collection), 157 (Collection of Howard and Judie Ganek); **Tim Fieldstead** 179, 180, 181; photo courtesy Gagosian Gallery, New York 70; **Courtesy galerie b 15, Munich** 53r; **Thelma Garcia and Diego Medina** 98, 99; **Claire Garoutte** 76ar; **Collection Frank Gehry** 15b; **Frans Grummer** 86l (Courtesy Garth Clark Gallery, New York), 86r (Collection of Lisa and Dudley Anderson); **Linda Gunn-Russell** 135l, 135r; **Chris Gustin** 91l; **Robert Hall** 112l, 112r; **Brian Hand** 72l, 72r (both Courtesy Garth Clark Gallery, New York); **Takashi Hatakeyama** 53l (Courtesy Togakuda Gallery, Kyoto, Japan); **Emil Heger** 76b, 77; **Steve Heineman** 90; **Douglas Herren** 155al; **Jan Holcomb** 154al (Private collection); **Tom Holt** 91r; **Ayumi Horie** 163r (Courtesy Garth Clark Gallery, New York); **Imatge i Lletra, s.l.** 82 (Collection of Howard and Judie Ganek); **Barbara Kaas** 46a; **Jacques Kaufmann** 171br (Collection of Museum of Contemporary Art, Dunkerque); **Akira Koike** 186al; **Collection of Museum het Kruithuis, 's-Hertogenbosch** 22a; **Geert Lap** 55 (Collection of the European Keramik Werk Centrum); **Jean-Pierre Larocque** 163l (Courtesy Garth Clark Gallery, New York); **Ah Leon** 102b, 103al, 103br (all Courtesy Garth Clark Gallery, New York); **Bob Lopez** 36a; **Frank Louis** 171mr; **Marilyn Lysohir** 154bl; **James Makins** 73b (Courtesy Jaap van Liere); **Marer Collection at Scripps College, Claremont, California** 15a; **Beverly Mayeri** 154br (Private collection); **Robert McKeever** 71 (Courtesy Gagosian Gallery, New York); **Photo courtesy Mobilia Gallery** 134; **J. J. Morer** 84br (Courtesy galerie b 15, Munich); **Patrick Muller** 42l, 42r (both Courtesy Garth Clark Gallery, New York); **Thomas Naethe** 44, 45; **Kohei Nakamura** 118 (Private collection); **Kenji Nakano** 52 (Courtesy Togakuda Gallery, Kyoto, Japan); **Barbara Nanning** 168al, 168br, 169a; **Abbas Nazari** 51l, 51r (both Courtesy Anthony Ralph); **Andra Nelki** 50l (Collection of Inge Peters), 50r (Private collection); **Arthur Nelson** 31a (Private collection); **Richard Notkin** 107b (Courtesy Garth Clark Gallery, New York), 108r (Collection of Pamela and Stephen Hootkin); **Jeff O'Brien** 138 (Private collection); **Pekka Tapio Paikkari** 171al; **Courtesy Franklin Parrasch Gallery, New York** 167a, 167b; **Jan Pauwels** 100, 101 (both Private collection); **Courtesy P.P.O.W.** 162 (Collection of Stephen and Pamela Hootkin); **Courtesy Prime Gallery, Toronto** 142br, 143; **Courtesy Max Protetch Gallery, New York** 58; **Fritz Rossmann** 46; **Royal College of Art, London** 20b; **Paul Sanders** 73a; **Richard Sargent** 94bl, 94ar; **Sylvia Sarner** 54b (Collection of Pamela and Stephen Hootkin); **Christian Schluter** 47b; **Roger Schreiber** 36r, 37; **Paul Scott** 113a; **Susan Shutt Wulfeck** 136al (Courtesy Frank Lloyd Gallery, Los Angeles); **Bobby Silverman** 74, 75; **Gert Skaerlund Anderson** 33a, 33b; **Richard Slee** 109bl (Private collection), 109br; **Van Sloun & Ramalkers** 79; **Don Tuttle** 38l (Courtesy Garth Clark Gallery, New York), 38r (Collection of Paul Hertz), 39 (Collection of Museum het Kruithuis, 's-Hertogenbosch); **Peer van der Kruis** 130l, 130r (both from the Europees Kermisch Werk Centrum series); **Johan van der Veer** 158; **Eric Van Eimeren** 187ar, 187bl; **Irene Vonck** 87b (Collection of Carol A. Straus); **Donald Waller** 183; **Kevin Waller** 185br; **David Ward** 62a; **Steve Welch** 185al; **John White** 31 (Private collection), 54al (Collection of Professor Del Kolve and Larry Luctel), 59r (Courtesy Max Protetch Gallery, New York), 61b (Courtesy Garth Clark Gallery, New York), 63l (Collection of Caren and Walter Forbes), 64l (Collection of the Arthur M. Sackler Gallery, Smithsonian Institution, Washington, D.C.), 64r (Private collection), 67al (Private collection), 108l (Collection of Martin Davidson), 119r (Collection of John Axelrod), 120 (Private collection), 124l (Collection of Karel Reisz), 124r (Courtesy Garth Clark Gallery, New York), 127al (Courtesy Garth Clark Gallery, New York), 127bl (Collection of Pamela and Stephen Hootkin), 127br (Collection of Pamela and Stephen Hootkin), 129r (Collection of the Carnegie Museum of Art, Pittsburgh), 131a (Collection of Caren and Walter Forbes), 139 (Private collection), 140 (Private collection), 141al (Collection of Martin J. Davidson); **Courtesy White Cube, London** 22b; **Margita Wickenhauser** 189; **Arnold Zimmerman** 175 (Courtesy John Elder Gallery, New York)

Index